# The Hard Yards

# The Hard Yards

## A SEASON IN THE CHAMPIONSHIP, FOOTBALL'S TOUGHEST LEAGUE

### Nige Tassell

**SIMON &
SCHUSTER**

London · New York · Sydney · Toronto · New Delhi

First published in Great Britain by Simon & Schuster UK Ltd, 2021

Copyright © Nige Tassell, 2021

The right of Nige Tassell to be identified as the author
of this work has been asserted in accordance with the
Copyright, Designs and Patents Act, 1988.

1 3 5 7 9 10 8 6 4 2

Simon & Schuster UK Ltd
1st Floor
222 Gray's Inn Road
London WC1X 8HB

www.simonandschuster.co.uk
www.simonandschuster.com.au
www.simonandschuster.co.in

Simon & Schuster Australia, Sydney
Simon & Schuster India, New Delhi

The author and publishers have made all reasonable efforts
to contact copyright-holders for permission, and apologise
for any omissions or errors in the form of credits given.
Corrections may be made to future printings.

A CIP catalogue record for this book
is available from the British Library

Hardback ISBN: 978-1-3985-0446-2
eBook ISBN: 978-1-3985-0447-9

Typeset in Bembo by M Rules
Printed and bound by CPI Group (UK) Ltd, Croydon, CR0 4YY

*To Ma*

*'The hoops and the stripes*
*The halves and the quarters . . .'*

— HALF MAN HALF BISCUIT

# Warm-up

Sometimes the highest view isn't always the best.

Take the Eiffel Tower, for instance. Visitors to the landmark have a range of altitudes from which to admire the Parisian skyline. Those with the sturdiest constitutions will make a beeline for the great glass elevators that take them to the tower's peak – its summit, its zenith.

Aside from the occasional chink of glasses in its champagne bar and the wind whistling past sightseers' ears, the summit is a quiet place. It's detached from the city, distanced from the scramble of the streets far below. Nearly six hundred feet lower down, the second-highest viewing platform is where it's at. It's a busier, more popular vantage point; the architectural splendour of Paris can still be gazed upon from a more than decent height, but it's one where visitors can also feel closer to the throbbing pulse of the capital.

Now consider the English football pyramid. The rarefied air of the Premier League might always be the ultimate goal for those with a head for heights, but it's the second tier, the Championship, that matters most for many. Life here doesn't operate in a bubble. It's raw and real. Down here you can hear the hustle, feel the bustle.

Ever since its inauguration, the Championship has been an extraordinarily competitive league. It's a division so tight that the line between being within a sniff of the Premier League promised land and falling through the trap door into lower-league ignominy is often a perilously thin one.

The Championship's formidable nature is almost universally acknowledged by those who have played and managed within it. Gus Poyet once declared it to be the toughest league in England. Neil Warnock went further, believing it to be the tightest division in Europe. That wasn't enough for Norwich boss Daniel Farke, who went further still: 'The Championship, without any doubt, is the toughest league in the *world*.'

Compared to the predictability of the Premier League and its near-inevitable top-six domination, England's second tier is a meritocratic free-for-all – any team on its day and all that. It redefines the concept of consistency. No Championship team will ever come close to a defeat-free Invincibles-style season. The league's innate combativeness, its undying competitive nature, are the checks and balances placed on each of its twenty-four teams. The ferocity of each club's desire – to be automatically promoted, to squeeze into the play-offs, to avoid the exit chute down to League One – is what keeps its playing field more level than that of any other league.

There has yet to be a Championship season that hasn't offered a full-throttle, blood-and-guts campaign that refuses to draw breath until the very last ball has been kicked. Take Wednesday 22 July 2020, for instance, the final round of matches of an interrupted season. Clubs that looked set for promotion suddenly derailed themselves, while those who had already accepted the near-certain fate of relegation performed barely believable great escapes. All the clubs that had sat in the bottom five places at the start of the month avoided the drop into the third tier just three weeks later.

As gripping as the events of that particular day were, this was no outlier. Fans of the Championship know that high drama is par for the course. It's inescapable with the stakes being so high.

Forcing your way to the top table of English football, where the cash supposedly falls like rain, is the ultimate bounty, regardless of the goldfish bowl they'd be forced to swim in.

And it's a league that means different things to different people. To the late-in-the-day, former top-flight pros, it's an irrefutable signal that they're coming down the mountain from their career peak. To eager young pups, it's a high-profile crucible – the proverbial shop window – in which to forge reputations and turn heads. To well-seasoned managers, it's confirmation that they've found their level, the madness of the Championship being a strange comfort zone that matches their talents. And to the new breed of bosses, it's both baptism and audition.

To meet these people, and to taste the relentless chaos of the Championship, I set nine months aside to dive deep into the molten heart of English football. And the 2020–21 campaign turned out to be unlike any other in history. Yes, those trademark dramatic moments came fitted as standard, but the ongoing peaks and troughs of a worldwide pandemic – and its stadium-emptying abilities – produced the kind of season that no one would ever wish to repeat. It was more chaotic, more intense, more relentless than any Championship campaign ever. Not only did it kick off just thirty-nine days after the previous season ended, but it was compressed into eight and a half months, more than a month shorter than normal.

I was fortunate to be able to travel to all four corners of this league – from Bournemouth to Middlesbrough, Swansea to Norwich – watching games and speaking to the protagonists, be they players, managers, chairmen, backroom staff, broadcasters, journalists and, far from least, fans.

The latter were, of course, largely absent through no fault of their own. This would be the season when their devotion was tested like never before, when they could only watch from a distance, their eye up to the telescope like those Eiffel Tower sightseers.

This nine-month odyssey – this inside view of a particular, *peculiar* season – is for them.

# September

*'The bookies haven't got a lot of faith*
*in us, but they didn't last season either'*

— ALAN PARRY

You can squint all you like. You could even slip on a pair of rose-tinted glasses. But there's no way you could mistake Hillbottom Road for Wembley Way.

Adams Park, residence of Wycombe Wanderers for the past thirty years, is located at the far end of an industrial estate, one that's home to window fitters, biscuit manufacturers and purveyors of part-worn car tyres. Glamorous it ain't.

On Saturday afternoons during the football season, when these industrial units are shuttered up for the weekend, the scene is at least enlivened by the snake of Wycombe fans passing through en route towards their field of dreams, each wearing the two-tone blue of their affiliation.

On this particular Saturday, however, the snake is in enforced hibernation. With coronavirus restrictions demanding that all EFL matches continue to be played behind closed doors, this first match of a brand-new, box-fresh season feels eerie. The roads are quiet. The burger van is doing no trade at all. A dribble of journalists and broadcasters have their accreditation checked and their temperatures taken. This is how match days look and sound in a pandemic.

Light industry only dominates one side of the Adams Park perimeter. The remaining three sides boast a bucolic backdrop of hills and woodland. Today the woodland's most conspicuous residents – the local red kite population – fly high above the pitch, tracing circles in the sky. They've got a sense of occasion at least, even if coronavirus has shown scant regard for what is one of the most significant days in the club's 133-year history – if not *the* most significant day.

Last season, Adams Park was the home of Wycombe Wanderers of League One. Today, it's the home of Wycombe Wanderers of the Championship. This afternoon will see the Chairboys' first-ever match in the second tier of English football.

At the point at which the regular 2019–20 EFL season was curtailed in early June due to the pandemic, Wycombe sat in eighth place in League One, outside the play-off places. However, they'd played fewer games than all those teams above them and, after the clubs voted for the final standings to be decided on a points-per-game basis, Wycombe's ratio elevated them right up to third place. A 6-3 aggregate win in the two-legged play-off semi-final against Fleetwood Town took them to Wembley, where a 2-1 victory over local rivals Oxford United confirmed their heavenly ascent.

And here they are now, at an altitude higher than ever before. For the club's long-serving captain Matt Bloomfield – a midfield stalwart whose sixteen years at Adams Park have rightly earned him the title 'Mr Wycombe' – it's all a bit surreal.

'Who would have ever thought that Wycombe Wanderers would be a league above Ipswich, Portsmouth and Sunderland?' he asks. 'But we've not been given this on a plate, despite what some people would try to have you believe. We deserve to be in this position because of the results we've had. Over three-quarters of the season we got the third-best average points in League One. We deserve to be here on merit. We've done it through sheer determination and hard work – and no small amount of quality along the way. We didn't win a raffle to get here.'

That the side he leads now sit higher up the pyramid than Ipswich is particularly poignant for Bloomfield. A native of Suffolk, he came up through the youth ranks at Portman Road (during which time he was called up for the England U19s) before being released a couple of months ahead of his twentieth birthday. 'I made one appearance for the first team, a cup game away to Notts County, which we lost. Maybe that had a bearing on my future. If the result goes against you, you sometimes get caught up in that and people make judgements off the back of it. Unfortunately, there was never a second appearance. A lot of my friends – Darren Bent, Darren Ambrose, Ian Westlake – were signing new contracts, but I was called into the office and told that I could leave.'

As a central midfielder, there was too much competition for places, with the likes of established internationals like Jim Magilton and Matt Holland being immovable fixtures of the first team. 'My route to the first team was very clogged. It was apparent that, to make a career in the game, I'd have to go elsewhere.

'I was getting ready to go out to have a Christmas meal with the youth-team lads and I got a call from [then Wycombe manager] Tony Adams. I got out of the shower to an answerphone message from an England legend! I rang him straight back. He asked whether I wanted to come down to Wycombe to have a look around. "I'll be there tomorrow morning . . ."'

Bloomfield's subsequent signing kicked off this long – and still ongoing – tenure in Buckinghamshire. 'If I'd have stayed at Ipswich for too much longer without playing football, I could have been in danger of missing the boat. I'm extremely grateful for what happened and when it happened. I see boys these days who play for Premier League U23 teams and who have nice contracts and nice cars, but they get to the age of twenty-three with just five first-team appearances under their belt. League One and League Two managers will just say, "Well, I've got a lad here of the same age, but he's got two hundred appearances." They know which one they can rely on.'

As a still-raw teenager, Bloomfield's departure from Portman Road was timely, allowing him to learn his trade in the cut-and-thrust of league football, rather than the sterility of the U23 game. By dropping down the pyramid, he quickly matured on the field and soon became that reliable, battle-proven young player for a procession of Wycombe managers. Not that the flame of ambition to play at a higher level was ever extinguished.

'I didn't come here meaning to stay this long. I saw it as a stepping stone. I signed an eighteen-month contract but, having dropped down from the second tier, I wanted to step back up again. But I soon got my feet under the table. I loved the club. When the opportunity came to leave when I was twenty-one, I didn't want to. So I stayed here for less money because I loved being here so much. And after sixteen and a half years, I'm still having the time of my life.'

Bloomfield's overarching aim throughout his career had been to return to the Championship. But the seasons kept ticking over, and the birthdays too, with it never really looking like he would achieve that goal with Wycombe. Indeed, the club seemed more likely to slip out of the league altogether. As he descended deeper into his thirties, Bloomfield had surrendered all hope. After all, another club was highly unlikely to make a play for his signature, to lift him upwards two divisions from the depths of League Two. 'It was no longer on my radar and I'd made peace with that.'

Bloomfield acknowledges that, back in 2014, when Wycombe

only salvaged their league status with a dramatic win on the final day of the season, 'the Championship would have been just a pipe dream. Getting to League One was obviously a more realistic ambition, but still an extremely tough ask.' Four years on, promotion to the third tier was secured and two seasons later came that play-off win at Wembley and the fulfilment of that career-long ambition.

'My career does not mirror a stereotypical Championship footballer's career. I've done the hard yards in League One and League Two. The life of a lower-league footballer isn't always an easy one. I didn't sign a sixteen-year contract with Wycombe. There have been lots of times when I've been out of contract and life has been uncertain. The sacrifices and the knocks and the injuries along the way made for the euphoria and the emotion at Wembley in July. It was an outpour of emotion that wasn't about one game, one final, one promotion. It was all about the back story. It was all about finally achieving a life ambition to get to the Championship.'

The compromises Bloomfield has made to family life throughout his career continue to this day. His wife and daughters live in Felixstowe, meaning – in a regular week during the season – he sees them two days out of seven, doing the 125-mile M40/M25/A12 shuttle on Sundays and on a midweek day off.

For the remaining five days, Bloomfield lives in a rented house in High Wycombe, one he shares with a few other first-team players. It's not surprising that – for someone whose immaculately side-parted hair is rarely out of place, even in the heat of battle – he's the man of the house, the one who sets the tone. And, presumably, the one who draws up the cleaning rotas. 'I'm the elder statesman,' he confirms. 'There are no dirty plates or dirty washing lying around the place.'

But, despite his seniority, Bloomfield is not content to embrace the dying light of his playing career. His enthusiasm remains undented; he's as evangelical about the game, and about the club, as he was the first time he drove through the Adams Park gates. 'I hate leaving the family every Sunday evening when I have to do the drive back up, but I love getting up in the morning and going into the club. I jump out of bed. I can't wait.'

He's also a man who won't be content for his Championship adventure to be fleeting.

'For me, the euphoria of Wembley lasted about two or three hours before my mind started wandering. I knew I now needed to be better. I knew *we* now needed to be better. I certainly didn't want to go into the Championship but come back down at the first time of asking, having rolled over and handed out three points in each game. We want to be a match for everyone, every week. We're here and we want to establish ourselves in the Championship. We want to write a new narrative for us this season. It would be naïve and silly of us not to have that mentality.'

That mentality is visible on the pitch as the Wycombe players warm up ahead of making their second-tier bow. Each and every one exudes focus and commitment. From up in the press enclosure in the Beechdean Stand, the gathered journalists study them, familiarising themselves with any fresh faces who've joined for the new season. The blond hair of winger Daryl Horgan, a summer signing from Hibernian, makes him particularly easy to spot. A handful of his new team-mates – suited and booted on the touchline, with injury ruling them out of this historic match – gaze on with envy.

If Matt Bloomfield's long association with the club has bestowed upon him the honour of being 'Mr Wycombe', a certain former football commentator currently sat among the press corps can claim an even deeper affiliation. Despite being a Liverpudlian, Alan Parry's connections go back nearly half a century, two decades of which he served as one of the club's directors.

'In 1975, I was a rookie reporter with BBC Radio in London, having just come down from Liverpool. They asked me to cover the FA Cup Third Round tie between Wycombe, who were then in the Isthmian League, and Middlesbrough, who were joint-top of the old First Division. Jack Charlton was their manager and players like Graeme Souness were in the side.

'I said, "Where's High Wycombe?" I'd never heard of it and had to look it up on the map. I got the train down from London and followed the crowds up to the old Loakes Park ground in the town centre by the hospital. It was full that day and people were so friendly and approachable.

'A few months later, I moved to the area and started going to games. One thing led to another and, as I played a bit of football back then, I asked if I could train with them one night a week, on a patch of muddy ground behind the stand at Loakes Park. So I started training with them, then began to go to games more regularly. Someone said, "We've got a vacancy on the board. Do you fancy applying for it?" I didn't think it was my scene, but then I thought about the divide in football between the fans who watch, the players who play and the directors who sit in comparatively luxurious comfort and who don't really connect with the other two. I saw it as an opportunity to bring those three factions together.

'So I stood for election. I'd never done anything like that before. I remember saying, "I know more about team sheets than balance sheets, so if you're looking for someone to help the club financially, don't vote for me." I got voted on and that led to more than twenty years as a director, from the Isthmian League to the Vauxhall Conference to the Football League and to where we find ourselves today.'

One of Parry's achievements while on the board was helping to persuade Martin O'Neill to take over as manager in 1990, the same year that the club moved to Adams Park, here on High

Wycombe's western outskirts. O'Neill got the club promoted to the Football League from the Conference, then a further promotion into the third tier just twelve months later. It wasn't long, though, before O'Neill's ambitions showed themselves to extend beyond what could be achieved at Adams Park and he left to take over at Norwich City. Mention of the Ulsterman's departure is met with an involuntary Parry sigh.

'That was a big blow, clearly. We had a few years of, as the cliché has it, mid-table mediocrity, where we weren't really going anywhere. But we gradually got to grips with league football – enjoying promotions and suffering relegations. The moment that any Wycombe fan will never forget was at Torquay six years ago. It looked as though we were going out of the league. We lost to Bristol Rovers here in the penultimate game of the season and everything was set up for us to get relegated. We were away to Torquay in the last game and Bristol Rovers were at home to Mansfield. Bristol Rovers were pretty cocky. They thought, by winning here, they had put us down. But they lost and we won, so we stayed up.

'The feeling of euphoria then was greater than anything – at least, anything before we won promotion to the Championship. The club's whole future would have been in doubt. There were big financial problems behind the scenes. Relegation would probably have led to administration and, who knows, it would have probably meant at least a few seasons of just ticking over in the National League. But we survived. Since then, Gareth's gone from strength to strength, taking the club with him.'

'Gareth' is Gareth Ainsworth, manager of Wycombe since September 2012 and a man deemed untouchable in this corner of the Thames Valley, having guided the club away from the trapdoor of relegation into non-league to being just one tier down from the Premier League. He is the longest-serving manager at any of the ninety-two league clubs.

Like that of O'Neill, Parry had some influence in Ainsworth's appointment too. After the dismissal of Gary Waddock early into the 2012–13 season, the chairman asked Parry for his thoughts. His response was automatic, explaining how the still-playing Ainsworth would make a perfect caretaker manager, one who came with the backing of the dressing room fitted as standard.

'I said, "He's your man for next Saturday." But never in my wildest dreams did I think he would go on to achieve what he has achieved. He's just been unbelievable. He's his own man. He doesn't care what people think about him.'

Right on cue, Ainsworth appears below us on the touchline, looking like no other Championship manager who's ever come before. With his shoulder-length hair, tight-fitting navy shirt and expensive-looking dark jeans, he looks every bit the Ford Mustang-driving, middle-aged rocker he is; away from the day job, he's the singer in covers band The Cold Blooded Hearts. And as he slowly wanders up and down the pitch, soaking up the sunshine, soaking up the anticipation of the occasion, a suitably classic rock soundtrack plays over the PA. As the last notes of 'Light My Fire' dissolve on the air, Ainsworth salutes the local journalists in the press box before slipping back down the tunnel, ready to give his pre-match instructions. The time to hesitate is through.

The confidence with which Ainsworth carries himself clearly drips down to his players and the supporters. This might be the first time Wycombe have ventured into the deep end that is the Championship, but there's a definite air of optimism about the place. Time will tell if it's misplaced. It's an optimism that isn't shared by the bookmakers, who have Wycombe at odds of 2/3 to go straight back down to League One. Any hopeless romantic who fancies the Chairboys to reach the Premier League come next May have the chance to get very rich. The odds on that happening are 75/1. Winning the Championship title is seen as a 500/1 prospect.

'I think we'll surprise a few people this season,' says Parry, looking across to where Wycombe's strikers are currently undertaking some shooting practice. Around half the efforts on goal are either high or wide. 'The bookies haven't got a lot of faith in us, but they didn't last season either. They had us being relegated then too.' Indeed, for the whole of last season, the wall of Ainsworth's office was decorated with a press cutting that predicted Wycombe would finish twenty-third in League One. It was both a daily reminder of other people's expectations and a motivating tool for the manager, one that resulted in that third-placed finish.

'Our owner has said that this season we'll have the lowest budget of any Championship club ever,' Parry reveals, 'and there's usually a correlation between budget and position in the league. So I can understand why the bookies have got us down for relegation. But we'll see. Some factors have come into play that will help us. For instance, games are being played behind closed doors. We showed in the play-offs last season that we could play in empty stadiums and succeed. So why not again?

'I think making a good start is absolutely crucial. If we cling on, fourth from bottom or whatever it takes to stay up, that would be a much bigger achievement than getting here in the first place.'

Whether the bookies have read it right or not, Parry is clearly excited about what will occur at Adams Park as the next nine months unfold. He very much applauds the unpredictable and meritocratic ways of the Championship, how – on their day and with a following wind – even the lowliest side can beat the runaway favourites. 'We're not going to be star-struck. We won't be autograph hunters. "Oh, isn't it fantastic? We're playing in these great stadiums. What a lovely day out." No, we'll be going all out in every single game. I don't think anyone will find it easy to beat Wycombe.'

Neither the commentary gantry nor the directors' box are Parry's domain any more, but he's here in the press seats legitimately. He's just been signed up as a columnist for the local paper, the *Bucks Free Press*, with metaphorical pen poised to wax lyrical or vent spleen about matters Wanderers. And there's an underlying purpose to the new role. Under the current Covid restrictions, numbers are severely limited when it comes to how many guests are allowed in. Those all-important sponsors are first in line, meaning there's no guarantee that the names of long-serving former directors will be on the list. So, becoming a newspaperman again (Parry's career started as a reporter on the *Liverpool Weekly News*) has its advantages.

A wink. And, underneath the face mask, probably a smile too. 'It's a way for me to get into games ...'

*

Close to kick-off, the classic rock has been replaced by a diet of younger-vintage Britpop ('Supersonic', 'Park Life') as the final preparations are made. The ground staff wipe down the goalposts with antibacterial spray, while Sky's touchline reporter, Bianca Westwood, makes some last-minute notes before going live to the nation. Up in the press box, the radio commentators test their ISDN lines, shuffle heavily annotated sheets of statistics and rearrange their highlighter pens into a rainbow of colours.

The anticipation, though, is slightly muted – not just by the absence of fans, but also by the workings of the fixture computer. For this most significant of days in Wycombe's history, the software could have selected one of the division's big boys. Double European Cup winners Nottingham Forest, for instance, or former title winners Derby County, complete with Wayne Rooney in their line-up. Instead it's Rotherham United, who've made the journey to Buckinghamshire, a team the hosts are very familiar with, having accompanied them on the passage from League One last season.

But Matt Bloomfield doesn't feel any sense of anticlimax. 'No – it's historic in my mind and it's historic in the club's mind. Of course, away to Derby or Forest in front of 30,000 people would have been a real welcome to the Championship, but it doesn't matter who or where we're playing. For me, it's about making my Championship debut at the age of thirty-six as the captain of my club, playing in the second tier for the first time in its 133-year history.'

Bloomfield leads the team out, not to the roar that everyone would like, but to a polite ripple of applause, mainly from the substitutes taking their places in the stand and the sponsors, guests and injured players in the Frank Adams Stand over on the other side of the pitch. Gareth Ainsworth's instruction in his programme notes – 'Let's get this place rocking' – is more than slightly optimistic.

Despite their talismanic, sixteen-stone striker Adebayo 'The Beast' Akinfenwa not gracing the occasion through injury, Wycombe very nearly make the perfect start to their Championship existence. Adams Park has seen just two minutes of second-tier football when the nippy forward Scott Kashket breaks away down the right and crosses for debutant Horgan. The Republic of Ireland international slides in but can't direct the ball into the empty net from four yards out.

Still, it bodes well for the remaining eighty-eight minutes. Perhaps.

History is actually made twenty minutes later, when Bloomfield becomes the first Wycombe player to receive a yellow card in the Championship, the referee adjudging him to have followed through in a full-blooded challenge on the Rotherham number four, Shaun MacDonald. The booking is met with hoots of derision and consternation from the Wycombe subs, now with the benefit of a grandstand view.

The rest of the first half passes without great incident, save for Wycombe defender Darius Charles hitting the post from a set-piece, and a high Rotherham boot that appears to make contact with Kashket's head but which is roundly ignored by the officials. At half-time, Ainsworth lingers at the entrance of the tunnel to discuss the matter with the referee.

In the week leading up to the game, an earthquake hit the Chilterns, but there's little danger of anything seismic happening today. After forty-five minutes of ring-rusty football, the match bears all the hallmarks of a goalless draw. 'This could go either way,' one of the radio commentators behind me tells his listeners. Or, of course, it could go no way at all.

The second half takes a similar shape to the first, and the Wycombe faithful – albeit in their limited numbers – are showing signs of stress. 'That linesman is useless!' comes a shout from the supposedly impartial press box. It's the unmistakable voice of the new correspondent of the *Bucks Free Press*.

After seventy-two minutes, Bloomfield makes another contribution to the club's history books, becoming the first Wycombe player to be substituted in the Championship. But there's no huffiness when his number's up. For a man who's done his coaching badges, and for whom a few decades in the dugout surely await, he stays on the touchline rather than heading up the steps to a seat in the stand. From here, he advises, cajoles and motivates his team-mates to both keep things tight at the back and take the odd risk upfront.

Next to him on the touchline, Ainsworth pogos up and down on the spot, trying to encourage his header-shy wingers to make an aerial challenge rather than be anchored by feet of clay. His frustrations have an air of prophecy about them. In the second minute of added time, Rotherham captain Michael Ihiekwe rises largely uncontested to head the winner from a corner. A point looked like it was in Wycombe's pocket, but it was then gifted away. It might prove to be a point of extraordinary value come May.

Over the past four seasons, Rotherham have shuffled back and forth between the Championship and League One. Down and up, down and up. During their last spell in the Championship, they managed just one away win all season – and that in itself had been their first away win in the division in forty-four attempts. The Millers have now equalled that tally on the very first afternoon of the new season.

Not that there's the slightest hint of annoyance on Gareth Ainsworth's face as he emerges from the tunnel having consoled his players. 'It's a sucker punch at the end, but I'm really pleased. We saw that some of our boys are not going to be out of place in this league. We've got some really differing styles to come up against and we'll have to work each one out. Certainly the chances you get in the Championship are few and far between. You don't see hundreds of chances in Championship games. So when they do come, be clinical. Make sure you put them in the goal.

'We'll learn plenty from this today and we'll go again, no problem.'

Ainsworth disappears back down the tunnel and Adams Park, much quieter all afternoon than it should be on a Saturday, now falls silent. Out in the car park, though, the sound of gunshots suddenly peppers the air. Its source is the paintball centre in the woods behind the ground, and there's a distant cheer as one of the amateur snipers successfully takes out his prey. Ainsworth would surely approve of their accuracy. Over the months to come, and in order to ensure their own survival, Wycombe Wanderers' professional sharpshooters will need to find the target with exactly this kind of precision.

*

Dan Gray knows his way. He could walk these streets blindfolded.

It's not the most direct route to the Riverside Stadium, but it's his favourite. Head north out of Middlesbrough station, up Cleveland and Durham Streets, with the most famous landmark on the town's skyline heaving into view and getting bigger with each step – the blue, four-legged triffid known as the Transporter Bridge. Or, as the poet Ian Horn called it, 'a giant blue dragonfly across the Tees'.

On reaching the bridge, there's usually a period of reflection as Gray gazes into the inky depths of the river ('thinking that my ashes would be in there one day – a very cheerful thought!'), before heading south-east across this flattened, post-industrial landscape. To his left on Vulcan Street is the elegant wall of the former Cleveland Salt Works, the only evidence of its existence that still stands. To his right, the teetering piles of long-dead cars stacked high on top of each other in a vehicle dismantler's yard. Bent, dented, burned out. Many have had their radiator grills ripped out and now resemble the toothless former Middlesbrough midfielder Nobby Stiles.

Gray's stride pattern gets quicker. He's close to his destination. Past the handsome Victorian clock tower that, in times of yore, would tell the dock workers whether they were late for their shift. Past Anish Kapoor's big, bold and mildly baffling Temenos sculpture. Over the pedestrian bridge.

Journey's end now. The Riverside Stadium. The cathedral of Gray's dreams.

Once there, there'll be another moment of contemplation, this time beside the entrance gates of the club's old Ayresome Park ground, rescued, relocated and rehung. Gray might also search for the brick bearing his and his dad's names, one of ten thousand laid next to those gates to form the Boro Brick Road.

Today, though, Gray's walk is much different from all those

hundreds of times before. This Middlesbrough native now lives in Edinburgh but, as a fan who bought his first season ticket thirty-odd years ago, he'll never become a victim of geography. However, the moment he stepped out of the station at 1.30 p.m., he could sense his old hometown was very different. It's a Saturday in September, but the streets are silent.

Gray – editor of the quarterly Scottish football magazine *Nutmeg* and author of a trilogy of wistful volumes that beautifully observe miscellaneous 'delights of modern football' – is the ideal person to articulate what has been lost as football grounds have been forced to keep supporters out. He understands the rituals and the routines of the fan – and the gaping hole that their removal has left.

'"Routine" is a word that comes up so much with football fans, and for a reason. Saturday mornings for me are the most wonderful time. Getting the train south, the same old scarf, the same newspaper in my bag, the same sandwich from the station … And I still get those feelings, even when we're in the middle of a terrible patch of form and playing terrible football. For me, it's a homecoming, touching down on my roots again, seeing people again. People can't believe I travel this far, but it's nothing to me. Two really enjoyable hours on the East Coast Main Line – one of the loveliest railways there is – and then the smoky train to the Boro.'

It's the third weekend of September, but Gray has not trodden these streets, not gazed at the Ayresome Park gates, since February ('a one-nil defeat to bottom-of-the-table Luton in the snow'). The pandemic closed down in-the-flesh football to the fans shortly after.

'It left a bigger hole than I imagined. During the lockdown in April and May, it was waking up on Saturdays with no train to get on, no ground to go to. It was a real kick to my routine and my equilibrium. And thousands and thousands of us feel like this. Not to be able to walk away after a match to discuss it. That valve of going for a pint afterwards. It was a real punch. The surety of the fixture list is very important to my life.'

It could well be a surety that's returning to Gray's life, starting from today. He's done that favourite walk not out of sentimental reasons, not to ease and assuage that yearning. He has a match ticket in his pocket. A real ticket for a real match.

Three days ago, the government gave the green light for a small number of EFL clubs to open their doors to a limited number of fans. In the Championship, three of today's matches – Luton vs Derby, Norwich vs Preston and Middlesbrough vs Bournemouth – have been singled out as these pilot games and each will be graced with the presence of one thousand home supporters. Here at the Riverside, Gray is one of the lucky ones whose name came out of the metaphorical hat.

After Boro were announced as one of the three games, their season-ticket holders were invited to log on to the club's website last Wednesday evening, where they were placed in an electronic queue. 'The romance of the queue outside the stadium it was not!' laughs Gray.

'About twenty past eight, there was a flash and I was in. Cue an almighty scramble to click on various seats, which kept greying out when they'd been taken by others. Tantrums and all the rest. Then I gave it one last refresh before I gave up and there it was: a block became available and I just clicked on any old seat.

'They were only issuing paper tickets, so then there was the wait for the postman. When he came down the path on Friday morning, I could have hugged him.

'I had the ticket in my pocket on the way down. It was a real Charlie Bucket moment. With only 1/34th of the ground's capacity occupied, I do feel privileged. And I feel a sense of guilt towards those who've missed out. But what can you do? It was a random internet generator that got me my ticket. I can't feel too guilty about that one.'

There's a further sense of privilege. The rest of North-east England – Northumberland, North Tyneside, South Tyneside, Newcastle, Gateshead, Sunderland and County Durham – were placed under tighter restrictions just forty-eight hours ago, controls that Teesside appears to have escaped. 'Everywhere my train stopped at after Scotland is under extra measures, but Middlesbrough isn't. I was expecting them to announce extra measures for us yesterday. They didn't. Then to announce it this morning. They didn't.'

On his walk to the Riverside, Gray hasn't seen a soul. 'That's so unusual. That would only happen if you went super-early on a match day. The club have encouraged everyone to drive, but I don't drive and don't own a car, so it's public transport for me. I've been the only one walking to the ground. There's no catering wagons, no smell of sizzling sausages, no programme sellers calling out. Yet I still feel something strong. It helps that I can still hear the Tannoy from outside.'

The local council are handing out face masks with the legend 'Up The Boro' on them, while the stewards ensure all attending fans sanitise their hands. Gray has taken extra steps today that will help to keep his distance from his brethren, particularly when it comes to using the stadium's facilities. Sometimes, before his pilgrimage to the Transporter Bridge, he might pop into town for a pint at the Twisted Lip. Not today. 'I've had just one cup of tea all day just so that I don't need the toilet.'

Gray approaches a Riverside turnstile for the first time in seven months and a steward welcomes him back. 'I've never been welcomed into a football ground in my life ...'

Two-and-a-bit hours later, after Boro and Bournemouth share the points in a 1-1 draw, Gray emerges to tell the tale of his game.

'It felt incredibly cathartic to be back there,' he gushes. 'Just that first glimpse of the green turf. It's not the most exciting stadium in the world, as any away fan will tell you, but it's our home and to be back, in whatever the circumstances, was quite special.

'I knew it was going to be an historic occasion, if not a happily historic one. But there was one moment when it really became almost normal. I didn't know whether we were going to be allowed to sing or to make any other noise. I hadn't read down to the seventy-ninth paragraph of the regulations. I'd just read the basic ones about social distancing and respecting others. The players were clapped off when they finished the warm-up, then came a shout: "Come on the Boro!" That gave me goose-bumps. It felt like we'd been given permission to let ourselves go. Once one Teessider with a foghorn voice had hollered, we were fine. We could all do it. We were all Spartacus.'

The ebb and flow of the crowd, the rise and fall of expectation, had been removed for the past few months. Matches had been becalmed. But a gentle swell was rising again.

'We found ourselves one-nil down, but were playing very well. Then a lovely bit of skill from Paddy McNair – a beautiful cross with the outside of his boot – and a header from Marcus Browne to equalise. I celebrated like I've celebrated big goals before. I didn't think I would. I thought I would be too self-conscious. I had three empty seats either side of me, so it wasn't like I was just blending into a big crowd with my mates. But I was back there. It was just wonderful.

'Some club staff were sat in front of me and they looked at each other with the most beautiful, proud looks, like a mum has when a child has brought her something they've made at school. "They've got their club back. Isn't it lovely?"'

The only disappointment for Gray – apart from the lack of a match-winning goal – was the absence of the Boro boss, Neil Warnock. He was isolating back home, 400 miles away in Cornwall, having contracted Covid-19. Warnock had been appointed as Jonathan Woodgate's successor back in June, so no

Boro fans have yet seen him in action on the home touchline. 'He's one of those figures you can't stand when he's managing someone else, but when he's at your club, you can't help taking to him. I was gutted not to see this combustible, passionate man on the touchline – seeing him in an empty-ish stadium so I could really hear his shouts.'

Still, there would be plenty of future opportunities for Gray to study Warnock over the coming months. Or so he thinks. Heading back to the station, he begins looking forward to the prospect of four home games in October, starting with the match against Barnsley in a fortnight's time.

But a handful of successful pilot games didn't help open the doors to fans. Three days later, the government slammed them shut again. 'We do want to, in due course, allow people to return to watch football and other sporting events,' Cabinet minister Michael Gove explained on *BBC Breakfast*, 'but it is the case that we just need to be cautious at the moment and I think a mass reopening at this stage wouldn't be appropriate.'

Just when there was light at the end of the tunnel, a landslip blocked the exit. The nation's football fans gave out a collective sigh of frustration.

The Championship, insulated to a degree by television money, wouldn't feel the effects of no income through the turnstiles as deeply as those further down the pyramid, many of whom faced grim futures – if they had any at all.

But whether Premier League billionaires or National League paupers, the hypocrisy of the entire situation struck home. Not one club would elect to keep its doors shut. And not one club would disagree with the angry words of Colchester United chairman Robbie Cowling as he penned an open letter to Boris Johnson.

Calmly setting out the changes to procedure that clubs had been making to ensure their grounds could safely welcome back fans, as well as confirming the ongoing safety processes that have been in place since he bought the club fourteen years earlier, the final paragraph of Cowling's letter revealed the level of incredulity – and the depth of despair – of not just him but the football world in general. It was a point with which few could disagree.

'Just so I understand it when I'm having to lay off even more staff, can someone explain to me again how I can safely sit in a confined aeroplane with three hundred other passengers and I can safely eat inside a restaurant or drink inside a pub until 10pm, but I can't safely attend a football match which is predominantly outside and has been certified as safe?'

Back in Edinburgh, Dan Gray would agree. The honour of being at that single pilot match had begun to properly crystallise. 'Privileged is definitely the right word. We don't know when we're going back.'

*

It's mid-morning and, at the studios of BBC Radio Sheffield, Andy Giddings is in work earlier than any employer would have the right to demand. As the station's sports editor, Giddings was down in west London last night commentating on an EFL Cup encounter between Fulham and Sheffield United. He arrived back at the studios at 1.20 a.m., dropped off the radio car and headed home, reaching his front door fifteen minutes later. This morning he's sanguine about such demands; this is what's required from the travelling-wide-and-far occupants of the commentary box. 'As trips to Fulham go, it was seamless. Craven Cottage is a lovely place to watch a football match and the traffic was excellent. It was just a long day. Caffeine and sugar are propping me up.'

Giddings is in work already because, when your patch covers a Premier League club, three Championship sides and a League One outfit, there's no room to pause, little time to come up for air. It's a Thursday, so there are three press conferences for him and a colleague to cover today. Then there's the preparation needed for the games the station is broadcasting live commentaries of come both Saturday and Sunday. Pray the caffeine works.

If Giddings and his two-man team only concerned themselves with matters on the pitch, their working days and nights would be full enough. But then there's all the off-the-field shenanigans that need reporting and analysing. And few places have witnessed the level of off-the-field shenanigans in recent years that Sheffield Wednesday Football Club has.

During the summer, Wednesday were docked twelve points for breaching spending rules, namely the inclusion of the sale of their Hillsborough Stadium in their accounts for the 2017–18 season, despite the sale – to their own owner, the Thai businessman Dejphon Chansiri – occurring a year later. In doing so, the club were able to post a pre-tax profit for that earlier season and thus avoid a points deduction under the EFL's profitability and sustainability rules.

In November 2019, the EFL charged the club with misconduct and, a full eight months later, Wednesday found themselves with a points deduction anyway. They probably, though, felt a strong sense of relief. They had got out of jail. Had the disciplinary panel's decision come in a more timely fashion, the deduction may well have been applied to last season, when twelve points taken off their total would have meant relegation to League One. (It would also have meant Charlton Athletic staying in the Championship; that the Addicks went down was met with no small amount of anger in south-east London when the punishment was meted out to the Owls.) Having reported on the whole saga from very close quarters, Giddings is ideally placed to measure the sense of relief across the blue half of the city that Wednesday had dodged a bullet.

'I think across the city there is a certain sense of disbelief that the administrators of the football club and the owner had put them in a position where this was even a possibility. Across the course of eighteen months, they had numerous chances to make this purchase between the two different companies set up by Mr Chansiri. They were afforded different meetings with the EFL, who the records show gave them various warnings and opportunities to get this sorted out before the deadline and then after the deadline. And they still didn't take them. Had the EFL not chased the wrong charge, Sheffield Wednesday would have been relegated.'

At least there are now forty-six games ahead to wipe out the deficit and also amass enough points to avoid that drop into the third tier. 'Most fans are in disbelief that they have a chance to get themselves out of it. In my personal opinion, staying up will be a major achievement. There is an element of the Wednesday support that likes to look on the club and the team with rose-tinted glasses, but I think most fans will be relieved if, come the final whistle on the last day of the season, they're still a Championship team. A lot of the fans would look at the recruitment, and the start to the season, and think, *Well, they'll be more than fine. Possibly mid-table.* But the more realistic supporters think that fourth-bottom, even by a single goal, come May is more likely how it's going to be.'

Wednesday's points tally might be in negative figures for a good few weeks, but their start to the season has offered glimpses of optimism, most notably a win over Cardiff and a home draw against Watford. However, at best, this season will simply mean survival as a Championship club. The biggest reward will be yet another season in the second tier. It's now twenty years since the Owls darkened the doorstep of the Premier League. It's not so much that the club is a sleeping giant – more that it's been in a coma for two entire decades.

The current Wednesday manager, Garry Monk, has been

in the job for a year and led the club to sixteenth place in his first season. That, to many Wednesday fans, would need to be improved upon were this a regular season. The points deduction, though, dictates it's anything but. And it gives Monk some breathing space, a little room to enact the 'cultural change' he's promised to bring to Hillsborough. Giddings agrees. 'The points deduction does help him. People will look on the circumstances with a degree of sympathy.'

Not that all Wednesday supporters will be cutting the manager too much slack, though. 'The fanbase is split on Garry Monk. A lot of the fans look at the squad, and look at the players who have been within that squad for some time, and say that because some of these players helped Sheffield Wednesday get into the play-offs some years ago, any manager who doesn't get this team into the play-offs is then by default a failure. But these fans are glossing over the fact that these players haven't played at their highest levels for several seasons. They are a couple of years older and a couple of years more injured. They still need a decent centre-forward or two. They haven't got one. Essentially, from back to front they're not bad, but finding a decent centre-forward is proving difficult. Any player who wants to join Sheffield Wednesday right now – twelve points behind everybody else – must really want to join Sheffield Wednesday.'

The ongoing circus at Hillsborough is set into sharp relief by the success of the red half of the city. Last season, Sheffield United, on their return to the top flight after an absence of thirteen years, finished an extremely creditable ninth. Their boss, Chris Wilder, was second only to Jürgen Klopp in the League Managers' Association Manager of the Year award. The blue half can only gaze on in envy.

'At the minute,' Giddings concludes before heading off for one of today's press conferences, 'Sheffield Wednesday are an average Championship team. The support is there and is wonderful. The people who have run Sheffield Wednesday don't really deserve it. The hope is that somebody one day will get it right. A lot of people – me included from a neutral's perspective – thought it would be under Chansiri. Sadly, everybody's still waiting.'

In his kitchen, a couple of miles west of the Radio Sheffield studios, one person has been waiting a long time. Jon McClure, frontman of the band Reverend and the Makers, is a lifelong Wednesday fan, but his patience has been sorely tested over the years. Over the decades, in fact. Born into a staunch Wednesday family on his mother's side, there would have been no escape from the pain even if he'd wanted to turn his back on the club. Choice and free will didn't come into it. 'My nanna danced with the players in the '30s when they brought the FA Cup back and my uncles were all Wednesday fans.' Sheffield United barely got a look-in on the family tree. 'Out of about fifty cousins, only two of them are Blades.'

McClure had his first season ticket as an eight-year-old at the turn of the 1990s and remained a season-ticket holder through-out that decade – 'that great period of Chris Waddle and John Sheridan. I had a bit of a hiatus when the band kicked off. I sort of lost it for a few years, but got it back around 2010. I've been back as a season-ticket holder ever since. I love it.'

Despite his celebrity, McClure would never be found sipping a latte or enjoying a customary prawn sandwich behind the glass of a hospitality suite. 'No, I always sit in the stand. I've never had any corporate hospitality from Wednesday. I think they're quite reluctant to throw their lot in with me because I'm quite honest about the chairman and about the way the club is run. I did get quite pally with [former manager] Carlos Carvalhal. He was quite a cultured gentleman, so me and him and my brother used to go and have a *cataplana* together at a local Portuguese restaurant. Other than that, I've always been on the terraces or in the stand with my friends and my brother and my cousin.

'I now take my little lad, who's five. I've told him he can follow any religion he wants, be any person he wants, be whatever sexuality he wants, but there are two things he has to do: be nice to his mum and follow Sheffield Wednesday. Do those and you're all right with me.'

After those comparatively successful years during the '90s, McClure admits that being a Wednesday fan has meant enduring a downward spiral ever since. For sixteen of the twenty seasons since the Owls last graced the Premier League, they've been mired in the second tier. The silver lining of the club's underachievement is that McClure has got to watch his team in his favourite league.

'I love the Championship. It's still got a bit of rough and tumble. It's the heartland of English football – Preston North End, Nottingham Forest, Derby County, Sheffield Wednesday ... I wonder to some degree whether the Championship is like what the old First Division was – and would still be had the Premier League never happened. It's harking back to how football used to be. You still get a bit of long ball. You still get some dodgy decisions. I know a few Man City fans and they all continue to talk about those years down in the Championship and League One with a real, genuine fondness. They've won titles and been in the quarter-finals of the Champions League, but love talking about Shaun Goater scoring for them away to Rochdale.

'In the Championship, football remains the people's game. I watched the Champions League semi-finals last month and it was an energy drinks firm versus a Middle Eastern dictatorship. That's not sport, is it?' That said, McClure would grab, with two hungry hands, the opportunity for Wednesday to exit upwards from the Championship. 'We all want our clubs to do as well as humanly possible. I'd love to hear the *Match of the Day* theme music and Gary Lineker introducing a match where we've tonked Liverpool. Can you imagine?'

For now, such a scenario does take some imagination. A proper leap of imagination. McClure still feels bruised after the whole affair of the stadium sale and the points deduction. And one man is in his sights to take all the blame. 'Our chairman is incredibly incompetent and he's lucky he didn't get us relegated to League One. He's the son of a successful businessman, rather than being a successful businessman himself. The difference is quite startling. For me, the guy is well-intentioned. I don't think he's an evil guy. But because we've never really had huge invest-ment, a lot of our fanbase pays him deference largely because he's rich. But wealth doesn't equal competence, does it?'

Despite Wednesday's position as one of those quintessentially Championship clubs, McClure remains positive about the task ahead. He cites incoming signings like the seasoned defender Chey Dunkley and Chelsea loanee Izzy Brown as reasons to be cheerful. And then there's the presence of Barry Bannan, a player recently given the captain's armband and arguably English football's tidiest midfielder outside of the Premier League. 'He's underrated on every possible level,' says McClure. 'He could go and have a game for Barcelona and he wouldn't look out of place. That's not an exaggeration.'

McClure is in the camp of Wednesday supporters willing to give Garry Monk a fair crack at the not-inconsiderable task at hand. 'Let's give him time. He seems like a decent fella. He was clearly annoyed at some of the players who were on the books and he's got rid of them now. A lot of the problems aren't of his making. I hope he's a good fit for Wednesday. But it's going to be two or three seasons before we get back into a position to challenge for those top places. We're a way off at the minute. I think we need to get behind him. It serves no purpose to slag him off. And the other thing is: who else are you going to get?'

If this season is to be a make-do-and-mend one on the pitch, it's the same off the pitch: supporters are having to show their love via an iFollow subscription. McClure clearly misses the match-day experience, meeting up with family and friends. And, of course, initiating his eldest son into the rituals and practices of Saturday afternoons. These can't be handed down in front of a television screen. 'No one wants a five-minute buffering episode, do they? It's like going to a gig and the guitarist reaching for, and then tuning up, another guitar in the middle of the set. You come back after a prolonged buffer and you're two-nil up.'

An ironic chuckle. 'Or, more likely, two-nil down.'

McClure is something of a soothsayer. A few days later – as he and his son honour their new routine of watching each match from the sofa rather than the stands, and quite possibly enduring another buffering episode – Wednesday do indeed go two-nil down in this, their last match in September. Today's opponents, Bristol City, are capable if unspectacular, and run out comfortable winners.

There are odd sparkles of consolation, of hope. On today's showing, McClure is correct about Barry Bannan. Despite his diminutive stature, he is head and shoulders above anyone else in this Wednesday side. Playing in a deeper-lying position than the number ten on his back might suggest – more in the quarterback role of an Andrea Pirlo – he's also reminiscent of Archie Gemmill in many ways: short, Scottish, strawberry-blond beard, thinning on top. Like Gemmill, he's also all left foot, but no matter. It's a left foot that would invariably be described as 'cultured'. Yes, he would know what he was doing lining up for Barcelona.

Anchored by Bannan, Wednesday are patient, not allowing that league position to panic them. Sharp in the challenge, they're particularly strong at forcing turnovers and regaining possession. What they're not strong at is scoring goals. As Andy Giddings indicated, they lack a potent edge upfront. Jordan Rhodes – scorer of more than 200 club goals across his career, including a particularly high-yield spell in the Championship

with Blackburn – is on the subs' bench today. Well, what quali-
fies as the subs' bench these days. He's in the stands, parked at
a Covid-safe distance from his fellow subs. In the warm-up
before the game, he was finishing in very tidy fashion, knocking in goals for fun. But, since first putting on the blue and
white stripes three and a half years ago, he's still yet to do it for
Wednesday. Today he comes on with just seven minutes left and
the Owls a goal down, leaving him little time to affect a match
against one of the league's most consistent teams.

Bristol City's second goal comes in stoppage time, leaving
Wednesday aground at the bottom of the table. That negative
balance is not budging. Even with a run of wins, it'll take a good
few weeks to clear, a good few weeks to get back into the black.

This is good news for Wycombe – and they're in need of
exactly this at Adams Park. That stoppage-time surrender to
Rotherham on the opening day of the season was far from
the worst it got for them in September. A five-nil routing by
Blackburn Rovers came a week later, followed by a two-nil
reverse to Swansea.

Perhaps those bookies have been right all along. Maybe
Wycombe are destined to be the league's whipping boys. Three
matches, three defeats. Not that the manager's optimism shows
the slightest dent. 'I'm sure we're not far away from our first
win,' Gareth Ainsworth breezily predicted after the Swansea
game. It was a brave statement, bearing in mind his side had yet
to score in 270 minutes of Championship football.

For now, though, the Chairboys could take a strange sort of
comfort from those three non-scoring defeats. They wouldn't
be going into October propping up the table. Still in negative
equity, still eight points away from ground zero, Sheffield
Wednesday held that ignominy. The soap opera continued.

*

## Championship table, 30 September

|  |  | P | W | D | L | F | A | Pts |
|---|---|---|---|---|---|---|---|---|
| 1 | Bristol City | 3 | 3 | 0 | 0 | 6 | 1 | 9 |
| 2 | Reading | 3 | 3 | 0 | 0 | 6 | 1 | 9 |
| 3 | Swansea City | 3 | 2 | 1 | 0 | 3 | 0 | 7 |
| 4 | AFC Bournemouth | 3 | 2 | 1 | 0 | 5 | 3 | 7 |
| 5 | Watford | 3 | 2 | 1 | 0 | 2 | 0 | 7 |
| 6 | Blackburn Rovers | 3 | 2 | 0 | 1 | 11 | 3 | 6 |
| 7 | Luton Town | 3 | 2 | 0 | 1 | 3 | 2 | 6 |
| 8 | Birmingham City | 3 | 1 | 2 | 0 | 2 | 1 | 5 |
| 9 | Millwall | 3 | 1 | 2 | 0 | 2 | 1 | 5 |
| 10 | Brentford | 3 | 1 | 1 | 1 | 4 | 2 | 4 |
| 11 | Queens Park Rangers | 3 | 1 | 1 | 1 | 5 | 4 | 4 |
| 12 | Coventry City | 3 | 1 | 1 | 1 | 4 | 4 | 4 |
| 13 | Norwich City | 3 | 1 | 1 | 1 | 3 | 3 | 4 |
| 14 | Rotherham United | 3 | 1 | 1 | 1 | 2 | 2 | 4 |
| 15 | Stoke City | 3 | 1 | 1 | 1 | 1 | 2 | 4 |
| 16 | Cardiff City | 3 | 1 | 0 | 2 | 3 | 4 | 3 |
| 17 | Huddersfield Town | 3 | 1 | 0 | 2 | 1 | 4 | 3 |
| 18 | Middlesbrough | 3 | 0 | 2 | 1 | 2 | 3 | 2 |
| 19 | Preston North End | 3 | 0 | 1 | 2 | 2 | 4 | 1 |
| 20 | Barnsley | 3 | 0 | 1 | 2 | 0 | 3 | 1 |
| 21 | Nottingham Forest | 3 | 0 | 0 | 3 | 0 | 5 | 0 |
| 22 | Derby County | 3 | 0 | 0 | 3 | 1 | 8 | 0 |
| 23 | Wycombe Wanderers | 3 | 0 | 0 | 3 | 0 | 8 | 0 |
| 24 | Sheffield Wednesday | 3 | 1 | 1 | 1 | 2 | 2 | −8* |

*Includes twelve-point deduction*

## Leading scorers

Adam Armstrong (Blackburn), 5
Bradley Johnson (Blackburn), 3
Jérémie Bela (Birmingham), 2
Tyrhys Dolan (Blackburn), 2
Lyndon Dykes (QPR), 2
Matt Godden (Coventry), 2
Lucas João (Reading), 2
Kieffer Moore (Cardiff), 2
Jed Wallace (Millwall), 2

## Manager of the Month

Veljko Paunović (Reading)

## Player of the Month

Bradley Johnson (Blackburn)

# October

*'I could never have imagined I'd be
on the same pitch as Wayne Rooney.
How quick the tables can turn'*

— TYRHYS DOLAN

It's raining in Lancashire, sheeting it down. The Ewood Park ground staff are out on the pitch, armed with forks, draining the turf. The floodlights are on full beam. It's three in the afternoon.

But a sustained downpour of biblical proportions is unlikely to dampen the spirits of Blackburn Rovers today. The visit of Cardiff City marks the home side's fourth league game of the season; the previous three have seen them score eleven goals – including five against Wycombe and four against Derby – while averaging twenty shots per match.

Their striker-in-chief Adam Armstrong might be the league's leading scorer, but today's eyes are on another member of Rovers' potent attack. Eighteen-year-old Tyrhys Dolan has, in little more than two full games as a first-team player, excited everyone who's seen him play. The teenage winger looks even younger than he is: short with curly locks and clear brown eyes. Indeed, during any one of the games thus far, the casual observer could have been forgiven for thinking that one of the ball boys

33

had slipped on an oversized first-team shirt and sneaked onto the field of play.

Lining up in the tunnel as the ground staff retreat from the pitch, Dolan trots on the spot, almost hidden behind the beasts of Blackburn's central defence, the man mountains currently trying, in a Canute-like fashion, to stare out the rain and make it cease.

But Dolan's size belies the stature he's carving out for himself at this early stage of the season. Having impressed coming on for his debut at Bournemouth on the opening day, he marked his first match at Ewood Park with a goal against Wycombe, following it up a week later with another against Derby. He's also, in a short space of time, proved himself to be a sure and ready supplier of chances, notching up as many assists as goals. Dolan's instant impact has earned him rapturous praise from the pundits on Quest TV's EFL highlights show and found him adorning the front page of the *Football League Paper*.

The story would be notable if this were the extent of it. But it's not.

After five years in Manchester City's academy, Dolan was released at the age of sixteen, whereupon he was signed by Preston, where he spent a further two seasons, among which was a short loan spell at Northern Premier League side Clitheroe. During the summer, though, he was again let go. Blackburn boss Tony Mowbray, who had previously seen him play against Rovers' U23 side and recalled the winger's stand-out performance, snapped him up, possibly scratching his head as to why the young man had departed Deepdale.

Dolan was more than happy to sign professional terms for Mowbray; the contract offered a chance to progress and develop in Blackburn's U23 set-up, with an eye towards knocking on the door of the first-team squad at some point in the middle distance. Perhaps a couple of seasons down the line. However, opportunity knocked much sooner. With several first-teamers out through injury, Dolan was invited to train with the big boys. Brimming with the confidence of youth, Dolan grabbed his chance, impressing Mowbray with his precocious talent and finding himself in the match-day squad for the Bournemouth game. From rejection to elation in two easy moves.

Further sparkling performances ensued. But, of course, when praise rains down like today's deluge, everyone suddenly knows about you. You're in plain sight. There's nowhere to hide. And this afternoon, at this sodden Ewood Park, the defenders of Cardiff City certainly know about Tyrhys Dolan.

Boasting one of the toughest, most battle-scarred back lines in the Championship, the Bluebirds soon make Dolan aware he's a marked man. They've read the headlines. They've seen the highlights. No space is given and challenges are strong.

But barely a dozen minutes in, Dolan's marker – the Cardiff left-back Joe Bennett, who's only just returned from a long lay-off – goes off injured, replaced by the Irish international Greg Cunningham. The Irishman, himself only recently back to fitness after an entire season out with a cruciate ligament injury, might be a worldly-wise campaigner, but he won't fancy the nippy Dolan running at him at speed for the next seventy-eight minutes.

Cunningham settles quickly, though, nullifying the danger. After half an hour, he and Dolan collide in an aerial challenge. Despite the latter's diminutive size, the Cardiff man comes off worse. He's suffered a sizeable cut that's seeping plenty of blood, so off he retreats to the touchline to have his head stapled.

Worse is to come. Within a couple of minutes of coming back on, Cunningham gets booked for a foul. The omens don't look good: he's been out for a year, his head's been stapled and band-aged, and he's now walking a disciplinary tightrope while up against one of the league's hottest young talents. Young, yes, but wise too. The next time Dolan receives the ball, within a minute of the yellow card being issued, he charges at Cunningham at full tilt. Jink, step-over, jink. The left-back has to hold back. He has to exercise caution. There's another hour of this to come.

Or not. Today, against the guile of the experienced opposition, Dolan does not produce another champagne performance. He's been neutralised, only able to pick out the odd through-ball to Adam Armstrong. Unlike Wycombe or Derby, Cardiff have had the measure of him. They've kept him under wraps. He won't feature in the headlines tomorrow morning. Not all games can be free-flowing goal-fests, after all.

Substituted on the hour mark, Dolan's last contribution is being fouled by Bluebirds midfielder Lee Tomlin, who picks up a caution for his efforts. This is not insignificant. Fewer than ten minutes later, Tomlin is given a second yellow for a wholly unnecessary chop on the edge of the Blackburn penalty area. In the stands, Dolan must be cursing, denied the opportunity to exploit the space that the sending-off creates. None of his team-mates are able to take advantage in the remaining twenty minutes. Rovers' high-scoring streak peters out into a flaccid, scoreless draw. Their motto is '*Arte et Labore*'; there's been more labour than art today.

But it's anything but a frustrated Dolan after the match. He reveals himself to be a considered analyst, a voice of reason, a wise old head on young shoulders. 'We did expect this to happen. Teams are going to notice that we're in good form, especially off the back of scoring nine goals in two games. We struggled to break Cardiff down, even when they went down to ten men.

'Being so young, I think I needed a tough game like that. It's not like a five-nil or a four-nil where it seems like the ball's in our court. There are going to be times when I don't go out and have a great game. Football doesn't work like that. Sometimes it works and sometimes it doesn't. But the knockbacks and set-backs help you. They allow you to appreciate the good times.'

Despite his upbeat outlook, the knockbacks and setbacks

of a fledgling career have left bruises. During his time in the Manchester City academy, Dolan would often find himself played out of position, considered to be a holding midfielder and thus in competition with the academy starlet Tommy Doyle. With pace to burn, Dolan felt he was being asked to fill the wrong hole. 'I felt limited, but I went into training with the right attitude. They could never question that.'

Those subsequent two years at Preston would in the end prove frustrating too. Although playing for the U23s in his more natural position out wide, Dolan's time at Deepdale ultimately encountered another significant obstacle. 'I thought I did well there and deserved a pro contract. When the phone call came, I didn't really get an explanation as to why not. "The club has decided not to give you a pro contract." That was it, really. There was no big speech.'

But the four games Dolan played out on loan for Clitheroe very much accelerated his development, ultimately helping him not to be intimidated when the hulks of Cardiff City visit Ewood Park. 'Coming from scholars' football, that was a shock. It's a big change to go into non-league football – to get battered and beat up. In the short time I was there, I had to mature really quickly as a player. I wasn't prepared for it being such a dog fight on the pitch. As a "fancy" player, I did get some welcome-to-non-league tackles, but I had to be willing to take the hits. And I think I adapted well. In those four games, I got two goals and two assists. I showed that I could do a job, that – even as a small player – I could mix it against older lads, as opposed to just playing against seventeen- and eighteen-year-olds.'

Dolan's confidence stood him in good stead when he made that rapid rise to Blackburn's first-team training sessions. 'I immediately realised this was a chance for me to go and show them what I could do. Some of the lads said, "Wow, who's that? Is that the new signing?"

'I just knew I couldn't let this pass me by. It was one shot and I might not get the opportunity again. Football's a brutal sport. You've got to perform on that chance you get, you've got to grab it with both hands. So when I was on my way down to Bournemouth, I realised that, after so many setbacks and rejections, I was here now. I couldn't let it go. I knew I just had to go out and play like I always had. There was no need to change my game or change who I was as a player.'

That second start for Blackburn found him, as a lifelong Manchester United fan, lining up opposite one of his boyhood heroes, Wayne Rooney ('I could never have imagined I'd be on the same pitch as him. How quick the tables can turn'). But Dolan wasn't intimidated, having settled into Championship football with smoothness and ease. One thing was possibly to his advantage, though. The empty stadiums dictated by the pandemic may have been playing into his hands; this is the same environment as academy football. It's not an alien landscape, as it would be to seasoned professionals for whom twenty-odd thousand screaming fans form the usual backdrop. The biggest crowd Dolan has played in front of was around a thousand at an FA Youth Cup tie when at Preston.

'I was actually talking to my dad about this just the other day. I told him I was glad that the first handful of games have been played when no one's been there. The nerves are still high obviously because I'm on the first-team stage, but there's no one on my back if I give the ball away. No one's there to slate me.'

That Dolan is able to dissect the whirlwind last few weeks with his parents over the dining table is a reminder that he's still a teenager. He lives at home in Altrincham, in the same bedroom he's always slept in. 'Nothing's changed at all. I can't get carried away. Yes, I'm on the TV now and people are talking about me, but I can't let it go to my head. There have been plenty of times when a player has come onto the scene but quickly fizzled out. I've got to make sure that I'm not one of them. "He could have been this He could have been that." I've got to reach that pinnacle. I've got to prove people wrong, those who said I'd amount to nothing and that I'd never get there.'

Certainly the management of Preston North End, for whom Tyrhys Dolan formed part of a summer clear-out, must now be kicking themselves. 'I don't want to say too much,' he offers, ever the diplomat, 'but I'd think so. As a club, you don't want to see an eighteen-year-old who you've let go play in the Championship the way I've been playing. It doesn't look too great.'

He smiles. 'But I don't want to crow.'

*

Sunday morning is a rare quiet time for professional football. No training, no transfer negotiations. Just a pause for breath before the lunchtime Premier League kick-offs.

Coming at the end of the latest international break, this particular Sunday morning should have been even quieter than normal, without a lunchtime game to spoil the peace. But quiet it turned out not to be. At 11.45 a.m., the *Daily Telegraph*'s chief football writer, Sam Wallace, unveiled an exclusive story with the potential to cause seismic tremors across the substratum of English football. Wallace revealed that two US-owned clubs, Liverpool and Manchester United, had been collaborating on a set of proposals that would radicalise the league structure. The leaked proposals, still a work-in-progress and going by the name of Project Big Picture, had many aspects to them, but two main thrusts dominated: to reduce the size of the Premier League, while also placing more power in the hands of its longest-serving member clubs; and to offer a significant long-term bailout to EFL clubs, many of whom had been down to their bare bones since the first Covid lockdown.

The seventy-two EFL clubs, including the twenty-four in

the Championship, would have little concern about the political manoeuvres and power struggles in the top flight. But they had plenty of skin in the game when it came to securing their medium-term financial futures. The proposals outlined an immediate £250m lump sum to be paid to the EFL to shore up the fiscal footings of its clubs.

Also proposed was the scrapping of parachute payments to clubs relegated from the Premier League, which would help the Championship's lesser clubs to compete on a more horizontal playing field. In its place was a guarantee that the EFL would, every season, receive 25 per cent of Premier League television money. For a pyramid whose foundations were crumbling at an alarming pace, this represented a major renovation project. (On this theme, another fund was also offered, one specifically ring-fenced for stadium development.)

For EFL clubs facing significant short-term uncertainty – if they weren't already howling into the abyss – this appeared to be a rescue deal worthy of deep consideration. EFL chief Rick Parry was interviewed for Wallace's exclusive about the effects the proposals would have on English football: 'What do we do? Leave it exactly as it is and allow the smaller clubs to wither? Or do we do something about it?' He noted how the balance of power among the Premier League's big-hitters was of little relevance to clubs in Leagues One and Two. 'The view of our clubs is if the [big] six get some benefits but the seventy-two also do, we are up for it.' (Not quite the seventy-two. Parry failed to acknowledge that the reduction of the Premier League to eighteen teams would mean two League Two sides falling out of the league, dropping the sainted ninety-two down to ninety.)

Championship chairmen queued up to express how impressed they were with what was being proposed. Another American owner – Wycombe's majority shareholder Rob Couhig, a New Orleans-based lawyer who had previously stood for election to be the city's mayor – was gushing in his approval. 'A lot of EFL clubs need money today,' he wrote in the *Daily Mail*, 'and if they don't get money in the next several weeks, there will be blood on the streets.' He saw no alternative to what was being proposed. 'It will enhance all revenues, and put in cost controls that are truly important if clubs are to get away from the current lottery system.'

Rotherham chairman Tony Stewart saluted how the proposals were a realistic way of redistributing wealth in the game. 'We are putting on a show for free out there,' he explained to the *Yorkshire Post*. Peter Ridsdale, advisor to the octogenarian Preston North End owner Trevor Hemmings, reported that there were 'no dissenting voices' among Championship clubs, while also declaring Project Big Picture to be 'a hallelujah for the EFL'.

The Premier League, and most of its clubs, didn't regard it as a hallelujah. With some having only learned of the discussions between Liverpool and Manchester United through Wallace's exposé, their backs were up immediately. The proposals sought to place more influence in the hands of the league's Big Six – those two, plus Manchester City, Arsenal, Spurs and Chelsea – along with the three next longest-serving clubs, at this point Everton, Southampton and West Ham.

Giving the elite clubs even more say as to the direction of Premier League football was, understandably, unpalatable to the remainder of the top-flight clubs. After a meeting held just three days after the leak, the proposals were dead in the water, the Premier League declaring that Project Big Picture 'will not be endorsed or pursued'.

Rory Smith of the *New York Times* observed that the proposals had not been 'an exercise in altruism' and that 'self-interest soaked some of its thinking'. Indeed, he also noted that those opposing clubs had specifically disagreed with the elements that 'threatened their place on a train laden with gravy'. There had, of course, been some degree of reaching out on the part of the project's authors, what Smith saw as 'a sort of *noblesse oblige*, a quid pro quo in which the Football League would be sustained in exchange for the right of the Premier League's dominant powers to shape soccer in England to their liking'.

Smith also acknowledged those who thought the speed at which the EFL climbed aboard with the proposals might have been a little hasty. 'They were simply grasping onto a passing lifeboat, the theory goes; they didn't have time to check if it was flying the Jolly Roger.'

Certainly Luton's Gary Sweet, one of the most considered club officials in the Championship, would have preferred the ideas behind Project Big Picture to have percolated for longer, rather than being poured away almost immediately. Writing in Luton's match-day programme less than a week later, Sweet noted that 'it came and went before we even had time to properly review it and pass comment on an informed basis. Having such an important proposal leaked prematurely wasn't ideal, of course, as it allowed critics to kill it before it was even born.'

Having since had the chance to dissect the proposals, Sweet believed 80 per cent of them to be excellent, highlighting the initiatives around supporter inclusion and facilities funding for special praise. 'The remainder needed working on. Maybe it needed too much work as it disenfranchised too many stakeholders in the opposing corners of the ring. But it's amazing that a topic as hot as this ticked so many boxes in its draft form.'

At the meeting at which the rest of the Premier League clubs put the kibosh on the project, there was at least an acknowledgement that EFL clubs needed emergency attention. A £50m bailout was agreed, taking the form of grants and interest-free loans. Not only was this a fifth of the instant handout put forward by Project Big Picture, but it could only be claimed by clubs in League One or League Two. Not a penny could go to the Championship clubs. The offer was rejected. 'The

EFL is seventy-two clubs, not forty-eight,' grumbled one Championship chairman.

As the pandemic lengthened, however, and as admission-paying fans continued to be kept at a distance, the crisis within the football pyramid was worsening. Gary Sweet called for urgent financial relief which, once the boat was back on an even keel, could precipitate talks on structural change. But all this had to come with one overriding condition.

'Egos and greed need to be put aside, temporarily at least. There's little point selfishly defending your place at the top table if the whole wedding is cancelled.'

*

'To be honest, I never really thought about becoming a manager.'

Jason Tindall sits in the first-floor meeting room at AFC Bournemouth's training pavilion, just beyond the south-east corner of the Vitality Stadium. Along with his office next door, this is the nerve centre of the club's footballing operations. Behind him, a tactics board shows squiggles and arrows and numbers – the coded hieroglyphics of a football coach. Before him, through glass double doors, are the training pitches upon which those squiggles get deciphered, where theory becomes practice.

This is Tindall's sole domain now. He's the one calling the shots. During the summer, the assistant manager assumed the position of top dog after the man he had so faithfully served for the past decade, Eddie Howe, called time on his long relationship with the club. For taking Bournemouth from the relegation zone of League Two to a five-year spell in the Premier League, Howe will forever have Mount Rushmore status round here – the true Founding Father of the club's recent glowing success.

The dutiful lieutenant has now slipped into both Howe's seat and Howe's shoes. And these are big shoes to fill. Yes, Tindall was a major contributor to Bournemouth's advances during the

Howe years, but his appointment still represents something of a gamble by the board; his only previous experience as a manager in his own right was a twelve-month spell as player-boss at non-league Weymouth more than a decade ago.

Not only will Tindall be judged in comparison to what his former colleague achieved, but he must also ensure that Bournemouth's slide from the Premier League is as far as they slip. Salutary lessons must be learned from other clubs – Sunderland, Leeds, Hull, Wigan – who fell from the top flight and just kept falling. Bournemouth need to grab the rope, find a foothold, and start the climb back up.

At the moment, in the glow of a season's very early days, Tindall is making a decent fist of it. The signs look good. Four games in, Bournemouth are third in the table, just a couple of points off Bristol City and Reading, both of whom boast 100 per cent records. The rope has been grabbed, the foothold found.

'When Eddie and the football club came to their decision, I had to sit down and speak to myself about what I wanted to do. Then I spoke to my family and my close friends. When I weighed everything up, there weren't really many options. I could have stepped away at the same time that Ed did, not knowing what the future would hold. There was no guarantee of what life would look like. Or, if given the opportunity, I could take on the role. After all, if I didn't do that, what else would I be doing?

'I think continuity was something that the club wanted – to see a familiar face leading the team. But you still have to earn the respect of the players. One minute they see you as someone else and all of a sudden you're the manager. Are you going to be the same person? Are you going to manage in the same way? These are all questions that players ask and that fans are thinking.

'I've tried not to change my character. When I took the job, I told myself that I couldn't try to become someone I'm not. I can't put on a front. I am me. I've got my own personality and my own way of doing things. I've always kept my distance from the players – I don't think you can get too close to them as a coach or as an assistant manager or as a manager. But at the same time, you need to be there for them and you need to communicate with them in the right way. You have to treat everybody with respect.'

Tindall was, possibly somewhat surprisingly for a rookie manager, given a three-year contract when he took the job. That suggests, should Bournemouth not make an immediate return to the Premier League, the board have a strong supply of patience. Not that Tindall is remotely easing himself in gently.

'We want to get promoted this season at the first time of asking. That's the pressure I put on myself. That's what I want to happen. And that's what the players want and it's what the club wants. We share this common goal. But it's not going to be easy. Only twenty-two or twenty-three per cent of teams who get relegated come back up in their first season in the Championship. It's tough to achieve. But we set out to win every single game. We don't go out there to be defensive. And that's probably helped the start we've got off to.'

For the time being, life is good on this stretch of the south coast – or, at least, as good as it can be in the midst of a pandemic. On this Saturday afternoon, the sun is shining here at the Vitality, ball games are being played in the park across the road, while one optimistic soul is trying to raise a multi coloured kite into the largely breeze-free air. Bournemouth are riding somewhat higher.

The only thing missing today is a snaking queue of fans inching their way into the stadium. The Cherries faithful are, like everyone else, having to applaud their side's success from a distance. It's an issue that continues to frustrate club chairmen. Echoing the words of Colchester's Robbie Cowling last month, in his letter in today's programme, the home chairman Jeff

Mostyn pleads for the application of logic and reason. 'If two or three thousand people can go to indoor arenas such as the O2 or the Royal Albert Hall and watch shows while social distancing, how can the government argue that is safer than watching football outdoors? All we ask for is consistency.' Tindall will once more be spinning his magic before empty stands.

Eddie Howe was far from the only departure from the Vitality during the summer. The blow of relegation was somewhat softened by the swelling of the club coffers through the sale of big-money players. Nathan Aké went to Manchester City for £40m, Callum Wilson to Newcastle for £20m and Aaron Ramsdale to Sheffield United for £18.5m – the very best part of £80m banked.

The wage bill was further eased with a few others leaving on free transfers (Ryan Fraser, Jordon Ibe, Artur Boruc) and a handful of battle-hardened veterans (Andrew Surman, Simon Francis, Charlie Daniels) being released into the wild, their futures yet to be defined. In all, around a dozen players moved on. 'Neither Watford nor Norwich have lost anything like that amount,' Tindall observes, 'and they'll have the same ambitions as us.'

Despite the near-constant swinging of the door marked 'exit', the Bournemouth squad continues to brim with high-end talent, players who've cut it in the top flight. These are names familiar to even the most casual *Match of the Day* viewer over the past five seasons of Premier League football – players like Asmir Begović, Dominic Solanke, David Brooks, Junior Stanislas, Steve Cook, Jefferson Lerma, Dan Gosling, Josh King . . .

It's a squad that, departures notwithstanding, is arguably still the strongest in this season's Championship, so much so that only two new faces have been brought in, both in on loan: the Spurs defender Cameron Carter-Vickers and the Atlético Madrid winger Rodrigo Riquelme, the latter a clear replacement for another loanee, Harry Wilson, who, having briefly returned to parent club Liverpool, was swiftly shipped back out to another Championship club, this time Cardiff City. Riquelme has swapped La Liga for time and experience in England's second tier. The glamour of the Spanish capital has temporarily disappeared from his life. Riquelme's kit is sponsored by West Way Motor Engineers.

Today's starting line-up oozes pedigree and experience, one able to cope with three players being out after the just-finished international break. Even if he hadn't played all three games for Norway during the break, Josh King may not have been in today's squad anyway. There is a squall of gossip currently swirling around the striker, that he's the next player to be heading away from the Vitality.

'Live Is Life', a hit for Austrian band Opus, is played before home matches here these days, a tune only otherwise heard during the past thirty years on Euro-pop oldies radio stations. They used to play 'Sweet Caroline' before switching, but no one quite knows why the change happened. The new song has vaguely inspirational lyrics about the past and the future, but there's no obvious connection to this corner of Dorset. Certainly no one's singing along in the press box.

When the song's strains fade and the two teams take the knee in support of eradicating racial inequality, not all the players from today's visitors QPR do so, rather surprising with half of their match-day squad being black. Those who don't are showing solidarity with the club's director of football, Les Ferdinand.

'Taking the knee was very powerful,' Ferdinand observed, 'but we feel that impact has now been diluted. In the same way "Clap For Carers" was very emotional for us all, it got to a stage where it had run its natural course and the decision was rightly made to stop it. Does that mean we, as a nation, don't care [about] or appreciate our NHS workers? Of course it doesn't.

'The taking of the knee has reached a point of good PR but

little more than that. The message has been lost. It is now not dissimilar to a fancy hashtag or a nice pin badge. What are our plans with this? Will people be happy for players to take the knee for the next ten years but see no actual progress made? Taking the knee will not bring about change in the game. Actions will.'

Ferdinand is here today, sat in the directors' box and sporting a handsome woollen cap. Down below him, his manager, Mark Warburton, limps around his technical area, nursing an injured knee. Warburton combines a sharp intelligence with sheer graft, an ethic derived from his previous career as a currency trader in the City, where he put in high-pressure fourteen-hour shifts, personally making deals worth billions of pounds on a daily basis. Negotiating a loan deal for a Championship hopeful could only be seen as small beer in comparison.

In the year that he's been at QPR, Warburton has created a team in his image: smart, well-organised and hard-working. They dominate the early exchanges, with the winger Bright Osayi-Samuel forcing Begović into a sharp save in the first couple of minutes. His team-mates know the threat he causes opposing defences; almost every QPR ball played forward is in search of the man wide on the right. The Hoops are energetic without the ball too, pressing with vigour and enthusiasm. They've done their homework. Bournemouth have had fifty-three shots on target in just four games. Today, though, the Cherries won't have a single one. Little space is given.

The closest the home side come to scoring is when, after half an hour, Dominic Solanke neatly brings down a long ball out of defence from Chris Mepham and sees his snapshot fly tantalisingly beyond the far post. This will be as good as it gets today.

You have to feel for Solanke. Unlike his team-mates, he wasn't the subject of intense transfer talk over the summer and now, with Callum Wilson gone and Josh King possibly departing, the burden of goalscoring will rest firmly on his shoulders.

It doesn't help that, back in the Premier League, the other Dominic – Calvert-Lewin, Solanke's strike partner at international level as the pair advanced through the age groups – is scoring for fun at the moment. Earlier today, the Everton man grabbed his tenth of the season in the Merseyside derby.

Bournemouth certainly need that kind of firepower upfront. Their midfielders are busy (especially Dan Gosling, who, after two goals against Coventry last week, wants to be involved in everything down the left-hand side), but the cutting edge further up the pitch has gone blunt this afternoon.

Tindall, the man in black prowling around his technical area, occasionally unfolds his arms to point out a deficiency, a defect, in Bournemouth's shape. He looks every part the self-contained manager, despite this only being his fifth Championship match as headmaster.

As the game progresses – or, more correctly, fails to progress – a super-sized dark cloud makes glacial-paced advance across the sky, a slow-moving metaphor for the home side this afternoon. Little of the second half's action is worth noting down. The more senior members of the press corps entertain themselves by swapping war stories about Harry Redknapp, who, of course, earned his managerial stripes here, back when this ground answered to the name Dean Court. Who knows? In years to come, the reporters of the future might be bathing Jason Tindall in a similar glow.

For now, the sun descends and the shadows lengthen. The clocks change in a week's time, a reminder of the dark, hard months to come. And this season – with the compacted fixture schedule and a potential second wave of the pandemic – may be darker and harder than ever before.

Still, any disappointment about today's nil-nil stalemate is assuaged by Bristol City and Reading both drawing too, their 100 per cent records over. Plus, fourth-placed Swansea lost, so

Bournemouth actually end the day in a better position than when they started it. Tindall is happy to take those silver linings however they arrive.

'I see myself as a positive person. I think my glass is always half-full. It's the way I've always been and I like being that way. I like to find the positives in every negative, in every situation. But it doesn't mean that I'm not serious or that I don't take things seriously. It means that I look at things differently.'

Having shared an office with Eddie Howe for so many years, Tindall can't name any aspect of his new job that has particularly surprised him. That partnership with Howe has stood him in excellent stead. 'I was part of almost every decision that was made, whether that was signing players or setting up training or whatever. Obviously when you're the manager, the buck stops with you. You end up making the actual decision, one that you feel is best. It might be leaving a player out of the team. It might be not renewing a contract. I've had to have those conversations and they're never easy. But you have to have them.

'I've not been surprised by, or fazed by, any situations that have arisen, but I'm always learning. Things pop up that you're not expecting and, as manager of the football club, you have to deal with them. I'm open and I want to learn.'

Tindall has been in the Premier League with Bournemouth for the past five seasons and so has had to reacquaint himself with the ways of the Championship, in particular the unrelenting fixture schedule, which demands eight more league matches than in the top flight. While it leaves little time for reflection, does this relentlessness also breed excitement?

'It is exciting, yes, and it works both ways. When you're winning games and doing well, you just want the next game to come around quickly in order to continue that momentum. The flipside is that if you lose a game, you've not got too long to dwell on it and feel sorry for yourselves. You've got to pick yourself up, dust yourself down and take the opportunity that's just around the corner to put it right. The only negative is that you don't get the chance to do a lot of quality work on the training field with the players.

'The next game is always right there.'

\*

Sixty-six minutes into that goalless encounter at the Vitality, the number 37 appeared on the QPR subs board, its digital display cutting through the dimming light. The club's latest signing was about to be unveiled.

Nearly a fortnight after signing on transfer deadline day, the thirty-something sub unzipped his tracksuit top and bounced up and down on the touchline, his adrenalin high. For although here was a man with more Championship experience than most, his latest move – the sixth time he'd signed for a second-tier club – had really made his heart sing. He was finally wearing the shirt of his boyhood team Albert Adomah had come home.

He hadn't always been a QPR fan. Up until his mid-teens, the Adomah family lived in Greenford, near Ealing, during which time he'd been a Manchester United fan. Then a house move a few miles east down the A40, to the borderlands of Shepherd's Bush and White City, saw him change allegiances. 'As a kid in the late '90s and early 2000s, I was a glory-hunter, but when we moved into west London from Middlesex, I thought I needed a London team. Chelsea, Fulham and Brentford were all in the vicinity, of course, but QPR were the closest, so I went for them.'

Loftus Road was just a five-minute walk from the Adomahs' new home. 'We used to get complimentary tickets from the youth centre I went to,' he explains, a little smile of embarrassment playing on his lips. 'But sometimes I sold my ticket for a little extra pocket money. I used to collect autographs too. I had

Paul Furlong's autograph, and then ended up playing with him at Barnet. I had a shirt that I tried to get all the players to sign, helped by a friend of mine who was a steward at the ground.'

While teenagers like Tyrhys Dolan are this season taking their first baby steps in the Championship, Adomah has experience oozing from every pore. His QPR debut against Bournemouth – when he almost scored with his very first touch in the blue-and-white hoops – was his 406th game in this division. Having been spotted by Barnet while playing for Harrow Borough in the Isthmian League, Adomah's Championship career started at Bristol City and has since touched down at Middlesbrough, Villa, Forest and Cardiff, during which time he forged a reputation as a pacy winger with an eye for goal. He's been one of the league's most consistent performers over the last decade, racking up the appearances while displaying an enviable ability to evade injury. Now, at the age of thirty-two, Adomah has belatedly got to sign for his boyhood club, after rumours of him joining had circulated on at least two previous occasions.

'About six years ago, I was linked with them while I was at Middlesbrough, but the fee was something like two million, which I think was too much for them to pay. Four years later, I was linked with them again and I thought it was going to happen. Again, though, it fell through for financial reasons. I really wanted to come back to London and to the team I supported. But it didn't happen.

'I guess it's third time lucky. I went on loan to Cardiff last season while I was at Forest, but went back to the City Ground at the start of this season. I had eight months left on my contract but they didn't want me there, so we came to a mutual agreement. This time I was a free agent, so there was no transfer fee to get in the way. It was my wages and that was it.

'But I didn't know it was happening. My agent rang me.

'"Guess what, Albert? Guess what club wants you?"

'"Cardiff?"

'"No, no. It's a London club."

'Straight away I knew it was QPR, but I was still in shock, in disbelief. "Are you sure?" And once I knew they wanted me, I didn't even ask my agent how much I was getting or anything. I just said, "Look, make it happen."

'I was actually in White City when I got the call. I'd gone to visit my mother-in-law, who lives opposite the stadium. I was actually going to go to the club shop that day to buy a new QPR shirt for myself. But then I got the call. I saved my money and got one for free . . .'

Over the last decade, Adomah has been the quintessential Championship player for a host of quintessential Championship clubs. On two occasions he's contributed to successful promotions to the Premier League – with Middlesbrough in 2016 and Villa in 2019 – but neither occasion led to a long stretch in the top flight for himself. Adomah has still only played twice in the Premier League, the opening games of Middlesbrough's 2016–17 campaign. Soon to head to Villa Park back in the Championship, those 121 minutes still taught him what separates the two divisions.

'The difference was decisive thinking,' he explains, snapping his fingers to emphasise his point. 'Teams think sharp. They pass forward quickly – three or four passes and then there's a shot on goal. In the Championship with Middlesbrough, it was slower. It was more like seven or eight passes.'

He's philosophical about that personal relegation, heading back to the Championship after just those two games. 'Reaching the Premier League with Middlesbrough was an amazing feeling, but sometimes in football it's business. I really wanted to stay there and I was supposed to get a new deal, but it didn't go to plan. They signed a few new players and rewarded them, whereas some of the players who worked their way up, and who probably deserved something, were told, "Okay, bye. See you later. You helped us get here but now we can get better players." That's how it felt to me.

'Sometimes it comes down to financial matters. It's my career, my job. Sometimes people don't understand that. But footballers have got bills to pay too. At any given time, anything can happen to you, so you have to make sure you're secure. You could get injured and it could be all over. What's your plan B?'

Like many players who rise into the professional ranks from non-league, Adomah has a grounded outlook and plenty of experience in the real world, something that few academy graduates possess. He has qualifications in painting and decorating, having studied at the same north-west London college as football's most famous electrician, Stuart Pearce.

'Working a nine-to-five apprenticeship woke me up. It made me appreciate working hard for my money. I came from non-league and worked my way up to the top, step by step, all the way to playing for Ghana at the World Cup. I was just playing local park football when I was sixteen or seventeen, but I thought if I worked hard, I could maybe one day play for my favourite club and for my country. I could see them building the new Wembley Stadium from my mum's flat. I could see it all lit up and I thought, *You know what? It would be amazing to play there one day.* And I've now had the privilege of playing there in three play-off finals.'

Adomah's experience and philosophy were clearly factors in Mark Warburton bringing him into the QPR dressing room. The current squad is a youthful crop, one that could benefit from a wise, old(ish) head. But despite that enviable Championship pedigree, Adomah is by no means guaranteed a starting place in Mark Warburton's side. The current sparkling jewel of the Rangers team is a man who plays in Adomah's position wide on the right: Bright Osayi-Samuel. The side's number ten, Ilias Chair, is also more than capable out on the wing, while Warburton recruited another winger/forward the same day he signed Adomah – the former Arsenal player Chris Willock, brought in from Benfica. But the elder statesman is positively relishing the struggle for supremacy within this crowded paddock.

'It's healthy competition. I've played at clubs where there's been no competition and it doesn't help you perform. You get comfortable. You get picked every Saturday whether you win or lose. Our wingers here all push each other. I'm a bit older, so my legs might not be as sharp as those of the younger ones, but I still want to start games. I want to play every game.'

The ambition doesn't end there. 'I still want to get my third promotion from the Championship. I've only played those one and a half games in the Premier League, and it would be great to play some more for the team that I love and support. That would be an amazing feeling. We all want to reach the promised land.'

Whether Adomah's track record will propel a QPR ascension this season is debatable; the club's name rarely crops up in discussions about likely promotion candidates. Nonetheless, they'll surely benefit from him knowing this league inside and out, from his familiarity with its possibilities and its pitfalls.

'The Championship is an amazing league. It's just so competitive. I've been here for ten seasons now and have played in the play-offs maybe six or seven times. And I've also experienced relegation with Bristol City, which was the lowest time. Every season is very open, no matter what team you are. Anyone can finish in the top six. And the beauty of the Championship is that there are two opportunities for promotion. If you don't finish in the top two and go up automatically, you have a chance to play in the play-off finals. And those play-offs make it even more exciting.'

And, having signed a two-year deal, Adomah has a couple of

opportunities to add another Championship promotion to his CV. With his family settled in the West Midlands, he's currently living in a hotel, spending his time away from the training pitch looking for a small apartment for himself. For a player happy to move around the country to advance his career, those feet itch no longer. 'Hopefully this will be my final club. If I can retire here on a high, that would be amazing.

'People say you dream to do things, but this wasn't a dream. This was meant to happen.'

*

How many stewards does it take to hold down a gazebo in a gale-force wind?

Four, apparently. One on each corner. But this then means that, for the past few minutes, no one's able to take the temperatures of those arriving at Adams Park. A queue of cars begins to build out of the gates and down into the industrial estate.

Storm Aiden has reached the Thames Valley. The resident red kites have decided to stay on their perches in the woods. No taking to the skies today. Anyway, for this afternoon's bottom-of-the-table clash between Wycombe and Sheffield Wednesday, you're more likely to see vultures circling overhead. The pessimists are calling this a relegation six-pointer. In October.

After a middling start to the season, Wednesday come into the game on the back of three successive defeats, making Wycombe the form team of the two, having gained their very first point of the season four days ago in a one-all draw with high-flying Watford. That impressive performance arrested a run of seven straight losses and, although it means the Chairboys only have a single point after eight games, there's still clear daylight between them and Wednesday. The visitors' points tally remains in arrears.

Unsurprisingly, Wycombe field an unchanged side following

the Watford game, although there is a casualty in the dugout. Assistant manager Richard 'Dobbo' Dobson takes charge, as Gareth Ainsworth underwent an emergency operation on his back yesterday. What with Mark Warburton's gammy knee, this management lark seems to come with its dangers. Or, in Ainsworth's case, has the rock'n'roll lifestyle taken its toll? Too much lugging of amps from the back of Transit vans over the years?

In recent games, several crucial decisions have gone against Wycombe. Twice, left-back Joe Jacobson has had goals disallowed direct from corners – his particular speciality. Against Norwich, a clear dive resulted in the late-in-the-game free kick that gave the Canaries all three points. But the team's resolve and unity – arguably among their greatest virtues – means their stores of confidence haven't been depleted. The intensity this afternoon's match is being played at makes it feel much more like a typical Championship game than that season opener against Rotherham. Plenty of blood and fire. The table might suggest otherwise, but Wycombe are definitely growing into their Championship clothes.

With Storm Aiden having blown himself out, Wycombe start bright and sharp, spearheaded by the complementary combination of back-from-injury Adebayo Akinfenwa and nippy Scott Kashket, his socks rolled down like the international futsal player he used to be. Akinfenwa does the heavy lifting, but Kashket puts in the yards, skipping around all over the place, comfortably covering three times the distance of his strike partner.

But it's another combination that breaks the deadlock in the second minute of stoppage time at the end of the first half, when a David Wheeler glancing header meets an in-swinging Jacobson corner. It's the last touch of the half. And its effect is immediate. At the top of the hill above the car park, a vantage point that gives a decidedly limited view of the Adams Park pitch, two

Wycombe fans are watching the game on their phones. They noisily show their appreciation of Wheeler's goal throughout the half-time break. 'Wan-Der-Rers! Wan-Der-Rers!'

Into the second half, the lead feels increasingly slender and fragile. Wednesday have noticeably upped their game, with – almost inevitably – the twinkle-toed Barry Bannan at the centre of things, pirouetting one way and then the other, with all the nimbleness of an aspiring *Strictly* contestant.

Wycombe know they're under the cosh and that they need to see the game out. One-nil will do just fine. When midfielder Dennis Adeniran, currently on loan from Everton, is replaced, he sets what is surely a new world record for the slowest walk off a football pitch by a substituted player. At this point, there are still thirty-five minutes to go. Those are going to be thirty-five very long minutes.

But the home side keep holding out, in particular thanks to some imperious defending from centre-back Anthony Stewart. The minutes slip by. Down on the touchline, Garry Monk is getting increasingly animated as the sun slips behind the trees and the skies darken – from sky blue to deep blue, from deep blue to black.

The six minutes of added time see Wednesday laying siege to the Wycombe goal. Each of their players knows full well what the points difference will be if the score stays as it is – a full eight points, with even Wycombe now making upward progress while the Owls sit mired in negative numbers.

At the final whistle, the celebratory roar comes at an impressive volume, bearing in mind how few people are inside the ground. Waves of applause rain down from the hospitality suites, while the cheers of those two characters at the top of the hill, now in the soot-black dark, ride the air currents.

Richard Dobson has done something that his boss hasn't yet been able to: lead Wycombe to a win in the Championship – and he's in the honoured position of giving the triumphant post-match interviews. In a manner that more than slightly recalls David Brent, Dobson recounts a development day that the first-team squad went on during the past week, aimed at 'cementing our culture for the new lads'. One of the classroom activities was themed around Captain Cook and his four ships: *Endeavour, Discovery, Adventure* and *Resolution*.

'We said, "They're all four traits that we're going to need going into this division." We have to discover; we have to learn very quickly. And the boys have. I think you've seen that from the start of the season to where we are now. We had to show resolve and endeavour to get the result today, which I think the boys did in buckets. And the adventure part is us still being excited after seven defeats to go into the next game. If people thought that Wycombe Wanderers losing games was going to dampen our spirit, I think today showed otherwise.'

Dobson and Ainsworth didn't speak during the game; the latter, watching online from his hospital bed on a strict diet of heavy-duty painkillers, gave his assistant all the keys to the shop. After the game, though, Dobson admits that Ainsworth 'was the first phone call. We've got a very happy guy in hospital at the moment.'

There are smiles in the stadium, and smiles in the hospital, but Dobson reveals a very different emotion fuelled the win after those recent near misses. 'The boys were angry and wanted to put something right. We have had a lot of big game-changing decisions go against us and that has fuelled the fire a little bit. The boys feel it's been unjust, which I agree with. Some of these big decisions have been very tough to take. But they've added to the spirit. The boys feel they've been hard done by and that they deserve to be on six, seven, eight points. Now we're up and running, with four points on the board this week. That fire in their bellies is still going to be there, though. I wouldn't expect anything less. But we'll be a more confident Wycombe now. That millstone of the first win has gone. It's not hanging around our neck any more.'

There are fewer smiles and less bonhomie when Garry Monk faces the press pack. He looks weary, with a slight silvering of his quiff and frosting on his chin hinting at the strain of being a manager in this fiercest of leagues.

At first, Monk's words trace the familiar terrain of a manager trying to make sense of a disappointing defeat. The vocabulary is within easy reach. 'The lads ran their hearts out today ... the team gave everything ... we dominated the game ... just missing that killer edge.'

Mike McCarthy, Andy Giddings' colleague at BBC Radio Sheffield, is the journalist leading the grilling. It becomes the kind of interrogation not usually encountered in the relatively benign environment of the post-match interview, the usual purpose of which is to fill airtime or column inches rather than dissect in any great depth. This was more akin to the penultimate episode of *The Apprentice*, the one where those wannabe entrepreneurs are interviewed by industry rottweilers, their lives and aspirations brutally deconstructed.

McCarthy questions whether there's something more than just a 'killer edge' missing, as a defeat at Wycombe – a fourth straight loss, of course – might suggest. He makes the point that Wednesday may now have to win half of their remaining games to have a chance of staying up. This is a rather tall order, bearing in mind that the Owls haven't won back-to-back games since last Christmas.

'Why do you think you are still the right man to do this job?'

Monk plays a straight bat, explaining the enormity of the challenge, of the 'mammoth task' that this particular season has served up. Still, he also accepts that, even without the points deduction, Wednesday would still be in the bottom half of the table, a situation he admits 'is not good enough for Sheffield Wednesday Football Club'.

'You've scored two goals from open play this season. It's a lack of killer edge that's gone on longer than this week, isn't it?'

The accusation is that today wasn't a one-off, a blip, an anomaly. Monk acknowledges that they've had a bad week, that they've not been creating enough chances of late, which he partly puts down to strong defending from the opposition. But it's also about making the correct decisions in the final third of the pitch. 'Of course that needs to improve.'

The interview then drops a couple more degrees. The exchange gets chillier.

'I'll go back to my original question. Given the record, why do you still believe you are the right man to lead them through this difficult challenge?'

'Because I believe in the work that I do. I've proved that I can win games in this league ... I'm not going to lose belief in myself and what I do.'

Monk doesn't lose eye contact with McCarthy, those steel-blue eyes focused on his interrogator.

'I take full responsibility. I have no problem with that. But asking me whether I feel I'm the right man for the job or not? Of course I do.'

'How much is this hurting you right now?'

'What do you think?'

'Well, I would say an awful lot but sometimes it ...' He pauses. 'Put it into words. What's your weekend going to be like now?'

'I don't think my personal life has anything to do with you. If you're questioning whether I'm hurting or not, have a think about what you're saying to me.'

'I didn't question *whether* you were hurting or not. I was asking how much. That's different.'

'Well, put it this way: I'm not going to have a great weekend.'

*

## Championship table, 31 October

| | | P | W | D | L | F | A | Pts |
|---|---|---|---|---|---|---|---|---|
| 1 | Reading | 9 | 7 | 1 | 1 | 17 | 6 | 22 |
| 2 | Swansea City | 9 | 5 | 3 | 1 | 12 | 5 | 18 |
| 3 | AFC Bournemouth | 9 | 4 | 5 | 0 | 12 | 7 | 17 |
| 4 | Norwich City | 9 | 5 | 2 | 2 | 12 | 8 | 17 |
| 5 | Middlesbrough | 9 | 4 | 4 | 1 | 9 | 5 | 16 |
| 6 | Watford | 9 | 4 | 3 | 2 | 8 | 5 | 15 |
| 7 | Millwall | 9 | 4 | 3 | 2 | 10 | 8 | 15 |
| 8 | Stoke City | 9 | 4 | 3 | 2 | 10 | 9 | 15 |
| 9 | Brentford | 9 | 4 | 2 | 3 | 16 | 11 | 14 |
| 10 | Bristol City | 9 | 4 | 2 | 3 | 12 | 10 | 14 |
| 11 | Birmingham City | 9 | 3 | 4 | 2 | 7 | 6 | 13 |
| 12 | Huddersfield Town | 9 | 4 | 1 | 4 | 10 | 10 | 13 |
| 13 | Luton Town | 9 | 4 | 1 | 4 | 8 | 10 | 13 |
| 14 | Blackburn Rovers | 9 | 3 | 1 | 5 | 18 | 13 | 10 |
| 15 | Barnsley | 9 | 2 | 4 | 3 | 10 | 10 | 10 |
| 16 | Preston North End | 9 | 3 | 1 | 5 | 11 | 12 | 10 |
| 17 | Cardiff City | 9 | 2 | 4 | 3 | 9 | 10 | 10 |
| 18 | Queens Park Rangers | 9 | 2 | 4 | 3 | 9 | 12 | 10 |
| 19 | Rotherham United | 9 | 2 | 3 | 4 | 8 | 10 | 9 |
| 20 | Coventry City | 9 | 2 | 2 | 5 | 9 | 18 | 8 |
| 21 | Nottingham Forest | 9 | 1 | 3 | 5 | 5 | 11 | 6 |
| 22 | Derby County | 9 | 1 | 3 | 5 | 5 | 13 | 6 |
| 23 | Wycombe Wanderers | 9 | 1 | 1 | 7 | 4 | 16 | 4 |
| 24 | Sheffield Wednesday | 9 | 2 | 2 | 5 | 5 | 10 | −4* |

*Includes twelve-point deduction*

**Leading scorers**

Adam Armstrong (Blackburn), 9

Ivan Toney (Brentford), 9

Lucas João (Reading), 6

**Manager of the Month**

Neil Warnock (Middlesbrough)

**Player of the Month**

Ivan Toney (Brentford)

**Managerial departures**

Sabri Lamouchi (Nottingham Forest), sacked

Gerhard Struber (Barnsley), resigned

**Managerial appointments**

Chris Hughton (Nottingham Forest)

Valérien Ismaël (Barnsley)

# November

*'We're in a hotel two or three nights
a week. You're pulling your hair out
because there's nothing to do'*

— BEN FOSTER

Bournemouth go into November still holding third place, albeit in the close company of the other two relegated sides. Norwich are level on points with the Cherries, while Watford have just a couple fewer. The fact that all three are secure in the top six, while the three promoted League One sides – Wycombe, Coventry and Rotherham – are all in the bottom six, more than hints at the inherent iniquity of the Championship.

QPR's Mark Warburton told it plain a few weeks back at the Vitality Stadium when he calculated that the sides coming down from the Premier League 'have parachute payments that are multiples of our own squad budget. That's a fact. Is it a level playing field? No, it's not. But life's not a level playing field. You have to deal with it. You have to apply yourselves and do the best that you can. We go into the league knowing the situation.'

Like Bournemouth, the soft landing afforded by the parachute payments has meant that Norwich haven't had to jettison all their prize assets over the summer. They did allow two of their star defenders to chase their dreams and stay in the Premier League – Ben Godfrey went to Everton, Jamal Lewis to Newcastle – but arguably the pick of their back four, the fabulously mobile right-back Max Aarons, stayed at Carrow Road, despite heavy interest from Barcelona. Norwich's two attacking midfielders, Argentine Emi Buendía and Norfolk lad Todd Cantwell, evaded the snares of bigger clubs, while goal machine Teemu Pukki remains employed as the team's deadly lone striker. That these four are still pulling on the yellow and green is reason enough for the bookmakers to make the Canaries favourites for the title.

There's no Cantwell for tonight's match; he's out with an ankle knock. This isn't a total surprise. For tricksy playmakers like Cantwell, avoiding sturdy challenges from less-than-dainty defenders is an occupational hazard. And not only on match days. Cantwell picked up the injury in training the previous afternoon.

He's not the only one to be avoiding the clear and very cold conditions inside Carrow Road tonight. With Eminem's 'Lose Yourself' booming out over the PA, the Canaries-supporting customers of Morrisons across the street are reminded of what they're missing. As they load their cars with groceries, they look longingly towards the floodlights with wish-I-was-there eyes. They'd love to lose themselves tonight, regardless of the plummeting temperatures.

Some fans are in the stadium, though. The Gunn Club, the supporters' bar named in honour of Norwich goalkeeping legend Bryan, tonight contains a hundred socially distanced fans who've gathered to watch the match. However, they can only do so on a big screen; a brick wall obscures any view of the in-the-flesh action. Indoor bars can be open, but the outdoor stands of football stadiums not. Several other Championship clubs – Brentford, Bristol City and tonight's visitors Millwall – have done similar, welcoming fans into their grounds, albeit out of plain sight of the actual action itself. Last week, Norwich co-owner Delia Smith wrote an open letter to Boris Johnson to appeal for the application of 'grown-up logic' to the issue of letting face-mask-wearing, socially distanced fans back into the stands, a set-up that has to be 'a far better option than six around a table watching a match inside'. The letter was to the point and inarguably logical. 'Please, Prime Minister, before the final whistle is blown, can we have our football back?'

In the warm-up and the first ten minutes of the game, it's abundantly apparent why Barcelona were sniffing around Max Aarons a couple of months ago. Boasting great skills, balance, awareness and anticipation, he brings to mind Camp Nou legend Jordi Alba – a short and speedy full-back who's ever keen to get forward. He doesn't misplace a single pass all night. On the one occasion he misses a tackle, such is his speed that he's back in position before the resultant cross comes in. If the Catalans had had their way, Aarons might have been lining up opposite Dynamo Kiev in the Champions League tomorrow night. But he's still here in chilly Norfolk instead. He's a patient lad, a good head on his shoulders. And he's only twenty. His time will come.

Pukki is another who's clearly a top-flight footballer playing below himself. Whenever he's released onto goal by a team-mate's through-ball, the Finn accelerates away, for all the world resembling his fellow bearded compatriot Lasse Virén, the multiple long-distance champion, kicking for the finish line on the home straight as he closes in on another Olympic title. Lean and hair-trigger-sharp, Pukki also possesses feet that were made for slotting a football beyond the despairing reach of a goalkeeper. That's exactly what he did twice on Saturday at Ashton Gate. Tonight, however, he doesn't add to his goal tally.

Aside from the retention of key players, Norwich also kept the services of their manager, Daniel Farke. He might have been the man who took them down, but he was also the man who took them up the season before. He's been charged with doing that again. Looks-wise, he could pass for being one of Roger Federer's brothers, albeit one who rejected an adolescence spent on the tennis court in favour of staying indoors and acquainting himself with the classics of European gothic literature. As the game progresses, Farke angrily snaps at his players. Ben Gibson, the loanee from Burnley partnering Grant Hanley in the middle of the defence, is a particular focus of his ire.

They might not have the usual gallery to play to, but neither manager fails to react in time-honoured fashion to decisions that don't go their way. The arms of Millwall boss Gary Rowett appear to be permanently fixed in the quarter-to-three position, whether pleading with the referee or detailing the latest perceived injustice to the fourth official.

The deeper the game goes, the more the visitors fancy they might be taking all three points away from East Anglia tonight. 'Ah, you fucker!' yells a Millwall midfielder when the through-ball he'd just released gets intercepted, his voice echoing around the empty stands. But they come again, with Norwich forced to put in a series of frantic blocks to keep the Londoners at bay. The hearts of the home side skip a beat when Millwall substitute Shaun Williams grazes the bar with a long-range effort late on. The final whistle. Nil-nil.

Norwich enjoyed 61 per cent of possession tonight, as well as creating twenty-seven chances, but even their A-class attacking players couldn't penetrate Millwall's stout defences. 'It's not what we wanted,' grumbles Farke. 'We are not dancing on the tables.'

Despite the draw, Norwich climb into third after this evening match, swapping positions with Bournemouth who – offering proof of the way that the Championship can level itself out – surrendered this season's last unbeaten record tonight by losing at Hillsborough. It's an unexpected result. Bottom-of-the-table Sheffield Wednesday had lost their last four matches, failing to score in their last three. The win takes them to -1 point. They're almost out of negative equity. The debt has almost been paid.

Perhaps the patrons of the Gunn Club have yet to see the Championship table as they silently, disappointedly, disperse into the night. A trio of fans of a senior vintage say their fare-wells out on the street. With new Covid restrictions coming into force in twenty-seven hours' time, which will see all pubs, bars and restaurants closing for a month (and quite possibly longer), this was the last chance for Canaries fans to collectively watch their team. 'I probably won't see you now,' says one, 'so have a great Christmas, Bob.' It is November the third.

A couple of dads, chaperoning three lads of around the age of twelve, are next to depart. The boys – presumably with the effects of two hours' worth of sugary drinks racing through their veins – dash out into the middle of the road. 'Where are you, Millwall? Where are ya?'

If they stopped shrieking, they could hear exactly where Millwall are. Ever since the final whistle sounded, a chorus of chants and songs has rung out into the night sky, disembodied voices coming from a series of adjacent, darkened windows of the Holiday Inn that sits in the corner of the ground. Some of the hotel's rooms offer views of part of the pitch; for a handful of Millwall fans, hiring a top-dollar room for the night is the only way of seeing their team in the flesh at the moment. And even then it's through a pane of glass.

If the voices weren't so happy, you could mistake the scene for a student protest, perhaps a sit-in at a halls of residence over rent prices. The Lions faithful aren't agitated, though. They're very content with a point away from home at one of the division's most fancied sides.

Aside from the chanters, there's also a small gaggle of Millwall fans down at ground level, smoking for England outside the hotel. One of them, Jon ('That's J-O-N. We drop our aitches in south London'), is trying to justify spending £180 on watching a goalless match through a hotel window. 'We could see most of the pitch,' he protests. 'And, you know, we didn't miss a goal.'

There's a twinkle in his eye. 'Still, I'm going to get my money's worth in the morning at breakfast, I can tell you.' He stubs out his last cigarette of the night and pulls his face mask back up. Then his wife informs him that their £180 hotel booking is on a room-only basis.

Upstairs, the chanting shows no sign of fading anytime soon. If Daniel Farke isn't dancing on the tables after the result, up on the fourth floor of the Holiday Inn, the men of Millwall may be doing just that.

*

If chanting from the open windows of an adjacent hotel is a decidedly unconventional way to show support for your team in the days of behind-closed-doors football, twenty-four hours later, Watford's exiled fans are showing theirs in an equally original way. It's through the medium of fireworks, let off in the streets surrounding Vicarage Road.

We're twenty-seven minutes into a home encounter with Stoke City and the Hornets have conjured up an equaliser after falling behind with just ninety seconds gone. The nature of Watford's goal has made a lively match even livelier. Acting captain Tom Cleverley has just smashed the ball onto the underside of the bar and down onto the line. In gathering the ball, Stoke keeper Angus Gunn appears to have been bundled over the line by the teenage Watford striker João Pedro, but despite Stoke's protestations – equal parts bemusement and anger – the goal stands. And it has spurred the local pyrotechnicians into action.

The immediate neighbourhood fizzes and crackles and bangs with the sound of fireworks being set off. Close your eyes and, the bone-numbing temperatures aside, you could just about imagine yourself to be sat in the Istanbul derby, with firecrackers and flares set off around your ears. Echoing across the empty seating, the bangs make it feel as though you're under attack from both sides. A shelling in stereo. Two particularly loud explosions make the press box jump as one.

It remains one-all until half-time, during which a smart-thinking soul plays Katy Perry's 'Firework' over the PA. Earlier on, Watford had trotted out to the theme tune from *Z-Cars*. They've been doing this since 1963, when then manager Bill McGarry adopted it after Everton had done so the season before and won the title. It seemed like an inspired decision; after its first play at Vicarage Road, Watford embarked on a twenty-nine-match unbeaten run. Its magical properties are needed tonight. The Hornets haven't won in their last three games.

Like the squads of Bournemouth and Norwich, Watford have retained plenty of experience in their post-relegation ranks. Tonight, the metaphorical subs' bench will be warmed by the backsides of seasoned campaigners like Troy Deeney, Andre Gray and Will Hughes. There's not even room for that dependable goalscorer Glenn Murray.

Stoke, too, boast a squad of seasoned depth, although tonight they're without stalwarts Joe Allen, James Chester, Ryan Shawcross and Tom Ince. Despite these experienced absentees, they've been finding their feet of late. Manager Michael O'Neill, a man who increasingly resembles a young Tommy Docherty, is leading a renaissance in the Potteries, as three wins and a draw in their last five testifies.

Into the second half, Watford show they're increasingly in need of some attacking variety. While their more athletic players flood forward in numbers, they achieve little penetration. They love their short passes, their triangles. These are undeniably neat and perfectly formed, but they don't advance the cause; they don't unlock Stoke's rear guard.

It takes a defensive lapse to breach the visitors' defences, with Ismaïla Sarr gifted a one-on-one against Gunn, who brings the Senegalese man down. João Pedro scores the penalty. Two-one. Stoke aren't done, though. Twenty minutes later, a long ball is pumped forward and nodded on, landing for Nick Powell to drill it low past Foster. All square again.

Into these last ten minutes, the effects of the neighbour-hood fireworks come to bear as a mist of smoke starts to descend on the pitch, a touch of sulphur in the nostrils. Still visible, though, stretched tight and taut across the seats of the Graham Taylor Stand opposite, are three giant banners. One depicts the familiar smiling and avuncular face of the former England manager and eternal Watford legend. The other two are devoted to quotes from him. One – 'Leave your mark at the club, not just by what you achieve but how you achieve it' – appears to be taken to heart by the home side. Rather than be content with a draw, they push on into stoppage time, forcing Stoke back.

Down the left, the Swedish midfielder Ken Sema turns his defender and gets to the by-line before pulling back for Sarr to side-foot it into the corner: 3-2 and three points. Just how important might these two extra points be come the end of the season? If they're the difference between getting promoted or not, they'll be worth in the region of £170m.

This third Watford goal, like the other two, is saluted by a hail of fireworks in the neighbouring streets. They saved some for the final whistle. The spirit of Istanbul continues on this dark Wednesday night in Hertfordshire.

While a week is a long time in politics, twenty-four hours is a long time in football, especially in the Championship. This evening, forty-odd miles south-west of Vicarage Road, leaders Reading suffer their second successive defeat, comprehensively beaten three-nil at home by Preston North End. Watford, the only side in the top nine to win during this round of mid-week matches, climb back into the top four at Bournemouth's expense. Ten matches in, the season's equilibrium is starting to find itself, but it remains as tight and taut as those Graham Taylor banners. Just seven points separate the top eleven.

There's plenty of intrigue in the lower echelons too.

During the first half of tonight's match came the breaking news that Sheffield Wednesday's twelve-point penalty has been halved on appeal. They're in the black to the tune of five points. The debt has been wiped out. These resurrected points, plus the Owls' win over Bournemouth the night before, cause an eight-point swing, putting Wycombe bottom.

Momentarily, that is. With Gareth Ainsworth still in post-op recuperation, the Chairboys played Birmingham away tonight and a win, their second in as many games, puts them on seven points and back ahead of Wednesday, just an hour after the Yorkshiremen had overtaken them. In fact, the win carries Wycombe above Derby, too. Ainsworth's army are now just a single point from moving out of the relegation zone.

Just ninety minutes are all that it takes to turn events on their heads in the Championship. And sometimes back again.

\*

In room 1251, on the second floor of the Bristol Marriott Royal Hotel, Ben Foster is climbing the walls. Or, in his own words, he's busy being 'bored out of my tree'.

It's late November. Watford play Bristol City at Ashton Gate this evening, but the Hornets arrived in town yesterday, more than twenty-four hours before kick-off. There are still ten hours to go, time that – other than a super-light stretching session – the squad will largely spend lounging around the hotel. Most of them can be found occupying various communal areas, playing games on their phones. The online version of *Countdown* is the game of choice of midfielder Tom Cleverley. Centre-back Craig Cathcart prefers *Super Stickman Golf 3*.

Isn't there a chance of being too relaxed? Is a day of lethargy really the ideal preparation for a need-your-wits-about-you game against the third-placed team in the league? 'Stop talking common sense,' warns Foster. 'It doesn't fly round here.'

There's nothing atypical about today, though. Irrespective of the kick-off time – and regardless of the distance to an away game, even if it's only a handful of miles down the road – Watford will always stay in a hotel the night before. That's only the half of it. It's a practice they even uphold for all home matches too. Whether a Saturday afternoon or a midweek evening, the squad will always have had a sleepover the night before.

'In this league especially, when there are games Saturday/ Wednesday pretty much every week, we're away an awful lot,' explains Foster. 'We're in a hotel two or three nights every week. You're pulling your hair out because there's nothing to do.' The weather in Bristol this morning is miserable too, so there's not even the prospect of a socially distanced, time-filling mooch to admire the architecture of the city centre's finer quarters.

This season, though, Foster has been relieving the boredom by setting up his own YouTube channel under the moniker of The Cycling GK. The twice-weekly videos he uploads cover both football and his other great sporting love, cycling. The football element takes viewers behind the scenes leading up to each match – luxury coaches, well-appointed hotels, temporary dressing rooms in Portakabins, lockdown haircuts and nightly Netflix choices. One of the more eyebrow-raising revelations is the amount that players eat before a match. After a generous meal on the Friday evening, a cooked breakfast will be enthusiastically polished off on Saturday morning, followed by, just a couple of hours later, the pre-match meal. Here – on Foster's plate, at least – a teetering pile of various delights from the buffet awaits.

He's a lively host on his videos, clearly one of the jokers in the Watford pack. A regular feature of each is the positioning of Foster's GoPro camera in the back of the goal, with the footage it records offering a fascinating study of his art. 'A lot of people said, "No, you can't put a GoPro there. You're going to get in trouble." But I gave it a go to see what it looked like and it's flown from there. The response was immediate. No one had done it before. It's a different, unique angle – the goalkeeper's perspective. Young, budding goalkeepers tell me they've found it so helpful: how I move around the goal, the instructions I give, the criticism I dish out.

'Strictly speaking, broadcasting any material from matches is against the rules, so we've been speaking to the EFL, who have been brilliant. There's not been a time when they've said, "No, you can't do that." They've always tried to help. They're big fans of the channel and they want to keep it going.'

These revealing videos have enabled football fans, deprived of seeing their team in the flesh, to keep the machinations of the Championship at the forefront of their minds. And they don't just appeal to Watford fans. Far from it.

'We're playing Bristol City tonight. Over the past week, I've had loads of comments online from their fans: "Can't wait for the Bristol episode." They want to see behind the scenes at their club. They want to see me walking around Ashton Gate. When we get off the coach, what entrance do we use? What do the changing rooms look like? They want to see all that stuff. It's peeling back the curtain to see things they'd never otherwise see. If they're watching on telly, the moment we disappear down the tunnel, that's it. The game's over for them, the show's finished. So I'll take the camera down into the changing rooms and they get to see what happens from my perspective. That's the bit they love. Football fans are nosy creatures. We all are.'

Even fans who've been around the block several times can be

surprised by what's behind the curtain. 'They'll say, "You stayed in a hotel for Wycombe away? That's only twenty-five miles!"'

After nineteen years as a professional at Stoke, Manchester United, Birmingham, West Brom and now Watford (along with eight caps for England), at the age of thirty-seven Foster knows how to avoid getting over-absorbed by the relentlessness of the season. He's discovered his pressure valves: not just shooting the videos, but also getting on board one of his fleet of road bikes to lose himself on the country lanes of his native Warwickshire. This is a chance to leave football aside – although, he admits, that's something he finds remarkably easy to do.

'Football is the last thing I think about, ever. The moment I leave the football arena, whether that's training or a match, not one thought about football passes through my brain for the rest of the day. I love that. And I'm good at it. Whether we win, lose or draw, as soon as I'm on that coach – maybe even as soon as I'm in the shower – I know that game's done. There's no point wasting any emotional energy on worrying about this or that. The moment to worry about your football is when you're in that moment. You can't do anything about it afterwards.'

As the wise elder of the squad, Foster can effortlessly decompress in a way that younger players are unable to. As products of the academy system, they exist in an all-pervasive football bubble. They've never had a paper round; they've never stacked a supermarket shelf (Foster trained as a chef before turning pro). They don't have much of a life away from the sport. As soon as they're on the bus after a match, they're reaching for the games console, ready to play their umpteenth game of *FIFA*. Football is all they know.

'It wouldn't be so bad if all they did was go and play *FIFA*,' explains Foster. 'That would be okay. But the second they get off the pitch and are back in the dressing room, they check their Twitter and Instagram feeds to see what people are saying about them. They'll never meet these people in their lives, but the words they say permeate these players. It goes in deep and it really affects them. I see it all the time. I say to them, "Lads, get off that shit. It's not important. Don't listen to people like that." But they live their life around that kind of stuff nowadays. The people they should be listening to are their coaches, their manager, their team-mates, their parents, their loved ones – not Joe Bloggs in his bedroom posting stuff on Twitter because he's bored.

'Some of these players have been in academies since they were seven, eight, nine. The ones who make it to professional level – which is a tiny, infinitesimal percentage – have always been the best player in their team. They've had people patting them on the back, blowing smoke up their arse all the way through their lives. "You're the best, you're the man." But as soon as they get into first-team football and the world starts judging them, they don't know what to do. They've never had to deal with that.'

If cycling represents valuable time away from football for Foster, it has also made a major contribution to his physical longevity. As he approaches his fifth decade on the planet – and despite all that hotel cuisine – his fitness remains extremely high, with his agility meaning he's arguably the best keeper in the Championship.

'I've had three cruciate reconstructions in my knee over the years. And, at ninety-three kilos, I'm a big guy, so running to keep fit has always been a problem as it impacts the knees and makes them swell up. I found cycling was the only thing that has no impact on the joints whatsoever. I've missed one game in four years which, for someone with my past injury record, is incredible. So the club are very at ease with me getting out on the bike. They trust me to know what I should and shouldn't be doing to make sure I'm ready for Saturday afternoon.'

The result is that Foster is sharp and refreshed, both in the brain and in the body, come 3 p.m. on Saturday or 7.45 p.m.

on a Tuesday or Wednesday. 'Match day remains my favourite time of the week. My competitiveness is stupid still. When that game kicks off, that's me in full-on work mode. Nothing gets in the way.'

In the autumn of his playing career, it would be easy to expect a degree of cynicism and world-weariness to have penetrated that cheery outer shell. But not even the descent into the Championship at the end of last season appears to have dampened his enthusiasm a drop. This is Foster's first season outside the top flight for fourteen years, so what does the goalkeeper with the record number of saves in the Premier League think of what lies beneath?

'I'll tell you the biggest difference straight away. There's no VAR. For me, that's an absolute godsend. I hate VAR. If the referee makes a wrong decision, I can live with that. That's not a problem, that's human error. Without VAR, the game keeps flowing. You know exactly where you stand. If you score a goal, you quickly look at the lino and you know whether you can run off and celebrate. That's the beauty of football. I don't think I've spoken to one player who would prefer to have VAR over not having it.

'And I love the unpredictability of this league. It's so competitive. We play teams who've been promoted from League One, we play teams who, like us, have been relegated from the Premier League. But you cannot predict what the result is going to be.

'In the Championship, teams don't tend to moan. They just get on with it. In the Prem, there's always a moan or an uproar: "This isn't fair, that isn't fair." In this league, it's more a case of, "It is what it is, so let's just frigging get on with it." Fair play to Wycombe, for instance. I loved the way they played against us a few weeks ago. Any ball on that pitch was getting shovelled up to big Akinfenwa upfront and he was just holding three or four players off and then patting it down for his team-mates to get onto. There are so many ways to skin a cat. It doesn't matter how you approach a game. If that's the way your team plays and everybody's on the same page, that's a powerful thing. You'll always have half a chance.'

Having been five years away, Watford are learning to re-adapt to this new life, to this different footballing culture. Their style of play is arguably a little more prosaic and pragmatic than in previous seasons, perhaps not surprising bearing in mind a couple of their more creative players – Gerard Deulofeu and Roberto Pereyra – both signed for Serie A side Udinese a few weeks into the season. The Hornets have also had a few senior players out through injury, most notably their bullish, talismanic centre-forward Troy Deeney. Foster is glad they're returning. 'We're welcoming them back now and I'm sure that once every-body gets into their groove, we'll start picking up win after win. If you win two or three on the bounce in this league, you are right up there. Or, on the flipside, if you lose two or three, you can be right down as well.'

Tonight at Ashton Gate, there's a fair chance that fake crowd noise will again be pumped out over the PA. Foster encountered that for the first time last week at QPR ('Proper annoying!'), but he has acclimatised to the otherwise quiet environment – fireworks, notwithstanding – that is behind-closed-doors football. Naturally, like every other player, he mourns the absence of fans, but there have been particular advantages to a hushed stadium.

'You can hear everyone talking. That's nice. And people are finding that so interesting. Family and friends of mine who've been watching the games on telly have been choosing not to have the fake noise put over the top of the action so that they can hear exactly what players and managers are saying. It's certainly rung a bell in my head to stop swearing so much. I've had to tone it down a little because there'll be kids at home watching without the crowd noise option on.

'But it's good to know that if I'm going to shout something to someone, they're going to hear it. Talking to your team-mates is the most helpful thing you can do. It's so important. The modern-day player is not very vocal at all. It's like a dying art.'

We're an hour closer to kick-off now, and blue skies have broken out over Bristol. Foster grabs his charged-up GoPro and escapes the four walls of his hotel room, heading off for a saunter around the cathedral next door to film footage for his next video. He's the host with the most, with hours to fill and hundreds of thousands of subscribers to entertain.

Later that evening at Ashton Gate, the GoPro will record another masterclass from its owner in that dying art of on-pitch communication. Orders and encouragement are constantly barked out in equal measure. 'Come on the boys! . . . Brilliant, Jeremy . . . Winner! Winner! . . . Hey, Andre, oi! . . . Love that! Love that! . . . Craig, no!'

The deeper into the game, the more Bristol City pile on the pressure. 'Too easy!' is a recurrent message from Foster to his defenders. Despite that pledge not to corrupt the young ears of the nation, his language gets coarser during the closing minutes. The bleep machine will be working overtime when this latest footage gets edited.

The game ends scoreless. After nearly thirty hours in Bristol and all those long periods of boredom, a largely uneventful nil-nil is the reward. But this latest excursion is but one piece of a forty-six-match jigsaw. In a couple of days' time, the routine is revived. Another luxury coach journey, another well-appointed hotel, another generous buffet breakfast, another equally generous pre-match meal.

Repeat, repeat, repeat.

\*

The writing was on the wall. Literally.

On Catch Bar Lane in the Owlerton district of Sheffield, just a goalkeeper's clearance from the main stand at Hillsborough, stands a short section of wall. No more than twenty feet long, it acts as a bulletin board onto which disgruntled Sheffield Wednesday fans articulate their concerns via the medium of the spray-can. The latest missive, in black paint and underlined for emphasis, appeared ahead of the home game against Millwall. It was brief. It was economical. Two words.

MONK OUT

Two days later, those words would be heeded by the board of Sheffield Wednesday Football Club. No matter that the Millwall game yielded another draw, another point in the slow climb to safety. No matter that, the previous Tuesday, Hillsborough had witnessed a victory over much-fancied Bournemouth, ending the Championship's only surviving unbeaten run. No matter that that twelve-point deduction had been halved on appeal. Objective eyes might see the turning of a corner, but the owner didn't. Garry Monk was sacked with immediate effect.

'Being out of the minus points and beginning the next phase of climbing the league,' ran Monk's statement, issued through his union, the League Managers' Association, 'it is a big disappointment to be unable to see the project through.' It wasn't the first time he had publicly expressed disappointment after a blade had fallen. Wednesday was his fifth management position in less than five years; four had now ended in his dismissal.

And, as at these previous clubs, it wasn't just Monk clearing his desk that afternoon at Wednesday. Four of his coaching staff were also out of work in an instant. This is par for the course, the expunging of an inner circle to leave no trace. The manager takes the ire and makes the headlines, but the same fate is handed out to this team of largely invisible men. They are the collateral damage.

One of Monk's quartet was more recognisable than the rest. Retaining his boyish features despite now being in his forties, James Beattie is fondly remembered for his goalscoring exploits for the likes of Southampton, Everton, Sheffield United and Stoke, which garnered him five England caps. In recent times, he's been brought in as second-in-command wherever in the country Monk has been appointed, whether Swansea, Leeds, Middlesbrough, Birmingham or Wednesday. The loyal lieutenant, the faithful footman.

That Beattie was removed from his duties on that particular Monday was, by anyone's standards, harsh. Although Monk had been in charge at Hillsborough for fourteen months, Beattie had only joined him in Sheffield three months earlier, having seen out the previous season working from home while still contracted to Birmingham City.

In those three months at Hillsborough, though, Beattie was effectively an invisible man to the owner/chairman Dejphon Chansiri. 'Being a faceless employee, trying to build relationships with people – especially with Covid restrictions – is difficult.' If the chairman is halfway around the world, only watching matches online, he's not seeing the way that the coaches interact with their players during training or during pre-match warm-ups. It's then easy for the entire coaching team to just be lumped in together in the chairman's perception.

'I'm grateful for any position that I have because there are plenty of people who haven't got that. Gratitude is a big thing that I have. But how does the chairman know about that? He doesn't know that I'm in the training ground at seven o'clock in the morning and that I don't leave until five. I'm trying to do the best I can so that he can realise his ambitions and his dreams to get the club back into the Premier League.'

The chairman–manager relationship is even more crucial. Often, their worldviews are diametrically opposed. The chairman wants success as quickly as possible, while there isn't a manager alive who doesn't want to be granted time and patience. 'It's difficult to persuade a chairman that it might take two or three years to succeed when he wants it in six months. It needs to be a two-way relationship. What gets a manager the time he needs is rapport between the pair. If you talked about things that weren't football, or if you found each other interesting, then the decision – made from four thousand miles away by someone the manager has hardly met – becomes that much more difficult.' Expendability increases with distance and absence.

'You could say the form since January hasn't been good enough, but is the chairman being pressured by somebody outside of the club to make a change? Who does he listen to? Does he read social media and take the opinions of the fans behind their keyboards into account without really knowing what work is going in and the sacrifices being made on behalf of him and his club?'

For Beattie, there's an easy way of improving relations: 'Pick up the phone and ask the manager about results. Don't just have a go at him. Don't go off the opinions of others.' Without a manager's explanation, the subtler forces at work get disregarded. It's the headline – for instance, bottom club beats Wednesday to register their first win – that catches the attention of an absent chairman. For him, the hard maths of the final score will trump the manner of the defeat. 'We had forty-three crosses against Wycombe,' sighs Beattie in his former team's defence. 'And we battered Millwall. We should have scored four or five.' But it would be the absence of goals in both matches that Mr Chansiri's eyes lingered on.

One initiative Beattie had suggested, with the approval of the club secretary and the head of media, was aimed at getting some fan interaction during the days of closed doors. He proposed wearing a GoPro on his chest for the entire day so that the supporters could feel connected to their club again, while also giving them a unique perspective on the life and actions of an assistant manager. It was planned for the week after the mass sackings.

'I was really up for doing it. You would never suggest it if your work ethic was lacking and the structure you have at work wasn't in place. But we were happy with what we were doing. And then the phone call comes and it gets shelved and nobody knows about it. It would have been so insightful.' Insightful for the fans, certainly – and, quite possibly, for the chairman.

Beattie is sanguine about the frustrations felt by managers and their immediate staff when a chairman's finger pulls the trigger. It comes with the territory. 'It was my decision to join. Wednesday proposed a contract to me and I signed it. I can take it. I'm a big boy. I'm not eighteen any more. I know what I'm getting myself into.

'It's always Garry who rings me. He'll be told by one form or another – one time he found out via Sky Sports News. But if clubs want to behave like that, you've got to stick to what you believe is right. How others behave is out of your remit. Control what you can do. I'm very resilient. I was told I would never be a Premier League footballer by my own manager. The best feeling ever is to prove someone wrong when they say you can't do something.'

Among Beattie's successes as a coach have been the upwardly mobile careers of two now-established Premier League strikers: Chris Wood and Ché Adams. Each player was sold for £15m apiece, by Leeds and Birmingham respectively, after he had worked extensively with them. 'I know that, without my input, those deals don't happen.' It's a confidence, and a track record, that Beattie can take with him when a chairman dispenses with his services. 'I accept it for what it is. I'm ready to move on because I know what I do is quality work. The next club that employs me will have a good asset.'

Beattie and Monk first met at Southampton as young players; Beattie was twenty, Monk a year younger. Their playing careers went separate ways but they stayed in touch. Monk began his managerial career at Swansea in February 2014, by which time his pal was already boss at Accrington Stanley. When Beattie left the Lancashire club that September after a year in charge, he was invited to join the team at the Liberty Stadium as Monk's number two.

'People will have seen it as me taking a step down to become first-team coach – "He didn't really fancy it" – whereas the truth is that I loved it at Accrington and I did a good job there with all the challenges I faced. I had started thinking about what type of manager I wanted to be. Did I want to be a Neil Warnock or a Sir Alex, a boss who didn't do any coaching at all and just managed the players? Or did I want to be the type of manager who spends time on the grass to make sure the players are getting the messages loud and clear? And that's who I wanted to be. So taking a coaching job was to improve my coaching so that I could become a better manager when the time comes, when I feel it's right for me to go back in as a number one.'

While he's been Monk's right-hand man almost ever since, Beattie is at pains to impress that this loyalty isn't blind and unthinking. He's no echo chamber, into which Monk throws ideas that go uncontested. 'We've always been the best of mates, but I'm not someone who's going to be agreeing with everything he says. We disagree sometimes, we have heated discussions. It's not that Garry says something and I go, "Yeah, yeah, yeah." I've seen a lot of yes-men in my time and I'm certainly not one of those. I'm sure he would agree.

'You have to have a diverse pool of thinking. I was an attacking player and Garry was a centre-half. So a lot of my ideas are progressive – "Can we attack?" Garry, though, will be more risk-averse. It's a good mix. But, ultimately, he's the boss and so, when he makes a decision, that's the way everybody goes. We're all behind it.'

Now out of work, Monk will inevitably be linked with any vacancies that become available. His name will be a fixture on the bookies' odds board. But should an appointment result, Beattie understands that there's no inevitability that he will follow. Being Monk's assistant isn't a job for life. 'I'm part of his team as long as he sees me as part of his team. But I go with Garry because I choose to. He always asks. He never assumes that I'm going to go to a new club with him. He knows I'm independent enough and intelligent enough to make my own decisions. If I think it's a good opportunity, I'll do it. And if it isn't right for me, I won't.'

Of course, there's also Beattie's intended return to management to factor in. 'My long-term ambition is within my hands. I know what I'm doing. I know where I'm going. Garry knows exactly what the position is long term. It's all open. It's all on the table. It's all been discussed with him. He knows.'

While he waits for Garry's next move, or for an opportunity to become a number one again, Beattie isn't sitting on his hands, staring at the phone, willing it to ring. He's currently doing his LMA Diploma in Football Management ('I'm having to write essays at master's level, which is a challenge . . .'), while also soaking up as much Premier League and Serie A football on the television as he can. Back home on the south coast with his wife Sarah and their three kids, Beattie has more than enough to busy him. There's an imminent house move, for starters.

'Being away from the family is the biggest sacrifice. Usually I would get a job and then get a flat. I'd spend my time during the week up there, fully committed to my job but speaking to the family at night on FaceTime or whatever. Then, whenever time allowed, I'd shoot home to spend time with them, before getting back on the road and being prepared for work come Monday morning.'

Time spent gear-jamming his way up and down the motor-way network is the pay-off for following career dreams. He once diverted from this practice, having believed his new chairman would grant the incoming management team sufficient time to enact their grand plan. 'When I went to Middlesbrough, the whole family moved to Harrogate. That was great. Sarah was happy, the kids were in a really good school, and Harrogate was a beautiful place to live. The job was going okay. There were some challenges, but we were going in the right direction. We'd just won two-one – at Hillsborough, funnily enough – but Garry got the call. So I was in Harrogate with my family, we'd rented a house for twelve months but I was out of a job. That was the last time the family came with me. The volatility of it was too scary.'

Recalling his time in the North-east prompts Beattie to emit a sigh. Just before the axe fell at Hillsborough, he had signed a nine-month tenancy on a flat in Sheffield. It now lies empty.

Still, an instant opportunity soon arises to possibly sub-let it. Four days after Monk, Beattie and the three other coaches were sacked, Chansiri fills the vacancy at Hillsborough by appointing Tony Pulis as manager. It's not the first time the Welshman has succeeded Monk, having replaced him at Middlesbrough three years earlier.

At his first press conference, Pulis reveals that, for the time being, he was happy to work with the coaches retained by Wednesday – Neil Thompson and Nicky Weaver – but would in time bring his own men in. Even so, he stresses how his management style wouldn't be as collegial as that of Monk. 'You need one singer and one song.'

It's a metaphor that could also be applied to the relationship between Wednesday's chairman and any incoming new boss. To what extent Pulis – manager number six of the Chansiri era – would be allowed to sing to his own tune remained to be seen.

\*

The merry-go-round was gathering speed. The day after Pulis's arrival in Sheffield, forty-five miles down the M1 another manager was on the move. The announcement came as no surprise. Overdue, if anything. 'Derby County Football Club and manager Phillip Cocu have parted company by mutual agreement with immediate effect.'

The language of the announcement was familiar, thanking the Dutchman and his also-released staff for their 'hard work' and 'dedication', and wishing them 'every success in their future careers'. It was the inevitable end-play, what with Derby anchored to the Championship seabed.

What was more surprising, what was unfamiliar, was the identity of Cocu's interim replacement. Or, rather, its structure. For the first Cocu-free match away to Bristol City a week later, a four-man group of caretakers, drawn from the first-team coaching line-up, would be taking collective charge: Wayne Rooney, Liam Rosenior, Shay Given and Justin Walker. Observers were unsure how this system could operate. Selection by committee, tactics by majority vote.

Speculation gathered pace all week as to who the permanent replacement might be. On the Thursday on 5 Live, Dalian Pro boss Rafa Benítez – back in the UK after the culmination of the Chinese Super League – tried to chill the rumours that he was the frontrunner for the job. His polite answer as to whether he was interested was, though, qualified with 'at the moment, no'. But how long is 'at the moment'? A year? A month? A couple of days? The bookies remained unconvinced, keeping him as 7/4 favourite for the vacancy, ahead of Sam Allardyce and John Terry.

Earlier that day, the interim management team had held their first joint press conference ahead of that weekend's match. It was an occasion unlike many before it. Sat next to each other in matching black tracksuits, Rooney and Rosenior were singing from the same hymn sheet as they both stressed how a spirit of collaboration was now needed. But each also came across as a fiercely ambitious individual who wanted the job for himself. The press conference became something of a job interview; both were outwardly committed to the collective effort, but the personal aspect was loosely tethered, barely hidden. Hats were thrown into the ring with gusto.

Rooney placed emphasis on the success that other high-profile first-time managers – Steven Gerrard, Scott Parker and former Derby boss Frank Lampard – had enjoyed in their early days as the number one. It was a thinly disguised claim that he didn't, despite the caution of fans and other onlookers, represent a gamble. Rosenior was quite clipped in his pitch, bordering on the passive-aggressive. 'It's one thing wanting the job and another thing being the right man for the job. I have no doubt that Wayne will one day be an outstanding manager, but I also think that I could be an outstanding manager as well.'

Both men had their merits. Rosenior, a year older than Rooney, boasts a full array of coaching badges. Rooney doesn't. But England's highest all-time scorer has the name, the stature and the profile that the club's prospective billionaire owners would love.

Whatever their individual strengths, come that first Saturday, it soon became clear that four into one didn't go. Broadcasters had already pre-empted it. In their pre-match previews and during commentary, they couldn't help themselves aligning the team with the biggest name of the quartet. For them, it was 'Rooney and his interim team', or 'Wayne Rooney's Derby County'. Even for this first game, very few could get their heads around a four-way division of labour.

One particular moment during the second half, with Derby a goal down and heading for their eighth successive match without a win, encapsulated the impractical nature of the set-up. With Rooney on the pitch in a continuation of his player-coach role, late on he was handed a note from Rosenior proposing a change in formation. The confused look with which Rooney greeted the note suggested disagreement with the idea. Or that Rosenior has indecipherable handwriting.

This short scene both dismayed and embarrassed Derby fans already intimate with their club's dysfunctionality. Like many supporters, Chris Parsons – the founder and co-host of the podcast Steve Bloomer's Washing – watched from home through metaphorical fingers. 'It wasn't a good look, was it? That picture of Rooney looking at the note and looking a bit puzzled – being one-nil down and not knowing how to get back into it. I know they need to communicate things to each other, but . . .

'The note didn't bother me as much as the performance, which failed to inspire belief that they could get us out of this. I know it's only one game, but there didn't appear to be much difference to what was happening under Cocu. The set-up was similar, we were trying to create chances in the same way, and players were still being played out of position.'

Having led Derby to a tenth-place finish last season, the pressure had been applied to Cocu to make the Rams serious promotion contenders, as they had been under Lampard. His methods had been dubbed Cocuball, a take on the Total Football concept that turned his native Netherlands into everyone's second-favourite national team in the 1970s. The overriding question, though, was whether English football's second tier was the appropriate crucible for his artistic vision. Chris Dunlavy, columnist for *The Football League Paper*, neatly argued that Cocu 'tried to play chess against opponents intent on playing Hungry Hippos'.

Parsons agrees. 'Cocu's methods didn't really translate to the ding-dong, huff-and-puff of the Championship. He wasn't great at adapting when things went badly; there wasn't enough up-and-at-'em as there was under Lampard, who seemed to have a better knowledge of what you need to compete at this level – and in English football in general. Also, I wonder if our players were good enough to fully execute the sort of football philosophy that Cocu had in mind. I don't think he had the proper squad to pull it off.

'Now we need a firefighter to get us out of this. Allardyce and Benitez are the ones who've got the fans talking the most, but they're also the ones who are least likely to be appointed.' Three days after the Bristol City defeat, Steve McClaren returned to Pride Park, this time as technical director after two spells as manager. His presence suggests the appointment of a more experienced boss, a contemporary, was now highly unlikely. McClaren would, though, make the ideal avuncular figure on whom a younger manager could lean. Like, say, a John Terry.

'I wouldn't be hugely overjoyed with Terry,' says Parsons, 'because of him as a person really. But there is an element of beggars not being choosers. Maybe Terry guided by McClaren isn't the worst prospect. But the issue isn't that we're terrible defensively. We don't need to shore up at the back. We can't score goals for toffee. That's the issue.'

And what of Rooney and/or Rosenior's own chances? 'For me, is appointing two complete novices – and I can't emphasise that enough – the answer to what we need when we're bottom of the Championship after twelve games and can't score? Again, with McClaren at the helm, their chances have probably improved, but I would prefer us to go with a more experienced head, someone who knows the division, who's been in this situation before, and who has definite ideas to get us out of this long term.'

Steve Bloomer's Washing (its name references the club

anthem 'Steve Bloomer's Watching', itself a reference to the Rams' record goalscorer) is a labour of love for Parsons and his two co-hosts. It sprang up four years ago when the trio needed to find 'a creative outlet for our discussions about the club, which are frequent and passionate and varied and detailed. We weren't sure how long it would last. We tried to do it every couple of weeks, as we figured there would always be something to talk about. But we never foresaw how bonkers the life of a Derby fan would be over the next three or four years – the last eighteen months especially.

'It's a challenge. It's a labour of love. It's a drain on my time when I have a full-time job and a young family. But our listeners seem to appreciate the time and effort we put into it: the research we do, the depth we go into, the guests we have on.

'It can be really hard work. There have been times when we've been due to do a podcast but one or more of us has taken real convincing to sit down and record it. We'll be in such a bad mood that it's difficult. One time, about eighteen months ago under Frank Lampard, we were on the train back from Villa where we'd been thumped four-nil. It was a complete disgrace and we were sick of it. One of us said, "You know what, lads? I can't be arsed with it tonight. I don't fancy it." But we convinced him and that particular episode turned out to be one of our most popular. We formulated our thoughts and got them off our chest. We ranted and we raved. It was cathartic. The podcast is a valve.'

The podcast is, of course, the twenty-first-century equivalent of the fanzine. The *raison d'être* remains the same – unofficial, no-holds-barred analysis of a beloved football club. It's just that rather than a photocopier and a stapler, a microphone and a recording device are the tools of the trade. Plus, podcasters also have the advantage of not having to stand on wet street corners touting their wares. Let the download take the strain.

For listeners, podcasts like Steve Bloomer's Washing (its name could even be that of a back-in-the-day fanzine) are like eavesdropping on a post-match pub conversation, thus providing a vital service in these times when the pubs are shut. In the absence of seeing events themselves during recurring periods of lockdown, it's an outlet that's more needed than ever. 'I like that we're part of their lives. I like the intimacy of being part of people's commute or their gym session or when they're cooking their dinner.'

Parsons might joke that the club never runs short of offering topics for discussion, but the current managerial vacancy, and the parlous league position, aren't the only concerns at present. There's also the not-insubstantial matter of the club's long-mooted takeover by Sheikh Khaled, who is a cousin of Manchester City owner Sheikh Mansour and who continues to be in protracted discussions with long-term owner Mel Morris. 'The main feeling among fans is that the takeover is needed. It's been a while coming and it's no secret that Mel has been trying to do this for some time. The pot is running dry, basically. But it's hard to say anything about these people because we know so little about them. All I know is that the group were linked with takeover bids with Liverpool and Newcastle.'

It goes without saying that the longer Derby are mired at the bottom of the league, the less attractive they are and the less likely the takeover is to go ahead. After all, if Liverpool were previously in their sights, a League One club won't be. A sighing Parsons knows this. 'With every day that goes by, we're all getting a little more anxious about how likely it is to happen.

'If we carry on the way we are, we'll either be in serious financial trouble or in the third tier for the first time since the '80s.

'Or both.'

*

On a bright Friday morning in November, Tyrhys Dolan made the short journey from his family home to St George's Church in Altrincham. Despite the sunshine, the occasion was a solemn one. He was to be a pallbearer at the funeral of his best friend Jeremy Wisten. They had been the closest of pals throughout school, as well as being team-mates at Manchester City's academy. They were like brothers, living in each other's pockets as they made their passage into adulthood.

Both had been released by City, but while Dolan had second and third chances to realign his career, Jeremy hadn't been so fortunate and had begun to drift away from the game, from his dreams. Three weeks earlier, he had been found unresponsive in his bedroom at the family home in Baguley, south Manchester. The paramedics couldn't revive him. Just a fortnight after his eighteenth birthday, Jeremy Wisten had taken his own life.

His death sparked numerous discussions about the treatment of young footballers after being released by their academies. Many national newspapers used his story to highlight the issue. It was an awful, ugly irony that Jeremy's footballing impact – he was, by all accounts, a stylish and extremely talented defender who could play right across the back four – came after his tragically short life was over.

Eleven days after the funeral, Dolan scored his next goal for Blackburn, their third against Preston on his first return to Deepdale. After the customary celebratory cartwheel and somersault, Dolan looked skywards and pointed his arms towards the heavens. The message was unambiguous. That was for Jeremy. And it would be forever after.

'I will always dedicate every single goal to Jeremy as a tribute,' he later told The Athletic. 'Every single time I step out on the pitch, it's for him.'

\*

# Championship table, 30 November

|  |  | P | W | D | L | F | A | Pts |
|---|---|---|---|---|---|---|---|---|
| 1 | Norwich City | 14 | 8 | 4 | 2 | 18 | 11 | 28 |
| 2 | AFC Bournemouth | 14 | 7 | 6 | 1 | 23 | 13 | 27 |
| 3 | Watford | 14 | 7 | 5 | 2 | 19 | 11 | 26 |
| 4 | Swansea City | 14 | 7 | 5 | 2 | 16 | 8 | 26 |
| 5 | Reading | 14 | 8 | 2 | 4 | 23 | 18 | 26 |
| 6 | Bristol City | 14 | 7 | 3 | 4 | 17 | 14 | 24 |
| 7 | Brentford | 14 | 6 | 5 | 3 | 20 | 13 | 23 |
| 8 | Stoke City | 14 | 6 | 4 | 4 | 21 | 18 | 22 |
| 9 | Blackburn Rovers | 14 | 6 | 3 | 5 | 27 | 16 | 21 |
| 10 | Middlesbrough | 14 | 5 | 6 | 3 | 14 | 9 | 21 |
| 11 | Millwall | 14 | 4 | 8 | 2 | 12 | 10 | 20 |
| 12 | Luton Town | 14 | 5 | 4 | 5 | 11 | 17 | 19 |
| 13 | Huddersfield Town | 14 | 5 | 3 | 6 | 18 | 19 | 18 |
| 14 | Cardiff City | 14 | 4 | 5 | 5 | 17 | 13 | 17 |
| 15 | Queens Park Rangers | 14 | 4 | 5 | 5 | 16 | 20 | 17 |
| 16 | Barnsley | 14 | 4 | 4 | 6 | 15 | 16 | 16 |
| 17 | Birmingham City | 14 | 3 | 7 | 4 | 10 | 12 | 16 |
| 18 | Preston North End | 14 | 5 | 1 | 8 | 17 | 21 | 16 |
| 19 | Rotherham United | 14 | 3 | 4 | 7 | 14 | 18 | 13 |
| 20 | Coventry City | 14 | 3 | 4 | 7 | 14 | 24 | 13 |
| 21 | Nottingham Forest | 14 | 3 | 3 | 8 | 9 | 17 | 12 |
| 22 | Wycombe Wanderers | 14 | 2 | 4 | 8 | 7 | 20 | 10 |
| 23 | Sheffield Wednesday | 14 | 3 | 5 | 6 | 7 | 12 | 8* |
| 24 | Derby County | 14 | 1 | 4 | 9 | 6 | 21 | 7 |

*Includes six-point deduction*

**Leading scorers**

Adam Armstrong (Blackburn), 13
Ivan Toney (Brentford), 12
Lucas João (Reading), 9
Teemu Pukki (Norwich), 7

**Manager of the Month**

Vladimir Ivić (Watford)

**Player of the Month**

David Brooks (Bournemouth)

**Managerial departures**

Garry Monk (Sheffield Wednesday), sacked
Phillip Cocu (Derby), mutual consent

**Managerial appointments**

Tony Pulis (Sheffield Wednesday)

# December

*'I need to bring in the right one. I thought
Pulis was the right one, but I was totally
wrong. I can't make a mistake this time'*

— DEJPHON CHANSIRI

It's a sight. It truly is.

Turning into King's Park Drive, the tree-lined approach to the Vitality Stadium, there are obstacles in the road, obstacles that haven't been there for months and months. These obstacles are adorned in black and red, and they wear beatific smiles. They are the blessed ones. Welcome back, fans of AFC Bournemouth.

In late November, the government announced that clubs that found themselves in either Tier 1 or Tier 2 when the second national lockdown was lifted on 2 December could open their gates to fans again; four thousand in Tier 1, two thousand in Tier 2. No Championship clubs were located within Tier 1 (unsurprising, given that it was an area covering only the Isle of Wight, Cornwall and the Scilly Isles), but nine were within Tier 2. Wycombe and Luton were the first to welcome fans back in on the night the restrictions were lifted, with Reading, Millwall, Watford, Norwich and Brentford doing so three days later. Now, a week on, it's the

97

turn of both QPR and Bournemouth to see their stands being partially occupied.

Here at the Vitality, socially distanced queues twist around the car park. Procedure and process are the name of the game today, with fans given staggered arrival and entry times to minimise congestion. Those with tickets to the North Stand are the first members of the congregation to be let back into the cathedral. They filter in, shyly moving along the nave of the stand, looking for their allocated pew.

Today will offer a different view to that normally enjoyed by each of these season-ticket holders, but no one's complaining. 'Normal' hasn't shown its face round these parts for nine months, not since Bournemouth hosted Chelsea on the last day of February. That was 287 days ago. These fans have been in withdrawal ever since. Their club was a Premier League side then, one that sat outside the relegation zone. Now they're a Championship club readying to play Huddersfield Town.

The other three stands open their gates in turn, all fans nervously taking their first steps back in the ground. It would have been logistically simpler to open just one or two stands to the fans today, but instead they've been allocated seats on all four sides of the pitch. This is a nice touch, an attempt to at least partially replicate the atmosphere of a normal match day. But it will undoubtedly feel surreal for everyone here, sat at neat intervals from each other. The experience, of course, isn't exactly as usual. Down on the stadium concourse, the food concessions remain shuttered, the deep-fat fryers mummified in dust, the pie ovens cold.

On the two big screens in opposing corners of the ground, a compilation of the many goals Bournemouth have scored from outside the area this season is shown. Modest cheers accompany each one, magical strikes from the boots of David Brooks and Jefferson Lerma and others. Further reserved cheers seep out when the starting line-up is announced, swiftly followed by a short singalong that breaks out among a handful of fans in the North Stand. 'Oh, Bournemouth, we love you ...'

There's still a timidity, an awkwardness, across all four stands. But, as kick-off approaches, the faithful are starting to remember what to do. Like lovers reunited after a separation, they're relearning, nervously at first, how to express their love. Asmir Begović is the first player out to warm up, reciprocating the warm applause he's receiving as he jogs towards his goal. Then, when the rest of the squad emerge, the roars start. Players and fans have missed each other. The warm up is watched more intensely, more fondly, than ever before. Absence can do that. There's a sense of quiet wonder in the air, beguilement that's soon broken by the furious barking of Huddersfield's sergeant-major of a fitness coach.

The PA announcer takes the opportunity to remind fans to visit the club shop to buy those Christmas bargains. He's not had anyone to make those sales pitches to for more than nine months. Never mind the fact that the shop isn't actually open on match days. 'Live Is Life' gets another airing, although this time – in the context of fans getting to see their heroes in the flesh again – the song seems to make a little more sense. Cherry Bear the mascot is in position too. He/she hasn't been seen for months either.

A lone voice in the crowd cries out, answered by 1,999 others. There's no need to pipe in fake crowd noise when there're real people in the place, even if there're only 2,000 of them. The players of both sides take the knee and are received by applause across the stands, in marked contrast – and a direct riposte – to the booing that greeted the gesture ahead of Millwall's home game against Derby last Saturday. The Lions supporters had waited the same nine months to see their team in the flesh again, but a portion of them chose to mark the occasion with ignorance and distaste. They were rightfully, and roundly, condemned by all in the football community.

This is the first opportunity that the Cherries fans have had to show their appreciation and admiration for what Jason Tindall has achieved so far during this first Eddie Howe-less season. Bournemouth are currently second in the table behind Norwich, but today they're the only top-six team playing at home. There's a decent chance that the lucky 2,000 might be treated to a table-topping performance today.

As ever, the chairman Jeff Mostyn strikes a pitch-perfect note in the programme. 'Your challenge this afternoon will be to make enough noise for the friends, family and fellow supporters who can't be with you in the stadium today. Yes, I mean all 10,000 of them. The boys just can't wait to perform for you.'

He's right. The boys very quickly start performing. After just seven minutes, David Brooks puts Dominic Solanke through and his deft dink over the advancing Huddersfield keeper causes an eruption of noise. One-nil already. Within five minutes, Solanke doubles the advantage, slotting home for his eighth goal of the season. He's finding his feet. 'Easy! Easy!' come the shouts.

If this sounds a tad premature, Solanke soon tees up Brooks, whose measured left foot finds the net from twenty yards out. They're three up after just twenty minutes and looking every inch the Premier League side they were before the fans were forced into exile. Brooks certainly looks a player who should be operating at a higher level. With his sleeves pulled down over his hands to keep out the cold, he looks more skinny indie kid than battle-hardened Championship warrior. He's a graceful player, beautifully two-footed. The fans know his capability. Every time he gets the ball, 'Shoot!' is the cry.

The three-goal advantage has evaporated the fans' nerves. They can relax and have a little sport, whether it's winding up the Huddersfield keeper or laughing at an opposing player's lack of control. The ironic cheers ring out when a butter-soft shot rolls gently into Begović's arms. And when a wild shot from the visitors ends up in the proverbial Row Z, we hear laughter and jeers, rather than the empty sound of ball on stanchion. The cabaret is back. This is what we've been missing.

We've also been missing the call-and-response between fans. A single voice cries out. 'R-E-D A-R-M-E-E!' The response is instant. 'RED ARMY!' No matter that Huddersfield have possibly seen more of the ball in the first half; the scoreline doesn't lie. Thunderous applause greets the half-time whistle.

Brooks is substituted after an hour – the game's safe, so no point risking an injury to a player whose fleet-of-foot skills are irresistible to the prosaic attentions of opposing defenders. But Bournemouth don't relent. Junior Stanislas skips off on a long, mazy run which ends with him slipping the ball home for the Cherries' fourth. Huddersfield, without leading scorer Josh Koroma, have largely matched Bournemouth in every department except goals, but Stanislas's effort sees the raising of the white flag. Substitute Sam Surridge adds a fifth a few minutes later.

Referees have had it comparatively easy so far from the side-lines this season, with just the obligatory ire of each dugout to contend with. But, with fans back, the stands now resonate with the sighs and grumbles of collective indignation. And, despite their team being five up, there's still some vitriol in the tank, angrily voiced when Huddersfield win a soft free kick. Here, a fortnight before Christmas, it's all part of the panto.

At the final whistle, 2,000 very happy souls are in heaven. Tindall leads the players on a lap of honour, a parade to all four corners of the ground, soundtracked by the obligatory playing of 'Sweet Caroline'. They're bouncing in the stands. Good times never seemed so good. It's like they've won the league. Maybe that's to come.

While Tindall walks the perimeter of the pitch, his opposite number, Carlos Corberán, has long disappeared down the tunnel. Today, he's wearing black skinny jeans; some suggest this is the problem. The fan blog Terrier Spirit had got its calculator out and deduced that, in games when the Spaniard wears his white chinos, Huddersfield have collected an average of 1.67 points per game, but this reduces to a single point per game when he doesn't. But the scoreline this afternoon isn't the result of a wardrobe choice. It was down to the presence of the home fans, and the desire of their team to do right by them.

The fans slowly, reluctantly, make their way out of the stands and back down King's Park Drive. One of them, Sue, is ecstatic. She forgot that the concessions would be closed this afternoon and neglected to bring a flask instead, but no matter. The five-star performance has warmed her to her bones. She reveals that her daughter is expecting a baby in a couple of months. It'll be Sue's first grandchild. After this afternoon's performance, she's going to suggest that, if it's a boy, he be called Dominic.

The fans might be delighted with their return, but so too are the players. Cherries captain Steve Cook was equally effusive later on, applauding the club's decision to dot the crowd around the ground. 'As soon as we walked out to warm up, you could tell they were up for it. I had a few pre-match nerves. I haven't had them for a long time. It was just because we were going out into the unknown again, having our fans back.

'It was lovely when you heard them after the first goal. We spoke about that in the changing room. We wanted to come out and give them something to cheer. You want to hear that noise. It makes you feel warm inside. That's what you play football for.'

Towards the end of the game, Cook briefly got carried away by the occasion. Urged on by the faithful, he brought the ball out of defence and embarked on an Alan Hansen-esque surge up the pitch, only running out of gas once he reached the Huddersfield area. Up in the stands, two voices would have been roaring him on more than most; they belonged to his two young sons, able to finally watch their dad at work.

The Vitality falls quiet and the car park darkens. At the gate, the stewards seem more than satisfied with some kind of normality returning for the time being. 'Without the fans,' one of them observes, 'it's been like watching black-and-white telly. With them back, this afternoon was in high definition and with surround-sound.'

His colleague, making reference to fans occupying all four sides of the ground, offers a single-word review. 'Quadraphonic,' he beams through a curly silver beard.

*

When a football club unveils its plans to build a new stadium, the odds are high that it will mean a move to the outskirts of town, close to a motorway or trunk road, and with the almost-certain prospect of having branches of TK Maxx and Frankie & Benny's as neighbours. Meanwhile, the site of the old stadium, close to the town centre and thus of prime value for property developers, usually disappears under the bricks and tarmac of a new housing development.

Not so Rotherham United. When they moved into the New York Stadium in 2012, the club found themselves even more centrally located, wedged between the railway and the River Don on the site of a former foundry, just a few minutes' walk from the town's minster. Nor did their old stadium, Millmoor, get converted into housing. In fact, a full twelve years after the club moved out, following a failure to agree a new lease with the landlord (they played on the other side of the M1 at Don Valley Stadium in Sheffield for four seasons while the new stadium was built), Millmoor still exists, a couple of stone-throws from the Millers' new home. Its outer wall is topped by generous coils of fierce barbed wire, there to repel anyone who might fancy liberating a souvenir of days gone by or climbing its still-standing floodlight pylons. With its peeling paint and broken signage, the old place looks across jealously at the relative newcomer on the other side of the tracks, every bit the modern stadium, every bit the younger model.

This particular lunchtime, on the far side of the car park at the New York Stadium, several early-arriving journalists sit in their respective cars. Most of us are tucking into our packed lunches while watching the backroom team of today's opponents, Derby County, unload equipment from their Transit vans. Our attention might be occasionally diverted by a train or tram gliding past. The sandwiches are fresh and the sky is blue. It's a beautiful day for football.

Or so we think.

Another journalist walks across the car park towards where we're collectively parked. He's on the phone and runs his finger across his throat – the internationally recognised signal that someone or something has been terminated. Four words, loudly offered in our general direction, confirm this.

'Game's off. Positive test.'

Texts are hurriedly sent, Twitter feeds get checked. Most sit tight in their cars until there's official confirmation. And here's the Derby team bus now, parking up just in front of us. Perhaps rumours of this game's demise have been greatly exaggerated. I get out and wander across towards the bus. While all the players are obliged to stay on board, three men dressed head to toe in black – Wayne Rooney, Steve McClaren and goalkeeping coach Shay Given – are having a whispered conflab next to the bus's open door. It's impossible to tell from their neutral body language whether the rumours are true. Rooney has a scarf pulled up over his nose; you can't read his face. But the fact that the Derby bus is here at all – and showing no signs of leaving at the moment – suggests we might yet see a game.

A small swarm of photographers soon surround the trio. If there is to be no game, these snappers need something to show for their day. The steward nearest to me explains that a final decision has not yet been made, that there's still a possibility of the fixture going ahead. A few journalists have already left, though, trusting their sources when it comes to the veracity of the rumours.

They clearly have good intel. After ten minutes of limbo, while we wait for an announcement, the Derby staff begin loading their gear back into their vans and into the luggage hold underneath the bus. A few minutes later comes the official word, via the Rotherham website:

'Rotherham United can confirm that this afternoon's Sky Bet Championship fixture against Derby County has been postponed following a positive test of Covid-19 for a member of Paul Warne's squad, with further players within the first-team bubble showing symptoms of the virus at present.'

Betty Glover, the 5 Live reporter seconded to this corner of South Yorkshire today, has parked her bright-blue Skoda Fabia next to the Derby bus. Sat inside, and via her phone, she prepares to update Mark Chapman and his listeners about the state of play here at the New York Stadium. Or, rather, the state of non-play.

If the postponement is a frustration to Rooney, his scarf masks his reaction. Since Derby's misguided decision to experiment with four joint-managers died an early death, he's been solely employed as the interim manager pending the club's takeover (which in itself is pending). Today he would have been keen, against one of the league's more misfiring sides, to extend Derby's impressive six-match unbeaten run under his steward-ship. Nonetheless, it's been a decent week for him. The Rams beat high-flying Swansea on Wednesday night; the following day, his ten-year-old son Kai signed for Manchester United.

The luggage hold of the bus slams shut and its engine starts up, while interim manager and technical director stride off towards their respective 4×4s. Rooney points his Range Rover in the direction of the northbound M1 and will arrive home in Cheshire a few hours earlier than expected. The bus goes the other way, heading southbound back to Derby.

Fifty minutes later, after negotiating the winding lanes of mid-Derbyshire, the bus arrives back at the club's training ground in Oakwood on the very outskirts of the city. It's now five minutes to three, exactly the time at which the players should have been taking their positions on the New York Stadium turf. Instead, they disembark and head for the fleet of high-performance sports cars and 4×4s in the car park. It's a rare Saturday afternoon where they can relax at home, taking in football on the TV. Today they can be armchair fans, just as the rest of the nation has been forced to be this season.

*

'If we had carried on with that game of football and retrospec-tively something had happened, as a football community we couldn't have forgiven ourselves.'

This season more than any other, Stephen Gilpin occupies a key role at Rotherham United, with the spotlight beaming brighter on the club's head of medicine than ever before. Three days after the Derby postponement, he's taking a phlegmatic view of the disruption that the pandemic is having on domestic football. 'We have to err on the side of caution.'

Gilpin is in his second spell at the New York Stadium,

having also worked his way through the medical staff ranks at Sheffield Wednesday and Hull City. He rejoined the Millers in the summer, headhunted for a newly created position. Also squeezed onto Gilpin's CV is the shortest of spells at Nottingham Forest.

'Five days into my tenure, I lost my job when Martin O'Neill and Roy Keane got sacked. Because I was seen as Martin's appointment, I unfortunately went with him, as is so often the case in football.'

Medical staff didn't always follow a dismissed manager and his coaches out of the door. Back in the day, a club's medical department didn't extend much further than a tubby middle-aged man running onto the pitch in an ill-fitting tracksuit while clutching the sainted magic sponge. He would be a permanent fixture at his club, a lifer surviving numerous regime changes, as Gilpin notes.

'In years gone by, being a medical member of staff at a football club meant your job was always quite safe. Unfortunately, nowadays, backroom staff – whether physios, sports scientists, nutritionists, psychologists or whoever – can also part ways with a club when the manager gets sacked. In the Premier League, and now into the Championship, job security is really, really poor. You're very dispensable. If a manager loses his job, the backroom staff will be wary until the next manager is appointed and their jobs feel safe.'

Managers increasingly have medical practitioners they favour. Over the course of these two spells at the New York Stadium, Gilpin has cultivated a very close working relationship with the Millers boss Paul Warne. 'One of my mantras is that you can never overcommunicate with the manager. Apart from my family, I think the person I speak to most is the gaffer. We have daily meetings both pre- and post-training, but I'll also be on the phone to him many times a day, even if it's ten or eleven at night. Yes, we've got the players in the building between the hours of eight and four, but after then things still crop up. If I have any news about a player – whether that be good, bad or indifferent – that gets fed back to the manager. And that can be a phone call at any hour of the day. I'm on call twenty-four hours a day, seven days a week. My phone could ring at any point.'

Just to emphasise the seven-days nature of his role ('it's relentless'), Gilpin runs through a typical schedule during a two-match week. At first, after a Saturday game, the demands are non-existent – for the playing and coaching staff at least. 'Here at Rotherham, the players always have Sunday off, even if we have a match on Tuesday. There's never training. Paul Warne sees Sunday as a family day. But if there is a Tuesday match, the medical staff will have to work with injured players on a Sunday. After the game on Saturday, I'll find out who's struggling with what. I'll triage those players that night and ring them up the following morning. This is all about giving the manager as much information come Monday morning – who's available to train, who'll be struggling for the game on Tuesday.

'We start later on a Monday. We'll have an afternoon training session then, as this allows players to travel back from wherever they disappeared to on Saturday evening. They'll be travelling in from all over the country – London, Manchester, Leeds, Newcastle, wherever. The later start allows players to travel back without having to wake up at the crack of dawn in order to be in for a morning session, which allows them to get the recovery benefits from sleeping in on Sunday morning.'

Mondays will see Gilpin, in association with Ross Burbeary, Rotherham's head of performance, assessing who might be available for the Tuesday game – 'which players we'll need to patch up and strap up to get them back out there and which players might benefit from needing a few days extra. Are any

MRIs or scans needed? Does anyone need to be ruled out straight away?'

Tuesday finds Gilpin and his staff rehabbing those ruled-out players while also keeping tabs on those they had earlier doubts about. Late fitness tests on Tuesday afternoon may well be held should any concerns still linger. 'Come kick-off, we need to know that the players we put out on the pitch are going to be able to get through a substantial chunk of the game.' The game itself is 'probably 0.5 per cent' of Gilpin's job. 'It's just the show-piece event – the culmination of all the work during the week.'

On Wednesday morning, the cycle restarts. It's another day off for the fit players who were involved the previous evening, but the crocked ones are back in to continue their rehab. And, of course, the medical staff are present and correct. 'Generally, if you're a fit player at Rotherham United, the manager will give you two days off per week. If you're an injured player, you'll be in six days per week. And if you're a member of the medical staff, you could be in all seven days.'

In a forty-six-game season, where everyone associated with a Championship club is putting in the hard yards, the medical staff are arguably putting in the hardest yards. 'I think people don't realise this about football. From the outside, it looks very glamorous. Yes, there are nice hotels and nice meals and nice buses. But when you peel things away and dive beneath the surface, the reality, the nitty-gritty, shows it's far from glamorous. It's very long hours, a lot of travel, a lot of time away from your family. That's the reality of working in football. It's a long season.

'And the pressure never dwindles. It's always on, but that's what we love about it. If I've got a player with a six-week injury and the manager says, "I want him back in five", that's the kind of pressure we live off and thrive off. If everything in football was calm and relaxed, it wouldn't be such an enjoyable environment to work in.'

As it's the week before Christmas, there are no midweek matches in the Championship, so isn't there time to come up for air? 'Injuries don't go away,' Gilpin sighs. 'But it will be a different kind of week. Instead of preparing and patching up players in order to go again on Tuesday night, we can have a slower start to the week. And we can get a chance to take stock a little of the crazy last month we've gone through.' A slightly easier schedule, but still no chance of a day off. 'It's never a day off. You're always needed for something. It's just a day away from work.'

A typical season is tough enough, but this particular season has presented further and deeper challenges. With a month lost at the start of the season because of the overrunning previous campaign, not only is the fixture schedule even more congested than ever, but players' fitness has been compromised by both the unrelenting waves of matches and the inadequate recovery time over summer. Many a manager has been complaining about the frequency with which their players are suffering muscle injuries.

Rotherham's first team, though, have been little affected in this way. As Gilpin explains, this is a result of the 2019–20 League One season being brought to an abrupt and premature halt. Rotherham played their last third-tier match in March and, sitting in their automatic promotion places, didn't have to return later to work their way through the play-offs. Those clubs who were playing in the Championship didn't end their season until late July (actually into August for the beaten play-off finalists Brentford) and thus had very little time for their players' bodies to be in peak condition for the season ahead – a couple of weeks on holiday and then a pre-season period of little more than three weeks.

'Having last played in March, we knew that a six-week pre-season for Rotherham wasn't going to suffice. We had to programme our players on a twelve-week pre-season. This was the only way to slowly build up their resilience to load and resilience to train. It was the only way to safely prepare the players for a season of Saturday/Tuesday, Saturday/Tuesday.

'As a result of the huge amount of work that the players went through during that twelve-week pre-season, we haven't picked up many muscle injuries this season. Our injuries have tended to have been caused by contact. Now, if I were head of medicine at a club that played in the Championship last season, I know this would be very different. They've had almost two seasons rolled into one. Players need a period of time completely away from football to allow their bodies to regenerate and recover in a period when they're not putting the usual stresses and loads through their joints. But that needs to be followed by a period of pre-season training – a carefully planned staged approach that would normally be six or seven weeks.

'So what you'll probably find is that, after Christmas, these clubs' players will find their bodies feeling like they would in March or April in a normal season. Clubs might be okay on their injury statistics and data now, but I'm predicting that when we come into the later stages of the season, players' bodies are going to be in an unknown realm. It's then that we'll see the effects of these two-seasons-into-one, where muscular and fatigue-related issues are going to become more prominent. It will be down to the skill and artistry of these clubs' performance coaches and medical staff to try to negate these issues or mitigate them as best they can. It's going to be really interesting to see how this plays out.'

The Rotherham treatment room hasn't exactly been a ghostly place, though. The Millers currently have five of their first-team squad out with long-term injuries, four of which have required surgery. That's a fifth of the squad not available to be selected by Paul Warne for a significant period of time. 'Sometimes you can go a whole season without long-term injuries,' says Gilpin.

'We've been unfortunate this season that we've picked up five. These aren't players out for four weeks. These are ten- or twelve-weekers. But it's a contact sport and this is why we have squads. And it's why it's so important how you train and treat those players who are normally on the periphery.

'Let me tell you one thing: in the Championship, you need everybody. If you're part of a twenty-five-man squad, at some point in that season you're going to be used, whether as a starter or from the bench. So those fourteen players outside of the manager's starting XI are absolutely crucial to the success of that season. They need to be physically on point at all times so they can slip straight into the team when needed. They can't get sloppy in their gym work. They can't get sloppy in their training. They can't get sloppy with their diet. They still need to be the best versions of themselves because they will be needed during a Championship season.'

Never mind the relentless fixture schedule. Never mind trying to keep as many players fit as possible. The lurking spectre of Covid-19 has heaped extra pressure on football clubs' medical professionals this season, as Gilpin's team has found since September, in particular during the last few days. After all, it's impossible to treat an injured player while social distancing. Only a very small number of players are allowed in the well-ventilated treatment room at any one time, while any manual therapy, administered by staff in full PPE, must last a maximum of fifteen minutes.

'We're asking players to come to work in a global pandemic, so they have to feel safe and feel comfortable in this environment. We take it so seriously. But obviously footballers go home after training and we can't live their lives for them. But we strongly advise them on who they interact with and what they do socially. If we hear of occasions when players might be mixing and we're not comfortable with it, we'll call them on it.'

Certainly extreme caution is applied at all times, as it was before the Derby game. The player who tested positive during the previous week was placed in isolation and all players who'd been in contact with him were tested; all came back negative. However, on the morning of the game, two players exhibiting Covid-like symptoms meant the brakes were put on straight away (although these players' subsequent test results weren't positive). Multiple tests – 'the best part of fifty people' – were then conducted.

The club's caution would prove to be justified. The day after Gilpin and I speak, the club announced a number of positive cases within the first-team squad, dictating that their Boxing Day match against Middlesbrough becomes their second successive postponed game. An already congested fixture list now got that little bit tighter, those yards a little bit harder.

*

On the afternoon of the Rotherham/Derby postponement, there was another notable announcement. Shortly after four in the afternoon, the Prime Minister addressed the nation, explaining that a new strain of coronavirus was raging across London and the Home Counties, and why this meant the region would now be placed in a new fourth tier of restrictions, just three days after it entered Tier 3. This latest move effectively cancelled anything approximating a normal Christmas for more than sixteen million people.

While a nation of football fans ruminated on how this might affect the progress of the season at all levels of the pyramid, the BBC's resident and longstanding EFL expert, Mark Clemmit, was busy analysing the day's Championship matches on 5 Live. Specifically, he was mulling over the inconsistency of Watford – or, at least, their inconsistency when compared against their main rivals, the more dynamic and free-scoring Norwich and Bournemouth. Starting the day in third position in the league, the Hornets had been beaten two-nil at Huddersfield that afternoon, a defeat that saw them slip down to fifth place. They had also now won fewer than half their games. Clemmit was certainly part-joking when he observed that 'with their managerial record, you start to look at the situation and think, "Don't drift too far …"'

Another announcement came a few hours later. Watford's manager, Vladimir Ivić, had been relieved of his duties, despite the club being just four points off an automatic promotion position with twenty-six matches still left in the season. While some supporters had decried the team's more defensive approach in recent weeks – and there were plenty of rumours bouncing around about friction between the Serb and certain members of the first-team squad – Ivić had only been in the job for four months, overseeing just twenty-two games in league and cup. Most pointedly, he had been named Manager of the Month just eight days earlier.

Eight days.

Fewer than twenty-four hours after the sacking, the club, renowned for possessing the itchiest trigger fingers in the entire league, had appointed the Dinamo Tbilisi head coach Xisco Muñoz as Ivić's replacement. The Spaniard became Watford's fifth permanent manager in little more than a year.

A tweeting Gary Lineker neatly knitted together two of that day's announcements: 'Watford change managers more often than we change tiers.'

Still, Ivić's four months in Hertfordshire took the appearance of a long-term appointment when matched against Tony Pulis's time at Hillsborough. After just forty-five days as Garry Monk's successor, one more than Brian Clough famously managed at Leeds, Pulis was summarily sacked just after Christmas. True, he had recorded just one victory in ten matches in charge, taking a modest seven points from a possible thirty, but no one predicted the decision, especially as four of those points had come in Wednesday's last two games, suggesting a steadying of the ship. Wily old campaigners like Pulis, men of experience with the scars and medals to show for their decades of service, are usually given more time to bed down with their new troops.

The official statement from owner Dejphon Chansiri cited the points tally as the reason for his dismissal, while also hinting at something more fundamental: 'There are also other issues which have had a bearing on this decision.'

The instant inquest, conducted by confused journalists and frustrated fans, speculated that, with the January transfer window due to be opened in a few days' time, there was a certain disconnect between the manager's demands and the owner's supply. Pulis's last press conference, delivered on Christmas Eve ahead of a one all draw on Boxing Day away to Blackburn, was filleted for clues. One comment in particular took on added significance, all but confirming that the pair weren't necessarily singing from the same Christmas carol sheet.

'I've been in the game a long time and I've been promised loads by lots of people and ended up getting nothing. And I've been promised nothing by some people and ended up getting more than I ever believed I would get.' Getting the sack after a month and a half was probably more than he ever believed he would get too.

Rumours started circulating around Sheffield that Pulis had signed a two-and-a-half-year deal at Hillsborough on an annual salary of £2m, a figure that, depending on the wording of the contract, could also be the value of any severance package. If so, that worked out at more than £45,000 a day – or £200,000 per game.

On New Year's Eve, Chansiri – eager not to be portrayed as the silent, absentee owner – hosted quite an extraordinary online press conference. It lasted two hours, with twenty-five minutes alone devoted to the Pulis departure.

The diplomatic tone of the official statement had disappeared. 'He is the worst one in my club and tried to cause a lot of trouble.' This wasn't the usual measured, qualified appraisal of a departing manager. 'He could damage my club. I made the decision not to help him any more.'

And what news of his successor? 'I need to bring in the right one. I thought Pulis was the right one, but I was totally wrong. I can't make a mistake this time.'

As the clock ticked towards 2021, approaching the halfway point of a deeply troubled season, the manager's office at Hillsborough remained vacant.

*

'Welcome to the last match of 2020. What an awful year off the pitch, but a great year on it.'

To football fans in a particular corner of west London, Peter Gilham's voice may well be as familiar as that of a close family member. For the past fifty-one years, he's been Brentford's man on the mic, the PA announcer in the dual role of minister of information and rabble-rouser. He's seventy-three now, but age will not wither his love for his beloved team. 'I bleed red and white. I'm Brentford through and through. And to be this close to the club for all those years has been very special to me. I'm the luckiest guy alive.'

Gilham started supporting Brentford in 1954 when he was seven years old. As a young adult, he became involved with the social club and, in 1967, took a leading role in protests against the planned merger with QPR. With that threat to the club extinguished, Gilham graduated to becoming master of ceremonies in October 1969. He's the longest-serving PA announcer in English football, having picked up the mic a couple of years before Liverpool's George Sephton, aka the Voice of Anfield.

The number of matches that Gilham has been absent from over the last half-century can be counted on the fingers of one hand. 'I've only missed a couple of games in recent years. One was when I was going on holiday to the Maldives with my former wife, but we had a rearranged game against Colchester on a Tuesday night. I thought I'd rather be where I was going. In the end, the game got called off at half-time because of a frozen pitch. It was rearranged and I got to see it.'

Of course, almost all of those home matches ('I've never kept a tally') were at Griffin Park, Brentford's characterful old ground. Now boarded up – even if its floodlight pylons continue to draw the attention of motorists on the elevated section of the nearby M4 – Griffin Park hosted its last-ever first-team match in July. After that play-off semi-final second leg against Swansea, the club drew the curtain on 116 years of history by moving to a purpose-built stadium less than a mile to the east. Ahead of that final game, Gilham was the one charged with saying the goodbye, the one to bid it farewell. He added a personal element, quoting the lyrics of Madonna's 'This Used To Be My Playground'.

A pause. An intake of breath. 'Thank you, Griffin Park.'

'It had been a very emotional season, with every game meaning something to somebody. And I could feel the emotion building up throughout the game. It was incredible.' And this was with the stands empty, without supporters to say goodbye themselves. 'I felt honoured to have been there, to have represented thousands of Brentford fans.'

Gilham had already understood the honour bestowed on him during that splintered season, having been in the sainted position of attending matches once play resumed after that three-month, Covid-dictated break. He had feared that he might never set foot in Griffin Park again. After all, mascots weren't needed for behind-closed-doors matches, so why would a PA announcer not be surplus to requirements?

'Because of Covid, our social club had obviously shut down. An email was sent to staff explaining that there were lagers and Pepsi in the club that would be going to waste and inviting us to go in and take a crate. So I did. I went in on a Friday and got talking to the stadium supervisor and his assistant. They told me that, while we'd have no fans, they still needed a PA announcer. Would I be happy to do it? I was almost reduced to tears. The thought that I could carry on seeing my beloved Brentford meant everything to me.'

The absence of fans didn't alter Gilham's modus operandi. 'I gave it my all and shouted at the top of my voice. During those last few games, we did have fans outside the ground. They could hear me. They did their chants and then went off to the local pubs to watch the match.'

As the padlocks were wrapped around the Griffin Park gates for the last time, and anti-intruder paint applied to the walls and fences, it might have been the optimum time for Gilham, after more than fifty years' service, to bow out. Not a bit of it. While richly acknowledging and appreciating history, he's not an overly sentimental type. Clearly delighted about his services being retained ('I feel honoured and I feel privileged'), he's fully embraced his new workplace.

'We first started talking about a new stadium back in the mid-'70s, but this went by-the-by over the years. There was more talk around the turn of the century, but the financial downturn in the country made it get put to one side. So to see it come to fruition now just means everything. We all knew it would be very hard to leave Griffin Park, but to see this new stadium materialise in front of us is wonderful.

'To walk into here for the first time was almost overpowering.

It's absolutely magnificent. Even without a crowd inside it, there's something about it. It's a vibrant stadium. A few fans aren't sure about the coloured seats, but I think they make it look special. They make it feel as though fans are there. They give it an atmosphere of its own, which not many new stadiums have.

'And I love the fact that we've moved further towards central London. In the past, there was talk of moving out to Woking, out to all sorts of places. But we've been able to stay in our borough, unlike other teams we all know well. And it's our stadium. That says everything. It doesn't belong to the council. It belongs to Brentford Football Club.'

It took some imaginative thinking to consider how the original site — a scruffy triangular patch of land stranded within three railway lines — was suitable. 'If you looked at the site before building started, you'd wonder how on earth a football stadium could be put there. It was old garages and yards on a little link road between Kew Bridge and the M4.'

After sixty-six years of supporting the Bees, it would be very easy for Gilham to get misty-eyed about the closing of chapters, to believe that the club he adores was losing what they had, that their identity was being irredeemably reshaped. Instead, he's an evangelist for its brand-new tomorrow.

He certainly doesn't want Griffin Park to become the west London equivalent of Millmoor up in Rotherham, left to rust and decay. 'I'll be even happier if the floodlights at Griffin Park come down sooner rather than later. I appreciate all our history is there and we've brought that with us, but we're creating new history here.' This new history is immediate; eight days ago, Brentford beat Premier League Newcastle to reach the Carabao Cup semi-finals for the first time.

Some fans might not share Gilham's positivity and optimism. 'It feels like home to me already. But those people who loved

Griffin Park and who didn't want us to move haven't had the opportunity to see the new stadium. That's the biggest problem. Once they do, I think they'll fall in love with it. And with the team we've currently got, they're going to fall in love with them wherever they're playing.'

As with those last few games at Griffin Park, the empty stands at the box-fresh Brentford Community Stadium haven't altered how Gilham goes about his business. 'I'm shouting out in exactly the same way at the start of the game, at the start of the second half, and when goals are scored. The players want normality. With the fans not there, they need some kind of continuity.'

The brief reappearance of fans has now disappeared with London submerging into Tier 4 of Covid restrictions. For a frustratingly short time at least, both players and announcer were able to glimpse into a brighter future. 'Hand on heart, I was in tears. I stood in front of the tunnel, waiting for the players to come out. Pontus Jansson was the first player out, followed by Henrik Dalsgaard. I could see the look on their faces as they came out and heard the crowd. There were only two thousand there, but the sound of them made me lose it. Pontus said afterwards he felt the same – to suddenly see and hear fans. I reckon every one of those two thousand fans made a noise. It was magnificent. I can't wait until there are eighteen thousand in.'

Tonight, for the visit of Bournemouth, Gilham certainly doesn't hold back, despite the stands being empty. From his new perch directly above the tunnel, his performance remains the same as it's been for decades. 'Okay, Bees fans. Heeeeeeeeere they come!' Of course, there are no Bees fans to hear him.

With teams announced to a backing of The Prodigy, Gilham then unleashes his most famous battle cry. 'Come on, Brentfoooooooooord!' It's his equivalent of Noddy Holder yelling, 'It's Christmaaaaaassss!'

Gilham is right about the new place. It's a terrific ground, with old style floodlights and idiosyncratically shaped stands. And those coloured seats – alternately red, burgundy, dark grey, white and mustard yellow – give it a real sense of individual identity in the age of the identikit new-build stadium where you could be both anywhere and nowhere at the same time.

The new stadium isn't the only reason to be cheerful. Brentford are the Championship's form team, riding a fourteen-match unbeaten run that goes back to October. Plus, there's the not-insignificant matter of a Carabao Cup semi-final against Spurs in seven days' time.

They'll be sternly tested tonight, though. The Cherries' veteran keeper Asmir Begović has kept five successive clean sheets; it's been 472 minutes since a ball ruffled the back of his net. Bournemouth are pretty potent at the other end of the pitch too, as Dominic Solanke proves in the very first minute, having an effort cleared off the line.

On the touchline, Brentford boss Thomas Frank is putting in a serious claim to be the Championship's noisiest manager. Understandably agitated at the way that his side are being carved open by Bournemouth in these early stages, his screeching is drowning out both the middle-distant hum of the M4 and the planes overhead descending into Heathrow. He's tearing his hair out – and he's got plenty of it. If Gareth Ainsworth's shoulder-length locks are those of a classic rocker, Frank's suggest past membership of a turn-of-the-'90s indie-dance outfit.

Perversely, he retreats into silence when Solanke gives the visitors the lead after twenty-four minutes following a characteristically swift passing move. Having announced the goal in a decidedly matter-of-fact tone, Gilham's disappointment is hidden under his face mask. Next to him, the frustrated body language of his wife Linda is easy to translate. Almost as avid a fan as her husband, Linda used to operate the scoreboard at Griffin Park.

The couple's perch represents arguably the best seats in the house, a position that means Gilham doesn't have to pull out the opera glasses to be able to do his job. 'It's as close as possible to the players without being *with* the players. At Griffin Park, it was a nightmare as the dugouts were on the far side of the ground from me. Whether sunshine or floodlights, it was often difficult to pick out the numbers on the subs board. It's perfect now. The dugouts are here, right in front of me.'

The Gilhams' demeanour is turned on its head after thirty-six minutes when a Brentford header from a corner blemishes Begović's spotless record. The couple are straight on their feet. On goes the mic. 'Henrik Dalsgaaaaaaard!'

It's the right-back's second goal of the season, but his first at the new stadium, thus making it the first time Gilham gets to announce a goal here by the Dane. A more common pronouncement he's made this season has contained these six words: 'The scorer, for Brentford, Ivan Toneeeeeyyyy!' Eight times the striker has scored here in the league, a number matched by his tally away from home. Going into tonight's game, he's the leading scorer across all ninety-two clubs in English football's four highest tiers.

When the club sold Ollie Watkins, last season's top scorer, to Aston Villa in the summer, Bees fans may have been questioning the club's ambition on the pitch, as well as wondering where the goals were going to come from. But there was method at play. Of the £28m banked for Watkins, just £5m was invested in his replacement. A proven scorer for League One Peterborough over the past two seasons, if anything Toney has found the Championship even easier pickings. With sixteen goals to his name by Christmas, he's on course even to eclipse Watkins' total of twenty-six last time out.

'People across football recognised that Ivan Toney was quite special and scoring goals at Peterborough,' says Gilham. 'When he came on against Newcastle in the Carabao Cup – and the Sky commentators couldn't believe he wasn't in the starting XI – he caused their defence no end of problems. They didn't know how to cope with him. And he's come from League One. It's not as if he's stepped down and has Premier League experience. He has a phenomenal work rate too. Whenever we concede a corner, he and Ethan Pinnock are stalwarts at the back.' Despite being deployed as a lone striker, Toney's endeavour and application when it comes to defensive duties are abundantly clear tonight, a pillar of his team's own six-yard box when guarding against set-pieces. He might have only been in west London for a matter of a few months, but this is a man for the cause. That's five million pounds very well invested.

Toney doesn't get on the scoresheet tonight, but Brentford do manage a second goal when an unmarked Tariqe Fosu nods home at the far post after a trademark inch-perfect cross from Bryan Mbeumo. Bournemouth respond by sending both Josh King and Sam Surridge off the bench to join Solanke in a front three, but this roll of the dice yields no double six. It's been as lively and high-quality an encounter as you'd expect from a clash between third and fourth in the table, but Brentford hold on to take maximum points. It's now fifteen games unbeaten and they climb up to second. Kool and the Gang's 'Celebrate' rings out into the night sky.

Gilham makes his closing remarks over the PA as he and Linda offer a two-person standing ovation to Brentford's players as they head towards the tunnel, each and every one of whom looks up to acknowledge the couple. Gilham raises a celebratory fist and makes his final exclamation of the evening.

'Happy New Year!'

\*

## Championship table, 31 December

| | | P | W | D | L | F | A | Pts |
|---|---|---|---|---|---|---|---|---|
| 1 | Norwich City | 22 | 13 | 5 | 4 | 30 | 20 | 44 |
| 2 | Brentford | 22 | 11 | 8 | 3 | 36 | 21 | 41 |
| 3 | Swansea City | 22 | 11 | 7 | 4 | 25 | 12 | 40 |
| 4 | AFC Bournemouth | 21 | 10 | 8 | 3 | 36 | 18 | 38 |
| 5 | Watford | 21 | 10 | 7 | 4 | 24 | 15 | 37 |
| 6 | Reading | 22 | 11 | 4 | 7 | 32 | 27 | 37 |
| 7 | Stoke City | 22 | 9 | 8 | 5 | 26 | 21 | 35 |
| 8 | Barnsley | 22 | 10 | 4 | 8 | 27 | 28 | 34 |
| 9 | Middlesbrough | 21 | 9 | 6 | 6 | 25 | 17 | 33 |
| 10 | Bristol City | 22 | 10 | 3 | 9 | 23 | 24 | 33 |
| 11 | Preston North End | 22 | 10 | 2 | 10 | 30 | 30 | 32 |
| 12 | Huddersfield Town | 22 | 9 | 4 | 9 | 27 | 39 | 31 |
| 13 | Luton Town | 22 | 8 | 6 | 8 | 20 | 24 | 30 |
| 14 | Blackburn Rovers | 22 | 8 | 5 | 9 | 36 | 27 | 29 |
| 15 | Cardiff City | 22 | 8 | 5 | 9 | 29 | 25 | 29 |
| 16 | Millwall | 20 | 5 | 10 | 5 | 17 | 18 | 25 |
| 17 | Coventry City | 22 | 5 | 8 | 9 | 20 | 30 | 23 |
| 18 | Birmingham City | 22 | 5 | 8 | 9 | 17 | 27 | 23 |
| 19 | Queens Park Rangers | 22 | 4 | 9 | 9 | 20 | 30 | 21 |
| 20 | Derby County | 21 | 4 | 7 | 10 | 14 | 23 | 19 |
| 21 | Nottingham Forest | 22 | 4 | 7 | 11 | 15 | 26 | 19 |
| 22 | Sheffield Wednesday | 22 | 5 | 7 | 10 | 14 | 23 | 16* |
| 23 | Rotherham United | 20 | 4 | 4 | 12 | 19 | 29 | 16 |
| 24 | Wycombe Wanderers | 22 | 3 | 6 | 13 | 15 | 32 | 15 |

*Includes six-point deduction*

## Leading scorers

Ivan Toney (Brentford), 16
Adam Armstrong (Blackburn), 15
Lucas João (Reading), 11
Teemu Pukki (Norwich), 11
Dominic Solanke (Bournemouth), 9

## Manager of the Month

Thomas Frank (Brentford)

## Player of the Month

Duncan Watmore (Middlesbrough)

## Managerial departures

Vladimir Ivić (Watford), sacked
Tony Pulis (Sheffield Wednesday), sacked

## Managerial appointments

Xisco Muñoz (Watford)

# January

*'I knew I was only sixty per cent fit. I was standing in bins of boiling water to warm my Achilles up before I went out'*

— MATTY JAMES

Neil Warnock first brought a football team to High Wycombe a long, long time ago. Back in 1984, his Burton Albion side rolled up in their bus for an FA Cup Fourth Qualifying Round tie at the old Loakes Park ground in the centre of town. This was six years before Adams Park was built. Gareth Ainsworth, Warnock's opposite number today, had started secondary school the month before.

Warnock has brought plenty of his teams here since – the likes of Huddersfield, Plymouth and Oldham – as he climbed the pecking order of English football management. Today, though, is the very first league encounter between Middlesbrough and Wycombe. (They did, of course, meet in the FA Cup back in 1975, the day that Alan Parry first set foot in this corner of Buckinghamshire.)

With a game in hand over their immediate rivals, Middlesbrough are nicely positioned in ninth place in the league, like a judicious middle-distance runner biding his or her time in the pack, ready to pick up the pace as the race nears its climax, ready to kick for home on the final bend. Wycombe, despite being bottom, come into the New Year with renewed vigour and hope. Their last match of 2020 was a 2-1 win over Cardiff that brought them within a point of both Rotherham and Sheffield Wednesday.

Further green shoots of recovery appear this afternoon when, within the opening three minutes, Wycombe's first attack bears a goal, the big striker Uche Ikpeazu cutting in from the right and curling the ball into the far corner. Thirteen years younger than Adebayo Akinfenwa, Ikpeazu is clearly his successor-in-waiting.

Warnock is uncharacteristically quiet on the touchline after Boro have fallen behind so early. Wisely keeping his mouth closed on a day when the temperature barely gets above zero, instead he intently chews gum to keep himself warm. But nor does he celebrate when his side equalise after half an hour, nor when they go in front five minutes later. Today, he's motionless and emotionless.

With ten minutes left, Boro score their third and those green shoots are already wilting. On the final whistle, after a brief chat with Warnock, Ainsworth leaves the pitch alone, blowing into his fists to warm his hands up, blowing some life into Wycombe's deflating season.

Warnock presumably told Ainsworth what he tells the assembled media ten minutes later. 'I would be proud if I was manager of both sides today,' he announces. 'His lads are so honest, and I wouldn't write them off. Don't write genuine lads off. There will be a few teams who don't fancy coming here.'

Ainsworth could take some comfort from the older man's words, but it would be cold comfort. They sounded like the words that opposition managers might have said near the start of the season, not at the halfway point. They were devoid of the inescapable context: that of a season unravelling at an accelerating rate.

Neither Matt Bloomfield nor Adebayo Akinfenwa captained

Wycombe today, although The Beast took ownership of the armband when he came on late in the game. Until then, it had been worn, with no small amount of pride, by left-back Joe Jacobson. At thirty-four, he's the next oldest in the squad, the third in command. Seniority here is clearly denoted by date of birth. 'I'm the spring chicken out of the three of us,' he smiles.

A couple of days later, Jacobson finds himself at home in Hertfordshire with a free day ahead of him and, rarely, no midweek match to prepare for. After the fury and flurry of the Christmas and New Year fixtures, it's a welcome chance to catch his breath. 'Not everyone's off. The gaffer's given the older boys an extra day at home, which is nice.' It's a chance to rest those aching, ageing bones.

Jacobson is a long-established member of The Generals, the five or so senior players 'who run the dressing room a little bit, who are the go-betweens between the other players and the staff'. That seniority is the product of a career spent almost exclusively in Leagues One and Two, a path that took a circuitous route via Cardiff, Bristol Rovers, Oldham, Accrington Stanley and Shrewsbury. He's been with the Chairboys since 2014.

(Not that his career can be seen in terms of lower-league anonymity. There are some notable notches on the Jacobson CV. For starters, he's a former captain of the Wales U21 side. Then there's the fact that he was the first Jewish footballer to play in the English leagues since former Crystal Palace and Manchester City midfielder Barry Silkman hung up his boots in the mid-'80s. Incidentally, Jacobson isn't the only Jewish player at Adams Park. There's also Scott Kashket, son of the celebrated tailor Russell Kashket, supplier of uniforms to the Royal Household, including the outfit worn by Prince William at his wedding. Scott chose to stitch up opposing defences instead.)

Unlike Bloomfield and Akinfenwa, Jacobson didn't make his Championship debut this season. That occurred a full fourteen years earlier, when he came on in the eighty-first minute for Cardiff in a home defeat to Norwich in April 2006. But that would be his only appearance in the division for his hometown team. Nearly a decade and a half passed before he made his second bow in the second tier.

'Those nine minutes were special to me and I still look back on them fondly. I was making my debut for the club I supported, the club I'd spent ten or eleven years at. My adrenalin was so high that day. I think I warmed up for eighty minutes of that game. I was so desperate to be out there, I was running up and down the sidelines, taking in the atmosphere. But when I came on, I started cramping up. I can't remember too much else. I remember fouling someone, but the crowd loved it. They got a great buzz from it.'

Today is the exact halfway point in the regular season. As many days have gone as there are to go. So it's the ideal opportunity for Jacobson to reflect on those days gone, to deliver his half-term report. At the start of the season, both Bloomfield and Alan Parry were resolute in believing that Wycombe wouldn't be the Championship's soft touches, but anyone glancing at the league table halfway through the campaign might very quickly come to that conclusion. However, despite being a fixture of the relegation zone, Wycombe have only been on the receiving end of one real tonking, that early five-nil defeat to Blackburn. Last weekend's Middlesbrough game was the first time they'd lost by more than a single goal in two months.

'We spoke about this at the club just yesterday,' agrees Jacobson. 'We haven't been the whipping boys at all. The gaffer has this never-say-die attitude and is all about giving everything you've got in every game. We don't give up. We stay in games. But we haven't had the best luck. Everything that could have gone wrong this season has gone wrong. But we're still within touching distance. We've had a few months' experience at this level now, and hopefully we can keep improving over the next few, learning how to win more games.

'The start was tough because we didn't know where we were at and how good the league was. We didn't have that belief. You lose one, you lose two, you lose three, and suddenly you're seven games in and you haven't picked up a single point. But we kept plugging away and the results started to come. Neil Warnock said the other day that it was one of the most competitive games Middlesbrough have had this season. We're getting a lot of compliments that people weren't giving us at the start of the season. Obviously we need to put more points on the board, but if we still have something to play for going into the last game of the season, I think everyone would take that.'

Perversely, Wycombe have tended to fare better against the more fancied teams: draws against both Watford and Brentford, and only single-goal defeats to Bournemouth, Bristol City and Norwich, the latter by a decidedly dodgy free kick. These are teams packed with players with hefty Championship experience; three were Premier League clubs six months ago. On paper, the gulf between them and newly promoted Wycombe should be wider.

'I don't know whether teams think, "Right, we've got Wycombe. That's an easy victory", and they step off a little. Bournemouth had £100m worth of players playing against us that night. We've probably only ever signed a couple of players for money. The difference is there, but we don't want to keep using that as an excuse. We want to compete on the pitch, to show we're good enough to play at this level. After the Watford game, I remember Ben Foster said to one of us: "We need some of your players who've got that heart and spirit and fight about them." And we have that in abundance. We just need to take a few more chances and to stop conceding sloppy goals. We're still there.'

The elephant in the room that the optimists of Wycombe are

avoiding is that this season could turn out to be – for the foreseeable future, at least – the club's only appearance in the second tier, a fleeting cameo. And the tragedy would be deepened by only three thousand fans getting in to see those two home games not played behind closed doors. Jacobson misses them so much, even if he admits the absence of big crowds at away games has meant Wycombe not succumbing to intimidation.

'It's been more of a leveller without them, but I just wish we did have fans. Wycombe fans have waited a hundred-odd years to get to this level and now they can't be there to support us. And, as a player, you want to play in these stadiums when they're full. That's the reason to get up to the Championship. There have been a few stadiums that I've managed to tick off this season where I'd never played before, like Derby. I just wish there had been twenty-five thousand in there all hating me, or shouting abuse at me, because that brings out the best in you.' Snapping and snarling opposition fans have been one of the many casualties of a peculiar season.

The hope that Jacobson has for the team in the second half of the campaign is framed and tempered by a worsening Covid situation where an increasing number of matches are being postponed following positive cases. What's it like playing under this threat? Are you taking to the pitch in a climate of fear?

'Once you're on the way to the stadium, you don't think of anything else but the game itself. You've got to trust that everyone else is doing things correctly. Yes, we're in contact on the field, but things are so strict at the training ground. We're doing all we can to stop the spread. But we're very fortunate. We're allowed to go to work and see people every day. My wife's been working from home since March and has barely left the house to see anyone.'

The EFL has just embarked on a ramped-up testing programme; Jacobson was tested yesterday while today league officials are inspecting the Wycombe training ground to check that the long and varied list of rules is being adhered to. Of course, increased testing will almost certainly produce an increased number of positive cases – quite possibly an avalanche that causes the government to suspend elite football, to implement a circuit-breaking hiatus to the season.

'I'm hoping that's not the case,' Jacobson concludes. 'Football brings a lot of joy and gives people something to look forward to. We've been lucky at the club with not too many cases. Touch wood it remains that way, that we can continue playing and not have games called off because of it.'

Jacobson didn't touch that wood firmly enough. Ten days later, after an impressive 4-1 win against Preston in the FA Cup, Wycombe are forced to call off their next league match due to a Covid outbreak at Adams Park. The next match, away at Sheffield Wednesday, is also postponed when a similar outbreak engulfs Hillsborough. And with an FA Cup tie against Spurs in the schedule as well, the Chairboys only manage to fit in two league games in the entire month of January. Their points tally coming out of December remains the same going into February.

Wycombe are starting to get left behind.

*

At the Trillion Trophy Training Centre, located where suburban Birmingham gives way to bucolic Worcestershire, there's one particular sound that is rarely silenced. Everyone is used to it. It's the white noise that soundtracks life in this particular corner of Birmingham City's training ground – a near-constant hum, a three-part harmony, that can be traced to the laundry room. A trio of industrial washing machines are the source. Large, silver and forever spinning, they are key cogs in keeping the football club in motion.

These machines are the tools of the trade of Jon Pearce and his team. Pearce, a chipper east Londoner with close-cropped ginger hair, has been Birmingham City's head kitman for seven and a half years now. The current Covid restrictions might have stripped back the workload with fewer of the club's various teams in action, but in a normal season Pearce and his small team would be laundering around seventy training kits a day. At weekends, up to ten teams would be in action across all age groups. The scale of the endeavour required a five-strong department that included an old stalwart called Phil, who exclusively cleaned boots all day long. With the pandemic demanding a smaller operation, this lunchtime finds Pearce himself removing mud from studs, turning filthy footwear into glass slippers. 'I could get an apprentice or a scholar to do them,' he explains, 'but their schedule doesn't necessarily align with that of the first team. So I just do them. It's easier.'

Being a kitman wasn't Pearce's initial career path. He did twelve years in the service of British Airways, working as a baggage handler at both Gatwick and Heathrow, but on hitting thirty, he realised he had to scratch 'a burning itch' to work in professional football. 'I'd always been around football people as my dad was stadium manager at West Ham. He did twenty-five years there; him and my uncle both ran the ground. A lot of my friends at school became professional footballers too, so I was always in and around the game. I had the chance of working as a football agent and did that for six months, but I didn't really enjoy it. It was too cut-throat. I didn't have that killer instinct.

'Then an opportunity came up at Birmingham's academy. A friend of mine – an ex-pro who's now sadly passed away – tipped me the wink about it, so I applied and got the job. We sold up and moved lock, stock and barrel from east London to Shropshire.'

As with becoming an agent, the kitman job was a route into football that didn't require exams to be passed or being in possession of a playing pedigree; 'I don't want to do the kitman's union a disservice, but it's not a qualified role.' However, Pearce's new job definitely shared similarities with those dozen years he spent shunting luggage around airport terminals. He was again being entrusted with getting people's property from A to B intact. On arrival at their destination, everything that should be there must be there. In this respect, there's little difference between a Championship footballer and the airline passenger in seat 16A.

'There was always pressure on us as baggage handlers. Everything in that job was time-critical. Every minute that a plane was left standing idle cost money. The kitman needs to be two steps ahead too. You have to have a clear mind. You need organisation and common sense. It's about nous. It's about life skills.'

It's also about putting in the hours. Each morning, when it's not a match day, Pearce will arrive at the training ground at around 6.30, having driven an hour from his home near Telford. Those three machines will soon kick into gear, thirsty to drink up the thirty-odd litres of liquid detergent his team gets through each week.

'Most things should have been laundered from the day before, but sometimes it's not been done, so you have to do a bit of laundry before you start proper. Then you've got to put everyone's kit out. Before training starts at half past ten, I'll have pumped up the balls and opened up the equipment sheds. Then I'll be outside on the training pitches – as soon as the players finish one task, I'll be putting away any equipment that's no longer going to be needed. That will take up until lunchtime, when we start re-laundering for the next day. Some players hang around longer, so they're in their kit longer and you obviously can't launder it when you'd necessarily like to. It's a full-on day. Within the department, there's a good chance that one of us will be at the training ground first and one of us will be here last.'

And then there are match days that come thick and fast.

Birmingham's most recent away game, the 400-mile round trip to Middlesbrough, came with the bonus of being a lunchtime game. Pearce arrived in his van the previous afternoon to set up the dressing room and, after a night in the team's hotel, was back at the Riverside Stadium the following morning to check everything was still shipshape and Brummie fashion ahead of the 12.30 kick-off. A one-nil win for the Blues meant the journey home wasn't too much of a chore, but his arrival back at the training ground at half past six in the evening didn't signal the end of the day. With the first team in for training the next day, a wash needed to go straight on, accompanied by a session of boot-cleaning. (Of course, had the Boro game been an evening kick-off, Pearce and his team wouldn't have arrived back at the training ground until around 2 a.m. And, depending on the schedule, they could well have been required to be reporting for duty at dawn the next day too.)

'Sometimes there's no recovery for us,' he sighs. 'It's endless – game/training, game/training, game/training. I was talking to Sheffield United's kitman yesterday and mentioned something about how late it was. He said, "Fans don't see us do this. They don't see all the unseen stuff that we have to do."'

The players are appreciative, though – even if this appreciation is often unconscious and thus silent. 'A good kitman is an unnoticed one. If the players don't need you, you've done your job. These boys are athletes. They don't need little worries about what their kit is looking like.' Even so, there's sizeable pressure not to leave, for instance, the star striker's precious favourite boots behind. 'I do a lot by memory. I don't forget things too often. But it's how you react to forgetting things. If you find you've arrived at a ground and you've forgotten something, whether minor or major, get yourself out of it. Find a way. Thankfully it doesn't happen too often.'

The kitman is usually the one to be relied upon to iron out

any metaphorical creases in the entire match-day operation. His job goes way beyond simple laundry. He's the problem-solver, the fixer, the last line of defence.

'Our job is like a blank canvas. It's very much "Kitman will know" or "Kitman can do that". Things fall on you and you have to adapt. It's a case of being on hand should anyone need something. During a game, it's almost like being a mechanic in the pit lane. Players might need their boots changing or their studs tightening. You're the guy with the stud tightener and the spare studs in your pocket. My pockets are always full up with everything, whether it's chewing gum or pliers or a spare captain's armband.'

The player coming to the side of the pitch is the F1 driver coming down the pit lane. Both need urgent assistance. 'They might call for a new stud, but sometimes with twenty or thirty thousand people around, it can be hard to hear. You've got to be alert as to when they need you.'

But it's not just finger-in-the-dyke fixes. There's a long game to be played by the kitman too. 'Some duties are so far in advance,' explains Pearce. 'When the season's just started in August and September, that's the time when we'll be ordering the kit for next season. And you're ordering blind because you don't know who's going to be there then. You might have totally new staff, you might have totally new players.'

The kitman, though, tends to be a permanent presence, a fixture of the backroom scene who's able to survive regime change after regime change. 'Hopefully, yeah. But you can never be sure. Things can change. Different people have different ideas. Football's an ever-moving circle, but you've got to hope that you're not being pushed out of the circle.'

As well as being football's equivalent of a pit mechanic, the kitman is the closest thing that the game has to a roadie. The arrival of the team on match day, with their kit and equipment laid out immaculately before them, is akin to a band rolling up at a venue to be greeted by the drums having been set up and the guitars neatly arranged in a particular order.

Johnny Green, the legendary former roadie-in-chief for The Clash, once explained the distinction between being a rock'n'roll star and being part of the support staff. 'They treated me with respect,' he told me, 'but equal is not quite right. You're never their mate. Even if it's the most shadowy of gaps that you can only slide a Rizla paper between, it is still a gap. They are the band; you are the roadie.'

While quite possibly a suitable analogy for the relationship between a football team and its kitman, Pearce nonetheless enjoys close contact with some of the Birmingham players. He's become a confidant, an agony uncle. 'Sometimes people come into the kit room to unload their problems and air any gripes they have. You form relationships, you gain their trust. You can be someone they can come to if they need to.'

Although obviously not active participants when it comes to tactical discussions in the dressing room, kitmen are privy to such briefings as they go about clearing up the dressing room. Their presence around the fringes of the inner circle inevitably demands trust and discretion. They don't make excuses and remove themselves, even in the tensest of times. They are not semi-detached figures. 'You're in there. You're part of it all. You'd become more noticed if you did become detached.'

And, of course, being in and around football's inner workings, becoming an artery that serves the game's beating heart, was always Jon Pearce's intention. It's why he jacked in the airport job, why he moved halfway across the country. The logistics might scramble the brain, the early starts and late finishes might be grossly antisocial, the constant hum of those washing machines might never leave his ears, but this is a man who's in hog heaven.

'I'm living out my dream of being in football,' he smiles. 'I wasn't a good enough footballer, so I became the next best thing.'

\*

He was already the talk of the Championship, the red-hot object of desire for Premier League eyes. But in expertly tracing the arc of a long ball forward over his shoulder to hit a first-time volley past the Barnsley goalkeeper, Emi Buendía showed he wasn't the kind of footballer to become unsettled by intense transfer speculation. And with that sweet strike, one worthy of his compatriot Lionel Messi, he might just have added an extra million or two to his perceived value.

Arsenal were the Argentine's principal suitors, a side eager to find an instant play-making replacement for the soon-to-depart Mesut Özil. But a major stumbling block was that the Gunners, reported to have just taken out a government loan of £120m to meet the financial shortfall caused by the pandemic, were not cash-rich. Indeed, they needed to lighten their wage bill by releasing players. With the transfer window opened wide for business, the rumours were strong that they would try to prise Buendía away from Carrow Road by offering a part exchange involving either Joe Willock or Reiss Nelson – or both.

Another stumbling block for Arsenal came in the shape of Daniel Farke. Even if Arsenal had the readies to meet Buendía's £40m valuation, the Norwich boss had no reason to sell. Yes, the Canaries were blessed with others in their squad – most notably Todd Cantwell and Mario Vrančić – who could step up to become playmaker-in-chief, but why jeopardise their push for an instant return to the Premier League by handing over their prize asset? If top-flight football translates to an injection of income in the region of £170m a season, why gamble this to pocket a sum less than a quarter of that figure? 'He is our player and will continue to be our player,' said an impervious Farke. 'He is on a long-term contract with the club, so we keep him.'

Arsenal were far from the only Premier League club looking to strengthen its ranks from the second tier. Rumour and gossip were rife. Throughout January, the machinery had been working through the gears, slow at first but building momentum as the month deepened.

For those top-flight clubs looking to surge either out of the relegation zone or into the European places, strikers and play-makers always represent the high-price items, the most valuable commodities. West Ham, with realistic ambitions of challenging for a Champions League spot in this unpredictable season, seemed to be the subject of much of the rumour-mongering. With the misfiring striker Sébastien Haller leaving for Ajax, the Hammers reportedly had several Championship players in their crosshairs, among them Blackburn's free-scoring Adam Armstrong and Watford speedster Ismaïla Sarr. The latter, wearer of a high price tag despite scoring just nine league goals in eighteen months at Vicarage Road, was a strange suggested replacement. He's more of a touchline-patrolling Saïd Benrahma-type figure, and West Ham already have one of those. His name is Saïd Benrahma.

Elsewhere, Michael Olise, the neat and creative puppet-master of Reading's midfield, was a more than visible presence on the respective radar of Leeds, Wolves and Aston Villa. Villa, of course, had struck gold over the summer by signing Brentford's top scorer Ollie Watkins. His replacement, the equally free-scoring Ivan Toney, was another who was turning the heads of several recruitment departments.

In the end, rumours remained rumours and these young guns stayed put – for now, at least. The Premier League was likely to be their playground soon enough. A steadier flow of human traffic was travelling in the opposite direction, though: experienced players dropping down to the Championship to reignite careers that had faltered through injury, lack of form or simply being the wrong-shaped piece for a team that now fitted together in a different way.

The most conspicuous of these moves was Charlie Austin's return on loan to QPR from West Brom. Having made just five league appearances for the Baggies this season and failing to score in any of them, he was off and running three days after arriving back in west London. It took him just thirty-nine minutes to get on the scoresheet on his second debut for the Hoops. An instant impact.

The same week that Austin headed back to London, another Premier League player rolls up at a Championship club, another temporary signing who needs as much out of the arrangement as his new team. In this case, the club requires a midfielder with guile to steer them away from the magnetic pull of the relegation zone; the player needs to find traction for a career blighted by prolonged and serious injury.

Before arriving at Coventry City, Leicester's Matty James had already spent the first half of the season in the Championship, helping to solidify Barnsley's upward progress towards the play-off places. He presumed he was going to be spending the entire season at Oakwell, but not so. Having swapped South Yorkshire for the West Midlands, tonight James is stepping out at the Madejski Stadium for his first start for the Sky Blues.

Tall and sturdy, he's built more like a putting-it-about centre-forward or a none-shall-pass centre-half than the deep-lying, dot-joining fulcrum of the Coventry midfield. This evening, he's almost playing a sweeper role *in front of* his back three, albeit one who's also always prowling the edge of the penalty area whenever Coventry have a corner or an attacking free kick. James might have spent a significant portion of his career on the treatment table, but he hasn't forgotten his trade. Indeed, so comfortable and assured does he look that you could believe he's been part of this Coventry team for years, not days. He has the feel of a captain, a leader.

James is in tune with his new team's cause straight away. This is no uncaring mercenary for hire. The passion is there. Early on, his head is in his hands when a header from Coventry defender Leo Østigård goes narrowly wide. His head is soon back in his hands when the back three are caught out in too advanced a position and Lucas João puts Reading ahead.

That James is showing such deep and instant commitment to the cause of a club he may only be at for four or so months is down to his medical record, that long and winding list of slow-curing ailments. A regular starter in Leicester's midfield during the 2014–15 season, their first back in the top flight for more than a decade, James ruptured his cruciate ligament with three games left to go. It put him out of action for fourteen months. This would be a blow to any footballer in his prime. For James, though, it was more than that. The injury meant he missed the entirety of Leicester's greatest-ever season: the fairy-tale Premier League title win.

'It was a difficult time as I had numerous operations that season. The lads were splitting left to the training pitch and I was always splitting right to the physio room. It was quite lonely. To watch the title race was, in a selfish way, difficult as I wasn't involved. But I was also over the moon because it was my club. It was a tough season but an amazing achievement.'

Understandably, James found it difficult to break back into the team the following season and was looking for a loan move to build up his game time, but manager Claudio Ranieri reassured him that he would be involved with the first team at the King Power Stadium. He turned out not to be. During the January transfer window, James headed to South Yorkshire for his first loan spell at Barnsley. It proved successful; he only missed one game for the Tykes, and that was for the birth of his first child.

With competitive football back in his legs, James reported for pre-season duty back at Leicester that July, but was soon consulting the club physio. Extreme soreness in one of his Achilles was impervious to injections but, desperate to avoid the stigma that an injury-prone footballer can bear throughout their career, James chose to mask the true extent of the pain.

'I was doing well in games, but no one knew what I was exactly going through, that I was in so much pain. I was standing in the tunnel in some of the biggest stadiums, and playing against some of the best teams and some of the best players, and I knew I was only sixty per cent fit – if that. I was standing in bins of boiling water to warm my Achilles up before I went out. And I'd wake up the next day and not be able to walk. By April, my Achilles was three times bigger than it was supposed to be. If I tapped it, I'd be in agony.'

James sought specialist help, which ranged from 'Let's cut you open' to 'There's nothing wrong with you'. He flew to Sweden to consult with Håkan Alfredson, the world-renowned tendon specialist. After several operations to remove excess scar tissue, James was – after a lengthy period of rehab – ultimately pain-free. He returned to Leicester's starting line-up for an FA Cup tie against Newport the following season, but in the warm-up James was struck by a feeling of *déjà vu*. His right Achilles now felt exactly how his left had done. 'I was running around in a daze, thinking, *This can't be right. I must be imagining it. It's got to be in my head.*'

And that wasn't the end of it. From overcompensating for the pain in his right Achilles, James had developed a stress injury in his left shin. If it never rains but pours, he was caught in a never-ending monsoon. Knock followed knock, setback succeeded setback. And the stigma of the permanently crocked footballer began to stick. In his head, at least.

'I was so embarrassed by the entire process. My body was letting me down the whole time. All I was thinking about, aside from the pain, was people's opinions of me. I thought that they were talking about me behind my back. They weren't, of course. No one at the club was. That was just my own mind playing tricks on me. And I thought I had had enough. *Am I going to play football again? Is retirement coming to me early?*'

James had again been hiding the severity of his injury – from his coaches, his physio, his family. It all came to a head in the manager's office when he broke down in front of Brendan Rodgers. 'I let everything out. I was in there for about forty-five minutes. But the emotional intelligence that Brendan has is incredible – the way he helped me, the way he calmed me down.' The pair agreed to one final bout of surgery in Sweden, while Rodgers also enrolled James on a course to get his UEFA B coaching badge in order to distract him. (Of course, were the surgery unsuccessful, it would prove a judicious next step in James's career.)

Alfredson's scalpel worked its magic, though, and by January 2020, James was turning out for the reserves. But then the pandemic hit, another obstacle on the road back to regular first-team football. Now pain-free for the first time in years, in isolation James got himself as fit as he'd ever been. 'I was running on a cow patch near my house, so I knew when I got back to Leicester and their immaculate pitches, I'd feel fantastic.'

However, when the 2019–20 season restarted after the first lockdown, James remained on the bench. A request was then made to go back out on loan at the start of the following campaign. 'That's when the stigma reared its ugly head. It was "Matty's been out too long" or "I really like Matty but when was his last game?"

'But then Barnsley came in for me. They were my only option. At the time they had no manager as Gerhard Struber had just left to go to New York Red Bulls, so it was the board, the owners and Dane Murphy, the chief exec, who wanted me to come in. Perhaps that was to my advantage. Had there been a manager there, he might not have wanted me in because of my injury record. For me it was, "Where's the dotted line? Where do I sign so you can't pull out?"'

Having first played in the Championship ten years ago, James has noticed certain differences in the second tier. 'Technically and tactically it's changed. Back then, it was very rare that anyone was playing three at the back. It was unheard of. It was 4-4-2 or 4-4-1-1 or sometimes 4-3-3, depending who you were playing. Certain teams now are more possession-based, Brentford in particular, but can they get out of the Championship doing it a different way to how other teams have done it in the past? Leeds certainly managed it last season. When I made my Championship debut, I was playing for Preston against Sheffield United. It was a battle. But that physicality is still there today too. There's a bigger mix in the league now, so clubs have to be more adaptable.'

Brought in to anchor the midfield of a notably young Barnsley team, James did so to strong effect, the team climbing the table under their new manager, the former Wolfsburg head coach Valérien Ismaël. By the end of December, and the end of James's loan spell, Barnsley were sitting pretty in eighth place. It was therefore surprising to all onlookers that his loan deal wasn't extended.

'My expectation was to stay. I knew the club, had settled in easily and was enjoying it. But there was no consensus at the club; the manager, the directors and the owners weren't in agreement about me staying. The manager wanted his young players to play. Herbie Kane had been bought for more than a million and I think the manager felt he needed to play him. It was the same with Romal Palmer, another very young player. I don't mind coming out of the team for form, but I don't want to be out of the team for politics. Ultimately the conversation is with the manager. Valérien was fantastic with me. I've got huge respect that he was so honest.

'So we made contact with some other clubs. Mark Robins at Coventry was desperate to get me there. I knew that Coventry's style of play suited me, whereas at Barnsley it had been quite direct and not what I was used to. And I was desperate to play. I didn't want to wait around until the end of January and miss all this month's games. I went straight into action.'

After just a couple of weeks with the Sky Blues, James is enjoying the latest reboot of a stuttering, spluttering career. The pause button has been released. 'I now feel like a twenty-one-year-old boy, running around and around with zero pain. As a team, we're very forward-thinking, very attack-minded. We just need to keep the back door shut as well.'

Out of contract with Leicester at the end of the season, it's highly likely that his time at the King Power is almost over ('I certainly imagine so'). Bearing in mind James has only played a single league game for them over the past three seasons, the Foxes' loyalty has been unparalleled. 'They've been fantastic. When people ask me about Leicester, it's not a five-minute conversation. I could talk for two hours about how good they've been to me. The fans too. It's a very special place.'

James intends to make as many appearances for Coventry between now and May to improve his reputation, to neutralise the odour that's trailed behind him for so long. Then a fresh chapter can be written come next season.

'I need to add some good years onto the end of my career. Over the last few years, not many miles have been put on the clock. I want to feel the excitement and adrenalin I'm feeling now for a long time to come.' Whether that's by signing a permanent deal with Coventry or heading elsewhere remains to be seen. For now, it's all about steady caution.

'I just need to get to the summer.' A self-deprecating smile. 'And that's not a given in my situation . . .'

Back in Reading, with Coventry now down to ten men and

three goals in arrears (that back door's been left open again), James is taken off late in the game. Despite the result, he's earned his keep tonight. His dark hair is matted to his forehead by the damp night, but also by eighty-odd minutes of endeavour. His manager Robins will be pleased with the energy and commitment of his latest signing.

At the exact point that James leaves the field, 140 miles away in Derby, another midfielder in the final year of his twenties and with plenty of Premier League experience takes to the Pride Park pitch. He too has dropped down a division in order to quell the anxiety of, and get a firm grip on, a career that's not quite lived up to its initial billing. It's time for a reboot for Jack Wilshere.

In those twelve minutes on the pitch, the former England man would get an instant lesson in what he had signed up for. Brought in to give Bournemouth a further push towards automatic promotion, instead he's first got to help arrest the Cherries' current slide. Tonight's defeat to the Rams is the first time they've lost two on the bounce this season. Even more worrying for Jason Tindall is that they've only won once in the last six. The promotion favourites have been downgraded to mere promotion hopefuls.

*

## Saturday, 30 January

*1.15 p.m.*

Little more than an hour after leaving her home near Bristol, Michelle Owen pulls into the car park at the Cardiff City Stadium, just as she's done scores of times before. She's a frequent visitor both to this car park and to the car parks of football stadiums across South Wales and South-west England. After seven years as a match reporter in the service of Sky's flagship show *Soccer Saturday*, this is Owen's home patch. She knows the route, she knows the routine.

Today's routine, though, takes the slightest of deviations as, now parked up, Owen sits tight for a few minutes. It's a bitterly cold day in the Welsh capital and there's no need to leave the warmth of her car just yet. In these pandemic days, the life of the football reporter has become a little more solitary. Under normal conditions, Owen would head straight inside to the press lounge for a cup of coffee and the chance to socialise and chew the fat with the rest of the press corps, whether broadcasters, print journalists or minute-by-minute online reporters. These days, though – after the mandatory temperature checks have been made and the medical forms have been filled in – it's a case of going straight up to her lofty perch on the gantry of the main stand. To get there, you head upwards to the very top until there are no more clanging metal steps left to climb. Owen is up in the gods. Her office is this divine viewing platform.

The set-up is a modest one, a two-person affair consisting of Owen and John the camera operator. Owen's stool is positioned facing the camera, at right angles to the pitch. Just below the camera is a small monitor, there in case any crucial action occurs on the pitch behind her when she's on air. 'It happens,' Owen admits. 'You can't do anything about it. And it's better to say what you've seen or what you've not seen than trying to blag it.'

*2 p.m.*

Owen heads back down to the press box below the gantry 'to see if anything's happening with either team that I might have missed, little stories that a local journalist might know'. Being an hour before kick-off, it's the time at which the two starting line-ups are released to the press. Here at Cardiff, though, unlike almost every other club, physical team sheets aren't handed out. A freshly printed A4 sheet, clearly setting out the respective starting XIs, is an essential, user-friendly tool of the match reporter's trade. Instead, Owen has to improvise, making scribbles on the squad lists on the back page of the match-day programme. From this, she then draws up the most likely formations of Cardiff City and today's visitors Millwall, intuitively guided by her intimate knowledge of Championship football. Today is Mick McCarthy's first home game as Cardiff manager and he's left the playmaker Harry Wilson – a fixture of the starting line-ups of previous boss Neil Harris – on the bench, so an element of second-guessing is needed to deduce how he's going to set his new side up.

Owen's knowledge of the second tier has been earned out in the field. She's on match-reporting duties at least three times a week, sometimes four. Just as a player like Joe Jacobson or a kitman like Jon Pearce feels the relentless burn of the unfolding season, so too do the gantry gang. 'With this season being more condensed, there's only been one midweek where I haven't done a game and that was because of an international break. It's relentless, but I'm grateful for the work.'

Rather astoundingly, though, Owen has yet to report on a Premier League game for *Soccer Saturday* in all those seven years. But, on further consideration, this is perfectly logical. Say there were five Premier League games kicking off at 3 p.m. (an increasingly unlikely scenario in itself with top-flight games being spread far and wide across the TV schedules), the studio-based pundits would take care of four of them, with the fifth going to the most senior of the on-location reporters, Chris 'Kammy' Kamara.

Owen doesn't mind. 'The Championship has become my bread and butter. It wasn't deliberate, but that's not a problem as I love the EFL. I really appreciate the quality of the Premier League and obviously this season is more enjoyable than most because it's so unpredictable, but we have that every season in the Championship.'

Over the course of the season, the quantity of matches that Owen works at does mean they start to merge in her memory. 'If you asked me what game I was doing on a Saturday eight weeks ago, I wouldn't know. You finish the game and you walk away. And you don't remember forgettable games.' This afternoon's match, between two of the more prosaic sides in the division, may well not live long in the memory. A feast of free-flowing football is unlikely to ensue, with Owen not called upon to deploy too much purple prose in her reports.

*2.40 p.m.*
After a quick soundcheck, it's now a waiting game for Owen and John as they watch both sides go through their final warm-ups on the pitch. The Cardiff players are all wearing T-shirts with 'Bamba 22' on the back and 'We fight with you' on the front – a show of solidarity with their team-mate Sol Bamba, recently diagnosed with Non-Hodgkin lymphoma.

The gantry is a quiet place before kick-off, with thousands of empty seats stretching out before it. Just as the players are affected by the absence of fans, so too are those on broadcasting duties. There's no pre-match buzz. 'You don't have that energy to feed off,' Owen admits. 'It's a real shame.'

*Soccer Saturday* doesn't require a pre-match report; its reporters are there in position pretty much to simply deliver goal updates. Today, trying to keep warm ahead of kick-off – and hopeful of plenty of screen time thanks to an avalanche of goals – Neil Mellor is at Ewood Park, Bianca Westwood at St Andrews, Alan McInally at Hillsborough and Guy Havord at the City Ground. Kammy has been dispatched to Rotherham to man the sentry post at the New York Stadium. This afternoon, all of their reports will reference the near-sub-zero temperatures. It's inescapable.

Although best known for her on-screen reporting for Sky

('My career is built off *Soccer Saturday*'), Owen is also gainfully employed by BBC Radio 5 Live for midweek games, on which she enjoys more airtime: there will be pre-match, half-time and full-time reports to give, along with regular updates and goal flashes throughout the game.

'Working for them is a real joy. When I really got into football when I was young, I used to balance a radio on my windowsill. We lived in the middle of nowhere and I was trying to get reception. I didn't have a TV in my room at that point, and we didn't have Sky because my family are not into football at all. So I'd listen to 5 Live's commentaries, and to broadcasters like Mark Pougatch and Ellie Oldroyd. I love doing *Soccer Saturday*, but to be working for 5 Live *as well* is a real privilege. If you'd told the eight-year-old me that's what I'd be doing in years to come, I wouldn't have believed you.'

This season has found Owen's already formidable Championship credentials being strengthened even further. She's become the first reserve when it comes to presenting the EFL highlights on Quest, Colin Murray's stand-in when he's off recording episodes of *Countdown* or presenting live snooker for Eurosport. It gives Owen a rare Saturday afternoon away from the gantry's wintry chill.

*3.09 p.m.*

Nine minutes into the game and Millwall give Owen a reason to broadcast to the nation. After their quicksilver winger Jed Wallace makes a speedy charge down the left, his cross is diverted into the net by Cardiff defender Aden Flint. Immediately, Owen gets in touch with her producer back in London.

'Goal. Millwall. 0–1. Own goal.'

'Okay, stand by.'

Owen removes her woolly hat and, back at the studio, presenter Jeff Stelling wastes no time in handing across to her, teeing up the report with reference to McCarthy: '... he's not enjoyed the happiest of starts today, Michelle.'

Like she's done thousands of times before, Owen then delivers a succinct, word-perfect precis of both the move that led to the goal and the balance of play so far, along with a little stat for context: 'the last six games between these two teams, Jeff, have ended in draws'. Thirty-three seconds and it's back to Stelling.

Sometimes, if there's been a slight delay before the studio has come to the reporter, there might be a chance to watch a replay of the goal before going live. Not this time, though. The replay of the Millwall goal only appears on the small monitor as Owen is halfway through her report. This makes her identification of the hapless defender all the more impressive. Despite her perch being seventy-odd yards from the goal, Owen instantly recognised the culprit to be Flint. It's impressive not only because he was slumped face-down on the turf as the ball slid into the net, but also because Flint's Viking-like features – shoulder-length hair, straggly beard – are shared by his defensive colleague Sean Morrison.

*3.46 p.m.*

The half-time whistle blows. No more goals here, no more moments deemed worthy enough of a live update. 'Sometimes they might come to you four or five times, even if it's a nil-nil. It's up to the producer's discretion. It's very subjective and depends on what's happening elsewhere, or the context of a particular match.'

With this afternoon's game both low on incident and – with both teams sitting mid-table – relatively inconsequential, there's been plenty of time to consider whether the temperature could plunge any lower. It's not a concern shared by the pundits alongside Stelling in the studio in London, basking under the warmth of the studio lights. These three ex-pros – Paul Merson, Tim

Sherwood and Joleon Lescott – are each watching one of the three Premier League 3 p.m. kick-offs. Ally McCoist, broadcasting on home turf in Scotland, is on Championship duties. He's watching a humdinger of an encounter between Brentford and Wycombe. It's two-all at half-time, with no shortage of incident. The set-up is faintly ridiculous, though. The match is taking place just a couple of miles away from Sky's studios in Isleworth, but is being watched, described and analysed by a man sat in front of a TV screen in Glasgow.

With no half-time summary to deliver, the break offers Owen the chance to see what people are saying about the game online, to analyse the first-half stats, and to catch up with the other scores across the Championship. Even though she has the programme coming through her earpiece throughout, what's occurring in the studio doesn't take her attention. 'I'm not that attuned to it as I'm concentrating on my game. Unless someone's shouting . . .'

Half-time is also a chance to defrost, to counter the elements. A cup of tea or soup might offer some defence, but really it's all about the clothing. Although Sky don't like their reporters to wear headgear while delivering their pieces to camera, Owen is somewhat known for her collection of woolly hats, usually teamed with a matching scarf. She's even had the odd Twitter follower offering to knit her a new one. It could take off: the wool-based equivalent of *Test Match Special*'s listeners baking cakes for the commentators.

During these bone-shaking winter months, the temperature is the main talk of the gantry, a place that seems to have a weather system all of its own. 'I see people with heated gilets, but I'm not convinced they stay warm for that long. And I'd be worried about electrocuting myself or something. I have been known to bring a hot-water bottle, though. Anyway, it's my legs that get the coldest, so I'm going to buy some salopettes. Fleece-lined waterproof trousers are the way forward.' Today, Owen has brought a blanket from home and wrapped it around her knees. 'It's making no difference. But it's whatever does the job, to be honest. The viewers can't see my bottom half, so I don't care.'

*4.31 p.m.*

The second half has largely been as lumpy and unrefined as the first forty-five minutes – until, that is, sub Harry Wilson threads an inviting ball through to Cardiff's leading scorer Kieffer Moore, who dinks it over the advancing goalkeeper.

The equaliser is swiftly followed by the voice of Jeff Stelling down the line. 'Cardiff are back on level terms against Millwall and what a big difference Kieffer Moore, fit and firing, might make to Mick McCarthy. Michelle Owen ...'

Owen might be momentarily hat-less, but there's no kidding the viewers. You can hear the cold in her voice. Her update is kept brief, all the salient information delivered in a whistle-stop, but thoroughly professional, twenty-six seconds.

And that's the last that the Sky-watching public will hear from Owen today. No more goals, no more reasons to report back to the studio. Cardiff press for a winner and there are speculative shots from Wilson and Josh Murphy, but rather than rustle the back of the net, these just send the empty pull-up seats in the Canton Stand spinning furiously.

Even if the producers wanted to come back to Owen in the dying moments as Cardiff's pressure mounts, there would be little time available, thanks to what's occurring at the Brentford Community Stadium. From the comfort of his Glasgow studio, Ally McCoist has been served up a treat. Not only has he seen nine goals (of which the hosts have helped themselves to seven), but the woodwork has been hit more than once. The odd moment of controversy has flared up too. While Owen's two reports totalled less than a minute on air – and the match finished in a thoroughly predictable seventh successive draw between the two sides – McCoist has been in near-constant demand this afternoon. 'I'm so jealous,' mutters Owen beneath a half-smile.

*5 p.m.*
Owen decamps to the side of the pitch, ready to lightly grill both teams' managers. The wind is fearsome down at pitchside, causing the Perspex advertising board, in front of which managers are contractually obliged to go through the clichéd motions of the post-match interview, to crash onto the turf. Ahead of the transfer deadline in two days' time, Owen was hoping to quiz Millwall boss Gary Rowett about his plans to sign a much-needed striker, but assistant manager Adam Barrett is deputising instead. 'The assistant is never going to answer those types of questions,' says Owen. 'We think that's why he sent him out.'

Then McCarthy, with Cardiff yet to lose under him, takes his place before the advertising board. The interview is perfunctory and pretty standard: he's still getting to know the players, he's happy with the starting XI, he's pleased by the impact of his subs. Like the match, the interview will soon be forgotten, if it gets used at all. One of McCarthy's predecessors here, Neil Warnock, remains Owen's favourite for final-whistle observations. 'I have a really good relationship with him, but you can guarantee he'll come out talking about the referee.'

*6.25 p.m.*
Traffic has been light back over the bridge and Owen arrives home in time for her toddler son's bedtime. Today might have been a comparatively easy day, with a shortish drive in either direction and just two updates to deliver, but the whole endeavour still translates into a sizeable effort all ways round for such a small amount of time on air.

'That's what makes *Soccer Saturday* unique. The bases are covered. Even if there's nothing happening at a ground, they know they've got someone there. You never know what *might* happen. It could have been four-all today. That's the beauty of live reporting and I love it. Even if it's a nil-nil and you only do one report, it's still great to be part of the country's biggest Saturday afternoon football programme.'

Now thawed out thanks to her car's heating system, the focus is on the next game. And the diary is busy. On Tuesday night, Owen will be back in the service of Sky for Coventry versus Nottingham Forest, before heading to Twerton Park in Bath the following evening for a WSL Continental Cup semi-final between Bristol City and Leicester, from where she'll supply regular updates for 5 Live. Owen will be reporting for the same station come Friday night for the tasty top-of-the-table clash between Swansea and Norwich; nineteen hours later, she'll be back on *Soccer Saturday* duty, delivering the goal flashes from the Severnside derby between Bristol City and Cardiff.

Five matches in little more than seven days. No wonder games can merge and congeal into a single mass.

Owen does at least have a day off on Monday as Sky's coverage of Transfer Deadline Day will, in these Covid times, be a largely studio-based affair. She won't be required to stand outside a club's training ground for hours on end, just to tell the nation that precisely nothing is happening. However, she does have to fit in the co-hosting of the latest episode of the Bristol City podcast Robins At The Gate at some point this week. It never stops. The pages of the calendar on the kitchen wall – at least those between August and May – are always full.

And, of course, still to be factored in is an emergency shopping trip for that pair of salopettes.

*

# Championship table, 31 January

|    |                       | P  | W  | D  | L  | F  | A  | Pts |
|----|-----------------------|----|----|----|----|----|----|-----|
| 1  | Norwich City          | 26 | 16 | 6  | 4  | 35 | 21 | 54  |
| 2  | Swansea City          | 26 | 14 | 8  | 4  | 33 | 15 | 50  |
| 3  | Brentford             | 25 | 13 | 9  | 3  | 45 | 24 | 48  |
| 4  | Watford               | 26 | 13 | 8  | 5  | 30 | 18 | 47  |
| 5  | Reading               | 26 | 14 | 5  | 7  | 40 | 29 | 47  |
| 6  | AFC Bournemouth       | 26 | 11 | 9  | 6  | 39 | 24 | 42  |
| 7  | Middlesbrough         | 27 | 11 | 7  | 9  | 30 | 24 | 40  |
| 8  | Blackburn Rovers      | 26 | 11 | 6  | 9  | 41 | 28 | 39  |
| 9  | Bristol City          | 26 | 12 | 3  | 11 | 27 | 28 | 39  |
| 10 | Stoke City            | 27 | 9  | 11 | 7  | 32 | 29 | 38  |
| 11 | Preston North End     | 27 | 11 | 3  | 13 | 31 | 34 | 36  |
| 12 | Barnsley              | 27 | 10 | 6  | 11 | 29 | 34 | 36  |
| 13 | Luton Town            | 26 | 9  | 6  | 11 | 21 | 28 | 33  |
| 14 | Huddersfield Town     | 27 | 9  | 5  | 13 | 30 | 38 | 32  |
| 15 | Cardiff City          | 26 | 8  | 7  | 11 | 33 | 31 | 31  |
| 16 | Millwall              | 26 | 6  | 13 | 7  | 22 | 25 | 31  |
| 17 | Coventry City         | 26 | 7  | 9  | 10 | 25 | 35 | 30  |
| 18 | Derby County          | 26 | 7  | 7  | 12 | 17 | 25 | 28  |
| 19 | Queens Park Rangers   | 25 | 6  | 9  | 10 | 23 | 31 | 27  |
| 20 | Birmingham City       | 26 | 6  | 9  | 11 | 19 | 31 | 27  |
| 21 | Nottingham Forest     | 26 | 6  | 8  | 12 | 20 | 29 | 26  |
| 22 | Rotherham United      | 24 | 6  | 5  | 13 | 27 | 35 | 23  |
| 23 | Sheffield Wednesday   | 25 | 7  | 7  | 11 | 16 | 25 | 22* |
| 24 | Wycombe Wanderers     | 24 | 3  | 6  | 15 | 18 | 42 | 15  |

*Includes six-point deduction*

**Leading scorers**

Ivan Toney (Brentford), 18
Adam Armstrong (Blackburn), 17
Lucas João (Reading), 15
Teemu Pukki (Norwich), 11
Dominic Solanke (Bournemouth), 10
Kieffer Moore (Cardiff), 10

**Manager of the Month**

Steve Cooper (Swansea)

**Player of the Month**

Matt Crooks (Rotherham)

**Managerial departures**

Neil Harris (Cardiff), sacked

**Managerial appointments**

Wayne Rooney (Derby)
Mick McCarthy (Cardiff)

# February

'The cold-blooded murder of the football club
was being committed in front of our eyes'

— GARY SWEET

It was both the first day of February and the last day of the
winter transfer window. And, as the evening lengthened and the
trading period narrowed, at Derby County the coffee machine
was doing overtime.

Throughout January, the club had been subject to a transfer
embargo, one imposed after the non-payment of players' wages
at Pride Park. Not a single new player could be signed. But,
with the outstanding salaries paid and the embargo freshly
lifted, the entrance door had been metaphorically propped
open, albeit just as the window was closing. Speedy business
was called for.

Not that Derby's recruitment team were panicking. The first
signing wasn't announced until four in the afternoon, but it was
a deal that showed the advantage of having Wayne Rooney as
boss, of revisiting a former club and using accrued goodwill as
leverage. That late-afternoon signing of the defender Teden
Mengi from Manchester United was a loan deal, a pattern to be
repeated for the rest of the proceedings. The Stoke striker Lee

Gregory was next, an arrival announced midway through the evening. But then silence.

The 11 p.m. deadline came and went, causing concern to page-refreshing Rams fans. No matter. The wraps came off three more loan signings before midnight: the winger Patrick Roberts from Manchester City, the Rangers defender George Edmundson, and the midfielder Beni Baningime, borrowed from another of Rooney's former clubs, Everton. The effect was akin to three late goals in stoppage time. Those fans could breathe again.

With eight deals done (there were also three departures from Pride Park, two of which even brought some money into the coffers), Derby were the busiest Championship club on Deadline Day. But they were by no means an outlier. While the media relentlessly moaned about the paucity of Premier League transfer activity – and despite promotion-chasing Reading not signing a single new player during the entire window – business was comparatively brisk in the second tier. The cash registers were quiet, though. Loans were largely the order of the day across the board.

Preston North End were another club whose officials were putting in a hell of a Deadline Day shift. Having already signed five new players in January, they made a further three loan signings on Deadline Day, as well as releasing three of their own to pastures new, whether temporary or permanent. The single permanent departure created one of the headline moves of the day. Their elegant, left-sided central defender Ben Davies was called upon to help fill the void in Liverpool's backline caused by the long-term injuries to Virgil van Dijk, Joe Gomez and Joël Matip. The deal was something of a throwback and marked an increasingly rare occasion in modern football: the reigning champions of England dipping into the lower divisions to add to their first-team squad, rather than either looking abroad or promoting from their own ranks.

There was another Championship-to-Premier-League move that made the headlines – and which went longer and later into the night than any of the Derby deals. Last January, a £20m bid for Bournemouth's want-away striker Josh King from Manchester United had been rejected; ever since, the Norwegian had been a fixture of the transfer gossip columns and rumour mills. None of the hearsay surrounding him throughout the last month – when his suitors reportedly included West Ham, Burnley and West Brom – had come to fruition. As Deadline Day dawned, it was a case of whether any club was willing to match his wage demands or whether, with his contract expiring at the end of the season, King was content to be a bit-part player for the rest of Bournemouth's season – a season, we should note, in which he had failed to score in twelve league appearances – before departing on a free.

At breakfast time, it had looked as if a move along the coast to Southampton might be the most probable, with Shane Long making the journey in the opposite direction. By lunchtime, Torino had apparently expressed an interest in signing King at the end of the season. By early evening – with Southampton reported to have jettisoned their interest, scared off by King's expected salary – it looked like a race between Everton and Fulham for his signature. These were new actors in the saga, not among those previously linked to the player. On hearing these developments, the journalist Adam Hurrey tweeted his tongue-in-cheek prediction for what would happen next: 'All 20 Premier League clubs set to sign 5% of Josh King each.'

King had a dilemma. Everton was the higher-profile destination, but despite the departure of striker Cenk Tosun back to Turkey earlier in the day creating room in the first-team squad, the form of Dominic Calvert-Lewin meant no guarantees for

King to be in their starting XI. He was more likely to be a first-choice player at Craven Cottage, but with Fulham mired in the bottom three and looking destined for a swift return to the Championship, this wasn't a strong long-term option. Indeed, the talk was that, having been offered a three-and-a-half-year deal in west London, King's representatives were insisting on a release clause should Fulham be relegated.

As the evening unfolded, Everton moved into the ascendancy and Goodison Park was increasingly believed to be King's most likely destination. Ten minutes before the window closed, unofficial word came that he was heading there on a short-term permanent deal, worth £5m to Bournemouth, depending on appearances and achievements in the next few months on Merseyside.

But it wasn't until a minute past 1 a.m., the hour of the nighthawk, that confirmation of the deal was announced. Even the late shift at Pride Park had clocked off by then.

*

Josh Marsh also worked late on Deadline Day, but things weren't quite so hectic at Huddersfield Town as elsewhere.

As the club's head of recruitment, Marsh had done most of his shopping in a relaxed and timely manner earlier in the month. On the final day, there was just one new arrival at Canalside, the training ground on the Leeds Road, half a mile north of the John Smith's Stadium. That new face, the former Middlesbrough and Blackburn goalkeeper Jayson Leutwiler, joined a handful of seasoned players brought in over the previous few weeks to consolidate the Terriers' Championship status. Marsh had deliberately targeted players who'd been around the block, who had plenty of miles in their legs. There was no point filling gaps in the squad with recent academy graduates from Premier League clubs. This wasn't work experience. This was no placement. This was about survival. A recent poor run of form needed arresting and any incoming player had to be familiar with the league, had to hit the ground running.

These seasoned professionals – the defender Richard Keogh, the midfielder Duane Holmes and the winger Rolando Aarons – were all brought in to plug vacancies caused by long-term injuries to existing players. Holmes and Aarons were fixtures on Marsh's radar; their arrival was just earlier than expected. 'They were both players we wanted to sign this summer,' he explains, 'but they got brought forward with more urgency. Richard Keogh wasn't a planned signing, but a short-term need popped up when three senior centre-halves got injured. A lot of players who are available in January on a loan or a short-term deal usually haven't played for six months or so. That's why they're available. So it was a rare situation with Richard as he'd played half of this season in League One with MK Dons.'

These experienced acquisitions didn't stop Marsh from burning the near-midnight oil on Deadline Day, though. 'We were still active until the end, but we weren't in a place where we were panicking that we needed to sign two or three players. It was good to be in that position. We tried everything we could to bring in another offensive player because of the injuries we'd had and because of the sheer number of games left in the calendar. And because we're not in the best vein of form at the moment. But the ones we tried weren't possible for various reasons, so that was that. But now that we're out of the window, there are still a few free agents that we've been considering on short-term deals.'

With the latest window shut, Marsh has the chance to come up for air. He's working from home in Cheshire today, without the distraction of travelling up to Town's match at Middlesbrough tonight – although his absence was forced upon him. 'Tickets are really hard to come by at the moment. That's been a big change this season. Live scouting has definitely become a little bit trickier. It's not ideal by any means. I've missed that side of things, being out and about.'

Marsh has been at Huddersfield for exactly five years, half of which as head of recruitment. Prior to that, he was chief scout, a position he took up shortly after his twenty-fourth birthday. That's a tender age to be appointed to such a significant position, but this is someone not lacking focus or ambition. He was in his second year as a ball-playing centre-half in Wrexham's academy when he realised he wasn't going to make the grade to play at the highest level. He studied for a sports coaching degree, a programme of study whose graduates tend to gravitate towards careers in coaching, sports science or analytics. Marsh instead cast his eye in the direction of scouting.

'Back then, and still to this day, the side of football I found most interesting was the off-field stuff, the side you don't see, the business side of things. I didn't have the appetite to stay on the grass and be hands-on with players. The stuff behind the scenes was what intrigued and excited me the most.

'This was about seven or eight years ago. At that time, scouting and recruitment were beginning to change in terms of how clubs were setting up their departments. It was emerging and developing, and not many people were getting into it.' A former coach of his at Wrexham, Stuart Webber, was by now chief scout at Wolves, so Marsh offered to scout for him on a voluntary basis. Six months later, the volunteer became a part-time employee. A further six months later, the part-time employee went full-time.

After two years at Molineux, and a seven-month spell at Southampton, Huddersfield came calling in the shape of his former boss Webber, who was now head of football operations at the John Smith's. 'I'd worked closely with Stuart at Wolves and built up his trust. He came knocking on my door and it was something I couldn't turn down.' The progressive German coach David Wagner had arrived in West Yorkshire two months earlier and a culture shift was underway at the club. 'It wasn't a complete blank slate, but the club wanted to do something different. It was a massive shift. And it was an amazing opportunity at the age I was.'

Currently, there is only one other head of recruitment at a Championship club who's also still in his twenties – Stoke City's Alex Aldridge. But, as Marsh observes, scouting is an increasingly popular vocation among the younger guns, quite possibly down to it becoming, over the past ten years, more of a laptop-based pursuit. Not that the heavy use of data analysis is necessarily applauded by all. 'Some of the older guys with more traditional footballing values might turn their nose up at it, but I've known others, who've worked as scouts for decades, who are really open-minded, engaged and enthusiastic about how things are changing and improving. Irrespective of age, you get a mixture of personalities and outlooks. I've had no big problems on that side of things.

'What you can't get away with now in the scouting world is that stereotype: turn up, have a cuppa and a chat with your mates, and leave on seventy minutes having not done a lot. Departments are much more professional these days.

'There's still a place for both methods. The ideal process is that you bring both together.' Marsh runs through a typical vetting process for a player he might be interested in. It's decidedly rigorous. At first, he'll be watched on video in a variety of scenarios: when he plays at home; when he plays away; when his team has suffered a bad defeat; when he's played out of position . . . Then comes data profiling, comparing the player's stats both against those of the club's current players and against the league's averages. Research will then be undertaken on his background and his personal life. His social media channels will be studied. Interviews he's previously done will also be watched to gather a feel for his personality.

'But, fundamentally, in an ideal world, you can only tick off a player by watching him live. Within the department, we would make sure there were at least a couple of live viewings of him, before I would do a follow-up viewing as a final check. Then we produce something called a player pack – the proposal that contains all the information in a single document. I then pass that to Leigh Bromby, the head of football operations. We'll have a conversation and if he's on board and likes the idea, we'll share it with the head coach. From the sporting point of view, the coach has the final say. We'll provide a number of options for a particular position in the team and he'll be the one who makes that final call. If he's not happy with it, it won't happen.'

Marsh and his six-strong team – an academy head of recruitment, a loans manager, two full-time senior scouts and a couple of interns – work on two transfer windows at a time. 'When we're making decisions in January, we'll also be considering how that might affect what we're looking to do in the summer. There are so many moving parts. We have to prepare for every eventuality. For instance, we might not want to sell our central midfielder, but if a club really wants him and puts $x$ amount on the table, our owner might feel he's got to sell. So we need to be ready with ideas on his replacement.'

In his five years at the John Smith's Stadium, Marsh has endured pretty turbulent times – promotions and relegations, as well as witnessing the frequency with which the exit door has opened. As well as working with David Wagner, he's also served Jan Siewert, Danny Cowley and the current incumbent Carlos Corberán. That's only the half of it. Marsh is now onto his fifth head of football operations.

'It's fair to say there's been a lot of change, which presents

both challenges and opportunities. There are different personalities, different opinions, different biases. Each time there is
a change, you have to adjust to work with them. You have to
understand their ideas but you also have to try to point them in
the direction of what the club wants to do.'

The theory is that a settled head of football operations (or
however a club describes the role: a sporting director or director
of football) will establish a culture and an identity on the pitch.
Any new manager would then need to fit the club's philosophy
and style of play, rather than the club readjusting to the incoming manager's system. For the scouting team, such continuity is
crucial when their work stretches over such a long time frame.
Otherwise, the type of player they've been studiously hunting
after might be surplus to requirements overnight following the
latest regime change. A new manager might want to cultivate
a team based on swift passing but the scouting department
have spent the past few months fine-tuning a shortlist of old-
fashioned lumpy centre-forwards.

'We've experienced that and, no two ways around it, it is difficult. You see it all the time across clubs. It causes real problems.
You have a squad of players, many on long contracts. You might
have only made several decisions a couple of months ago. Then
a coach with a very different outlook comes in and those players
become redundant, but you're contracted to them for the next
two or three years.'

Marsh's job is undeniably a pressured one, faced with delivering on innumerable tricky tasks while also attempting to
gain a foothold on constantly shifting sands. He at least has
one advantage over the manager, being a largely invisible presence to outside eyes. Marsh could walk through the centre of
Huddersfield this afternoon and no one would know him from
Adam. If he is the target of opprobrium, it's usually that fired
by the equally invisible keyboard warriors.

'If you read too much into the social media stuff, you'll go crazy. I don't read it, but I've been made aware of certain things at certain times. But when you hear comments or opinions, you have to remember that the people saying them don't know the intricacies and the details that you know. There's so much context around decisions, around why something happened or didn't happen. If things go well and players do well, it's all "Hail the coach and the players". If things go badly and players don't do well, it's "Who's in the background signing them?" It's one of those.'

The scrutiny given to a Championship club's head of recruitment is close and forensic, and comes from all angles. And, like many other positions in the second tier, it's a relentless slog. 'There's a real intensity to the role. It's a job that never sleeps. It's a 24/7 thing. In every game and at every training session, players are judged, so naturally your work is being judged too.'

Given he's worked under four managers and five heads of football operations, Marsh is clearly sufficiently resilient and thick-skinned. He's learned how to adapt and survive. And he's learned the limits of the recruitment department.

'You have an involvement in the player coming to the club,' he concludes, 'but the moment they sign, you pretty much wave them goodbye. Of course you still speak to them around the building, but you're not the one who's dealing with them day to day. You're not the one who's now putting in place their plan of development. You're not the one who's selecting the side.

'You can sign a player, but so much of whether that player is successful or not is completely out of your hands.'

\*

Shane Long wasn't the only arrival at the Vitality Stadium on Deadline Day. Following the departure of first-team coach

Graeme Jones to become Steve Bruce's assistant at Newcastle, the Bournemouth board appointed former Middlesbrough manager Jonathan Woodgate as Jason Tindall's number two. The pair posed for the cameras in front of the training pavilion, two men in black sharing a fist bump. Tindall was smiling a half-smile, possibly out of relief that the club had moved swiftly to replace Jones. He needed all the assistance he could get. The club had lost three games on the bounce.

Two days later, three became four when the Cherries capitulated at home to a rejuvenated Sheffield Wednesday. Now, at breakfast time the following morning, the news breaks. Tindall – a Bournemouth man through and through, going back more than two decades when he joined them as a young midfielder – has been dismissed. It seems a harsh decision, and possibly a rash one. Despite those four successive defeats, Bournemouth are still sixth in the table, still in the play-off places. But, after fewer than six months in the job, Tindall is cut loose.

'Recent performances and results have fallen well below the board's expectations,' the announcement read. 'We feel a change is needed now in order to give the club the best possible chance of achieving the goals that were clearly set out last summer.' It suggested that Tindall had been charged with achieving automatic promotion at the first time of asking, that only that would do. And all after an exodus of many of their best players last summer.

Conspiracy theories immediately emerge online. Was this the reason for Woodgate's move to the south coast? Will he now get a near-instant promotion to the top job this morning? Or, with Frank Lampard – the nephew of former Cherries manager Harry Redknapp, of course – having become the latest casualty of Roman Abramovich's itchy trigger finger a week ago, will there be an imminent high-profile arrival in town? The bookies seem to think so. Lampard is swiftly installed as 6/4 favourite for the vacancy.

There's no small amount of outrage among the Bournemouth fans that the board has acted in this way. After the calmness of the Eddie Howe years, it's very un-Bournemouth-like behaviour. Yes, taking one point from a possible fifteen is far from promotion form, but every team will experience a blip at some point in a season. That's simply the ebb and flow of football's tides. Even Jürgen Klopp's Liverpool are susceptible to it; they've just come off a run of four games without scoring.

But there's also a sizeable portion of Bournemouth fans, their opinions amplified through the bugle of social media, who welcome Tindall's departure. For them, it's not just the results. It's been the manner of the performances of late and the apparent absence of a clear tactical framework. Plenty of these voices moan that Tindall was never the right person to be given the job after Howe's departure anyway, that assistant managers rarely made strong successors. Of course, that wasn't the song being sung when Tindall took the Cherries top of the league earlier in the season.

On the morning of the first game without Tindall in charge, the former manager issues an open letter to the fans. While generous in spirit and devoid of the sourness that might be perfectly justified in the circumstances, he nonetheless can't resist reminding readers what he accomplished while number one. Not only did he achieve the best start for a first-time Bournemouth manager since John Bond fifty years earlier, but the side weren't out of the Championship's top six throughout his reign. He was far from a disaster.

However, in that first Tindall-less match, with Woodgate having stepped up as caretaker manager, the losing streak evaporates as Bournemouth come from behind to beat Birmingham 3-2, with Jack Wilshere among the scorers. It's their first home win in the league since a single-goal victory over Wycombe back in mid-December. That was a full fifty-three days ago.

Naturally, as sure as day follows night, at the final whistle the quote-hungry press corps want to know whether Woodgate has designs on taking the role permanently. The former Real Madrid man is smart enough not to get snared in the trap. His response is straight out of the lexicon of the non-committal football manager. 'My remit was to manage against Birmingham and that's as far as it goes.'

In a market where the supply of experienced managers will always comfortably exceed the demand, wise men will never say never.

*

Intrigue, gossip and rumour are also rife at Ashton Gate this lunchtime. Last night, less than a fortnight after Jason Tindall left the Vitality, another assistant manager promoted to the top job last summer – Bristol City's Dean Holden – was instructed to clear his desk. Holden's sacking was somewhat less controversial than Tindall's. After five successive league defeats in which they had scored just twice, the Robins' season was in free-fall. They had led the league at the end of September, but were now fourteenth in the table and dropping further down with each match.

After a six-nil battering by Watford the previous weekend that he described as 'a humiliation', City owner Steve Lansdown had taken to local radio to publicly challenge Holden to show a response in their next game at home to Reading. 'We've got to turn it around and make things better. And Dean's got to do that, starting tomorrow night.' The message was clear and direct. 'He knows what needs to happen and he knows the pressure he's under.'

That following evening, the response never came. City

mustered just a single shot on target as Reading eased to a two-nil win. Less than half an hour after the final whistle, Holden was an ex-employee.

While the local media and various online forums chewed over the decision the following morning, Dan Sparks was also dealing with the aftermath of the Reading game. But it had nothing to do with the vacant manager's office. Sparks is the club's head groundsman, a position he's held for nearly five years, despite him still being a couple of years shy of his thirtieth birthday.

While outside a few City fans lurk in the Ashton Gate car park hoping in vain to catch a glimpse of a new manager arriving (the more optimistic ones think Eddie Howe is the prime candidate), Sparks stands in the old home dressing room under the Atyeo Stand. The space is now the ground staff's storeroom and before him stand a fleet of mowers and rollers, primed and ready for action. The far end of the room still wears the old tiles of the players' showers. Across the corridor in the – naturally smaller – confines of the former away dressing room, sacks of fertiliser and vats of white line paint are piled high.

After the final whistle last night, Sparks and his team walked the pitch with their machines that vacuum up the loose debris. Today they're on divot-replacing duty. To do so, they'll be weaving around the lighting rigs that are currently hard at work trying to breathe life back into the turf. 'These are probably the best tools in our shed,' explains Sparks. 'They create artificial sunlight and, without them, we wouldn't have any grass at this time of year.'

These rigs are particularly necessary for the part of the Ashton Gate pitch that sees no sunshine, a ten-yard corridor along the near touchline that's cast into permanent shadow by the towering and imposing Lansdown Stand. In the months of late autumn and early winter, the darkest portion of the calendar, these lights are switched on for twenty hours a day, seven days a week. Now, as the first buds of spring try to make their presence felt, their time has reduced to twelve hours on, twelve hours off.

There are extra smaller rigs that top up the high-wear parts of the pitch; not just the goalmouths, but also the areas where the Bristol Bears rugby team kick for the corner and try to drive over the try line. For, of course, Ashton Gate has dual use: it is the home ground of both Bristol City and Bristol Bears. As at Swansea and Brentford, the football club has to share the pitch with the local rugby team. As if – in this concertinaed season where August was a write-off – it wasn't hard enough for a head groundsman and his team to ensure the best possible playing surface for a forty-six-game Championship season, Sparks has to double this up for the rugby team too.

'The biggest challenge is when they play double-headers,' he explains, 'when they play back-to-back, with rugby on the Friday and football on the Saturday.' This happened just a couple of weeks ago when the Bears played Sale Sharks on the Friday evening and City entertained Cardiff the following afternoon. The team had the matter of a few hours to make the pitch ship-shape and Bristol fashion. And, because of Ashton Gate being bordered by houses, the floodlights had to be switched off at 11 p.m., meaning the team could only work by internal lights that were obviously far less powerful. They eventually clocked off at 2 a.m. before returning early the next morning. But, nonetheless, the pitch was ready on time for Saturday afternoon, despite the tall order.

'Rugby produces more churned-up areas through scrums, through line-outs, through driving mauls in the corners. You do see more damage. You have to do a lot more hoovering and a lot more divoting. And those areas don't have natural time to recover. When there's a week's grace between fixtures, the grass can get back to some sort of normality.'

Brentford and Swansea have both had issues with their pitches this season; indeed, just before Christmas, the Liberty Stadium was ripped up wholesale and replaced with a completely new playing surface. So why is the Ashton Gate pitch in comparatively good shape after such a damp winter? 'We've had a lot of rain here this season, but Swansea have probably had double that. They've got it tougher.'

Despite his age, Sparks is the longest-serving member of the ground staff, with more than ten years' service under his belt. He was about to turn twenty-four when he got promoted to the top job. There's a clear similarity between his career trajectory and that of Josh Marsh at Huddersfield.

'The club could have put a job ad out and brought in an experienced groundsman, but it's kind of their philosophy to promote from within. I'm sort of the off-field version of an academy player getting a chance in the first team, rather than the club just buying another player. I'd been here for six years at that point. I understood the club, I understood the pitch, I understood the surroundings.'

Sparks does indeed know the pitch, fully aware of all the foibles produced by the stadium. He's like a dedicated pensioner who knows all the ways of his or her allotment. 'I know that in that corner,' he says, pointing to the far end of the pitch as an example, 'there's very little wind. In all the other corners, the wind swirls more. To us, this isn't a single, whole pitch. We see it as a collection of different areas.'

We walk down the middle of the turf towards that windless corner of the ground, one that's also permanently in the shade. It's pretty mild today, but Sparks explains that, on a frosty morning, the temperature can dip as much as three or four degrees in that far corner. It's a patch that also shows plenty of wear from the other code, where the Bears have regularly kicked for the corner for an attacking line-out.

Handily, both clubs share a preferred grass length of 25mm ('the Bears like to play a fast-running game, so they like it reasonably short'). However, that's not to say that an incoming manager might not want change. 'Whatever they want we aim to deliver. We did use to have a manager who wanted the grass a little bit shorter because he wanted the ball to move a little bit faster. So we cut it to 23mm. It doesn't sound like much but there is a noticeable difference in playability.' Football is increasingly a game of marginal gains.

'We've also changed the pitch width in the past. We brought it in a little to make it that bit tighter, as it was the then manager's preference to condense the play. But it's gone back to its traditional sixty-eight metres wide now, which is what the stadium's built for.'

Is Sparks expecting the new manager, when appointed, to make a beeline for the ground staff's storeroom to set out his needs pitch-wise? 'I've not had previous managers doing so in the first couple of weeks — or even the first couple of months. They're busy getting used to their new surroundings. But when they start looking at the finer details, that's when the pitch comes into it. So it'll be discussed in time. I'm certainly not knocking on his door straight away. "What height do you want the grass . . .?"'

More important than the grass length is the degree to which it's kept moist. While this can sometimes lead to a difference of opinion between manager and groundsman, the latter may actually be guided by the players. 'I used to have a very good relationship with one of our central midfielders who was the team's key passer of the ball. During the warm-up, I'd ask him if he wanted the water on or off. It was just a nod or shake of the head, but it was a key relationship. He was the one who needed the pitch to be how he wanted it.'

Sometimes, though, players aren't so respectful of the surface

Sparks has lovingly prepared. Aside from the continuing vogue for knee-sliding celebrations that gouge scars into the turf ('It's annoying,' he sighs. 'A frustration . . .'), higher crimes and misdemeanours can be spotted by Sparks while he's watching games. 'Once, a penalty had been given and, while the ref was in discussion, I saw one of the players scuffing up the penalty spot. He really did a job on it. We knew it wouldn't recover in a week or two. We'd have to put grass seed down and it would be a full four weeks before it was fully grassed again. We were pulling our hair out sat in the stand.'

Spark's professional devotion doesn't rest exclusively with the Ashton Gate pitch. Only two members of his staff are permanently based here at the stadium. The rest are tending pitches at various locations on the city's outskirts: the first-team training ground, the Bears' training ground, the academy training ground . . . This is no small operation.

As light rain starts to fall, we head back down the old tunnel towards the storeroom. What of the future for Sparks? Has he peaked too soon? Has he reached the pinnacle of his trade, realised his personal ambitions, before even notching up three decades on the planet?

'I'm a Bristol boy from just up the road and I used to come here as a teenager with my season ticket. So it's great to be standing here today, doing the job I do. But I'd love nothing more than to be here as Bristol City get into the Premier League and to produce a pitch for them to play top-flight football on.'

Sparks hasn't reached the pinnacle of his current role because the club hasn't reached their own pinnacle yet. And, once again, that's not going to happen this season. Whether it will finally come to pass in the near, or middle-distant, future will depend on the identity of the next manager. And, to the chagrin of the fans patrolling the quiet car park beyond Dan Sparks' storeroom, there's no sign of anyone arriving anytime soon. Not today, not tomorrow. And certainly not Eddie Howe.

\*

In 2004, the BBC broadcast an extraordinary episode of *Trouble at the Top*, the documentary series that offered fly-on-the-wall access inside the boardrooms of notable companies and industries. This particular episode focused on the events of the previous summer at Luton Town, a time when the carpets of Kenilworth Road were soaked in blood.

The main villain of the piece was an oily character by the name of John Gurney, a businessman who was the public face of an anonymous consortium that had reportedly bought the club for the nominal price of four pounds. Gurney had big plans for Luton – or, at least, for the large patch of arable land the club owned adjacent to the M1. Here, Gurney grandly announced, the club would build a Formula One circuit with a 70,000-capacity football stadium at the centre of it, located above the motorway on stilts.

Gurney, though, had zero support among the club's fan-base – either for his pie-in-the-sky dreams or for his day-to-day stewardship. Just three days after the takeover, the popular manager Joe Kinnear and his assistant Mick Harford had been sacked. Gurney had also revealed plans for the club's name to be changed to London-Luton FC. The disgusted fans voted with their feet. En masse, they refused to renew their season tickets while Gurney remained in his position. Without ticket income, and with no sign of the consortium depositing any operating capital into the club's coffers, the staff's wages were paid late two months on the trot. The situation was rotten. Bankruptcy beckoned.

However, the consortium's due diligence ahead of the take-over appeared not to have been that diligent. A debenture held by an offshore company called Hatters Holdings, the club's main creditor to whom it owed several million pounds, appeared to have gone unnoticed. The fans, in the shape of the newly formed Luton Town Supporters' Trust, saw their opportunity to outwit Gurney. By acquiring shares in Hatters Holdings – indeed, becoming its majority shareholder – the trust called in the debt, thus placing the club into administrative receivership. Gurney's control had been ripped from his hands. Despite his defiance – 'If they expect me to walk away from Luton with nothing,' he told the documentary-makers, 'I'll make very sure there's nothing to walk away from' – the turbulent fifty-five days of the Gurney era were over.

One of the founders and main movers within the trust, an articulate young man in a Luton home shirt with more than a faint facial resemblance to Richard Hammond, is still involved at Kenilworth Road eighteen years later. Very much involved, in fact. Since 2008, he has served as the football club's chief executive. His name is Gary Sweet.

And here he is now, sat in an empty boardroom ahead of the Hatters' home game against Cardiff. On the walls are plenty of pictures from the club's rosiest days. The 1980s are particularly well represented: here's winger David Moss, with his neatly clipped Second World War fighter pilot moustache; here's Welsh midfielder Peter Nicholas, his hands tucked smartly behind his back; and here's striker Roy Wegerle, standing on Kenilworth Road's famous/infamous plastic pitch in his pimple-soled boots. More recent times are also liberally commemorated, in particular the League One championship celebrations from 2018–19.

More room might need to be found on these boardroom walls soon. Luton Town are a club on a steady incline. A non-league outfit as recently as 2014, a series of promotions took them to the lofty heights of the Championship two seasons ago. This season, although currently occupying the anonymity of mid-table, the Hatters are already sixteen points better off than they were at the corresponding stage twelve months ago. Onwards and upwards.

'You can't deny the progress,' says Sweet. 'We're doing better than all right. We're doing really well. We're not sitting here bottom of the table sweating like hell. And if you look at this over a long-term period, which we always do here, in the scheme of things this is a really, really good chapter. We have ambitions of climbing up the table at the end of every game. A lot of people might think we've got ambitions above our station, but let's talk about that when we get to the Premier League.'

Big talk about the top flight would have been unthinkable in the dark days of the Gurney regime. Without the intervention of its supporters – whether withholding their season-ticket money or being involved at a more active level like Sweet was – Luton Town would have been liquidated. 'The cold-blooded murder of the football club was being committed in front of our eyes.'

Today's mid-table position represents an astonishing turnaround. But they wouldn't be here were it not for a decision made by Sweet and the board towards the end of last season. Twelve months ago, Luton were twenty-third in the Championship when football was put on pause as the nation went into the first lockdown. They'd been bottom-feeders all season and relegation seemed odds-on, so action was taken. Two and a half months into the enforced hibernation, one Jones was replaced by another as manager Graeme left the club by mutual consent, the vacancy being filled by his predecessor Nathan.

'Relegation just could not be something we experienced. We had to avoid it, so we brought Nathan back. He knew the players and we knew he would motivate them. There was always something very Luton about Nathan – apart from one decision he made which was very un-Luton.' Sweet is referring to the Welshman ending his first spell in charge at Kenilworth

Road by abruptly defecting to Stoke City midway through the 2018–19 season. He allows himself a smile. 'But we're forgiving creatures round here . . .'

The board's decision to reappoint Jones was vindicated when he steered the Hatters to just a single defeat in the last nine matches of the season, including wins in their last two matches. A final-day victory over Blackburn pulled them clear. It was the first time they'd been out of the relegation zone since before Christmas. Sweet's sense of relief must have been the equal of his sense of joy.

'The thing about supporting a club you work for is that when you see successes and failures, it actually hurts you every minute of the day, every day of the week. But you have to strip away that emotion to make the right decisions. An emotional supporter would buy a player even if we couldn't afford him. We can't do that. We have to be clinical.'

Knowing all the factors that inform the difficult decisions means that the emotions, when they're allowed to be displayed, are even more vivid. They're in Technicolor. They're quadraphonic. 'Once you've made those decisions and the games get played out, the emotion is amplified. And it was a deeply emotional day when we stayed up. Yeah, sobbing . . .'

After twelve years overseeing everything at Kenilworth Road, Sweet has had to shape-shift somewhat – and not always for the good. 'Before all this happened, I used to wear a suit to my old job during the week and wear jeans and a T-shirt to the match on a Saturday. We're fairly relaxed here, so I now wear semi-casual clothes during the week and the only time I wear a suit is at a football match. And I don't like that! I still want to stand in the stands and have a few beers with my mates.' He does still manage to have a Saturday beer, though – with the shareholders, directors and staff who are his mates now. 'We all share the same passion. We all cry the same tears of joy or sorrow.'

Having avoided the drop last season, remaining in the Championship meant Luton were in a more secure position to navigate the choppy waters continuing to be whipped up by the pandemic. Not that the club had the financial reserves to ride out the waves. A large proportion of its operational staff, as well as the entire academy, was put on furlough. There was no other way. 'The sensible clubs have had to downscale and trim the fat off a little. There's certainly no arguing that we're not a lean operation at the moment.

'It was clear this wasn't something that was going to go away over the summer. When you're in a crisis situation, my view is that you start with the exit. Where did we want to position ourselves to be after all of this? We didn't know what it would look like, but one thing that was clear was that we had to maintain, or increase, our nimbleness. We needed to adapt, to be fleet of foot. We were reacting to a pandemic, but we had to be proactive about how we came out of it. If you wait to see what's going on around you, that's when you sink. This is not a year when you want to be fighting financially. You want to get ahead of yourself.

'We believe in a model where you shouldn't have to rely on the generosity or the egotistical nature of an owner to constantly plough money into the business. We don't feel that's right in football. And we certainly don't think that's right for Luton. So, it doesn't matter what league we're in, we cut our cloth accordingly. We operate on something called an optimum loss model. You spend as little as possible on players to achieve your ambitions, because the more you spend on players, the more you ultimately have to charge your supporters. We don't want to rip them off. The opposite, in fact. We want to give them value. But that gives us an absolute finite limit on what we spend on our players. It's a really simple model. We don't make money but we don't lose money. If we've made money,

I've underspent and we could have used that to do better on the pitch.'

At the start of this season – and with no guarantee of being able to watch their beloved side in the flesh – 7,000 Luton fans diligently paid their season-ticket money to help keep the club bobbing on the waves. But with the pandemic lengthening beyond the finger-in-the-wind predictions of every politician, Sweet is a little concerned about the near future. 'Our supporters are fantastic, brilliant people who've stuck by us over the last year. But can I rely on them to give me season-ticket money next season to keep the club alive? I really think they will, but I can't hand-on-heart rely on that to put into a business plan.'

But while they languish in the bottom three of the Championship when it comes to playing budgets, off the pitch Luton hold big dreams. These are more than dreams, in fact. They are concrete plans being realised by the club's separate, independent property arm; central of these is the move to a new, purpose-built stadium.

To Sweet and everyone else at the club, it's symbolic that the stadium is being built on a site even more centrally located than their current home. A ground on the edge of town wouldn't do – and certainly not one hanging above the M1 on stilts.

'There's nothing else in Luton that connects that broad church of people, of characters, of backgrounds, of religions, of race, like Luton Town Football Club. We are the glue of all that. And you glue the hub, not the edge of the spindles.

'We want to be in the heart of the town,' concludes Sweet. 'More than that. We want to *be* the town centre.'

\*

An hour later, Nathan Jones is perched on the advertising boards in front of Kenilworth Road's old wooden main stand, his sharp Rhondda accent cutting through the Bedfordshire night sky as he urges his charges on against Cardiff. He's both an explosion of passionate advice and the owner of a full array of physical gestures. These leave the targets of his ire in no doubt that they've done wrong. Jones frequently spins on his heel and offers a semi-rhetorical question about a particular shortcoming of his side. Sat behind him in the stand, the Luton legend Mick Harford – a victim of the Gurney era but back at the club where he's currently employed in the dual role of assistant manager and head of recruitment – does his best to answer.

Rather extraordinarily, Jones is forty-seven. Looking younger than half his team, he has the stature and physique of a student intern. By heavy contrast, further up the touchline, his counterpart tonight has a professorial air about him.

With his spectacles and that distinguished – if increasingly untidy – silver hair, Mick McCarthy could pass for an approaching-retirement academic. That's if, of course, you can disregard the puffer jacket, the tracksuit bottoms and the liberal use of the coarsest Anglo-Saxon.

Out on the pitch, his eleven students receive close scrutiny. Sometimes the criticism is aimed at the whole team: 'You're bringing it on yourselves!' yells McCarthy when Cardiff repeatedly give away free kicks within shooting range. Mostly, though, individuals are singled out. After Josh Murphy is released down the right wing but opts to go to ground after the slightest of touches, McCarthy marches down the touchline to register his annoyance. 'Josh! Get up! Get up!' This is swiftly followed by further condemnation of the winger's defensive duties. Murphy will be looking forward to the second half when he'll be a pitch's width away from his boss's critical eye.

McCarthy's exasperation dissolves significantly once Cardiff help themselves to a two-goal lead shortly after half-time, the first goal being a particularly sublime Harry Wilson finish. Advice is still noisily given, but the frustration has left his voice.

It's more avuncular now, resembling the encouraging tones of an U12s coach. 'Kieffer, stay onside!' he reminds his top scorer. The young sub Joel Bagan gets praised: 'Good boy! That was good.' Even Josh Murphy gets a thumbs-up.

The most amusing moment, one straight out of youth football, is when Aden Flint leaves his defensive post in the eighty-ninth minute to lend support to the attack at a free kick. McCarthy, a former central defender charged with marking the likes of Gary Lineker and Toto Schillaci at Italia 90, can't believe his eyes. 'Aden! Aden! Get back here, you!'

Nathan Jones has been quieter since Cardiff's second goal, half-resigned to losing to the league's most in-form team. Up in the stand behind him, Gary Sweet sinks lower in his seat and pulls his orange, white and black scarf a little tighter. 'That's the way it goes,' he will shrug at the final whistle. 'If only we had a finisher.'

Cardiff's revival under McCarthy continues unabated. Yet to lose under him in six games, they're now up to seventh, having been transformed into serious play-off contenders. Their silver-topped leader is surely a shoo-in for February's manager-of-the-month gong.

Not that things are going disastrously for Luton, for whom this is only their second defeat in the last nine home games. For now, their place in mid-table seems relatively secure and is certainly a big improvement on last season's final-day escape from the relegation zone. Tonight's primary task, against the giants of Cardiff, was trying to match them physically, as a philosophical Jones admits afterwards.

'I picked the biggest, strongest side I could – apart from the groundsman, who's six-four. He's the only one I didn't put in the team . . .'

*

Twenty-four hours after Nathan Jones offered his last shrug of the night, another Valleys boy takes centre stage – or, rather, a position behind the desk set up on the concourse of the Liberty Stadium, the ad hoc location of press conferences in the ground these days. Pontypridd's Steve Cooper is shrugging too, but not because his Swansea City side have just lost after being outplayed by Nottingham Forest. His is a got-out-of-jail shrug because, thanks to a late Connor Roberts header, his Swansea City side have just *won* despite being outplayed by Nottingham Forest. As The Teardrop Explodes' 'Reward' fades from the stadium's speakers, he greets the assembled press with a wink and an embarrassed smile. Whether the victory was deserved or not, Cooper has learned to accept his reward. Bless his cotton socks.

'Listen, I'm not going to sit here and say we were brilliant in the game, because in parts of our performance we weren't, especially with the ball. We struggled to play with enough rhythm and intensity, especially in the first half. In the end, we managed to create a good moment to go and win the game. So, I'm delighted with the win, but knowing we need to play better in the next game. And we will.'

Cooper has enough emotional intelligence to always tell it like it is, to reflect reality, to not hide behind excuses. His open face and straight talking are always received well, by both fans and journalists alike. He'll accept criticism when his players deserve it, but he'll always speak up for them too when it's deserved.

'When you don't play so well, it's easy to get frustrated, to lose a bit of concentration or confidence. But there wasn't any of that. It was, "We're not at our most fluid tonight, but we're going to roll up our sleeves and make sure we do everything we can to go and win the game." That's keeping the ball out of our net and scoring. And we did both.'

Tonight's single-goal victory is even sweeter with the news that Brentford have lost at QPR. It's the second successive defeat suffered by their promotion rivals after a twenty-one-game unbeaten run.

Cooper isn't bothered by that additional serving of sweetness, though. 'We're not going down that road of looking at others. I know you're thinking, *There he goes, boring as hell.* But it's a dangerous game putting your focus elsewhere. That means you're not a hundred per cent focused on what you can control – your performances and your results. All I'm focused on is Huddersfield on Saturday. They played really well last night against Middlesbrough and we've got to be ready for it. I thought they were excellent.'

Still, Swansea moved back to third this evening and have two games in hand on both Brentford and table-toppers Norwich. Win both of those and they go top.

Steve Cooper is no stranger to winning, from looking down at others from the top of the pile. After all, he is the only Championship manager to have won a World Cup. After a spell as academy manager at Liverpool, during which time he developed the likes of Raheem Sterling and Trent Alexander-Arnold, in 2014 Cooper joined the England set-up. Three years later, he had led the U17s to World Cup glory, marshalling the not-inconsiderable talents of Phil Foden, Jadon Sancho and Callum Hudson-Odoi into a tournament-winning outfit. After taking Swansea to the Championship play-offs in his first season in charge at the Liberty, and with them among the frontrunners again this campaign, he's now showing he can do it at club level too.

What it is that Cooper brings to the role of manager is difficult to identify and define, with his modus operandi largely inconspicuous. He neither rants nor raves; his demeanour remains pretty neutral throughout. And he's meticulous, as shown earlier this evening. Very few managers are present at warm-up, preferring the creature comforts backstage as they prepare their pre-match battle cries. Tonight, despite it lashing down here in South Wales, Cooper was there on the touch-line – focused, alert, watching. But it wasn't his own players he was studying. It was those of the opponents. He was looking for any clues in Forest's warm-up routines that might suggest how they were going to line up against his high-flying Swans. No warming pre-match cuppa indoors for him. Out in the elements, head above the parapet. And when his team head back to the dressing room, there's a pat on the back for each and every one of his young substitutes.

Cooper's coaching and man-management skills are rightly lauded by many – and, if rumours are to be taken at face value, they've turned the heads of bigger clubs that might be considering regime change. Particularly impressive is the way in which he's successfully moulded a winning Swansea team from a range of raw materials.

Take Cooper's strike duo, for instance. He's fashioned a prolific partnership between Jamal Lowe and André Ayew, two players who couldn't come from more opposite backgrounds. Lowe's passage to the Liberty was serpentine, including spells at eight non-league clubs before being airlifted into the EFL by Portsmouth. Indeed, he's played at every tier of English football from the Isthmian League Premier upwards. Every tier except the Premier League, of course, but his goals this season have kept Swansea very much in the hunt for promotion to the promised land. Possibly because of this footballing past, Lowe is a player who gives everything on the pitch; a lively, loose-limbed striker who's always available to receive the ball, always willing to run and chase.

By contrast, Ayew's career path has been decidedly linear. A product of the Marseille youth system, he's both the current captain of Ghana and the son of Abedi Pele, one of the greatest players Africa has ever produced. Playing at the highest level always seemed to be his destiny – and one he's achieved throughout his career, playing top-flight football with Marseille, Swansea, West Ham and Fenerbahçe, along with two World Cups and six Africa Cup of Nations tournaments. Tonight, though, his most memorable contribution was the way his French-accented 'Fuck off!' filled the air every time he was on the receiving end of a perceived injustice.

Ayew wasn't the only underwhelming player tonight. Against a well-organised Forest side, Swansea showed little sign of why they're riding so high in the league. In possession, their play was broken and stuttering, strangely content to endlessly stroke square balls across the pitch. This is the sign of a team lacking in confidence and initiative, attributes that – unbeaten in eight before tonight, including comfortable victories over Norwich and Watford – they should be brimming with.

Tonight, with Ayew and Lowe unable to change the game, Cooper threw on Jordan Morris to create a three-pronged attack with which to pierce Forest's defence. Morris, a mid-season loan signing from Seattle Sounders, is an experienced player who first represented the US national team while still in college and who won the MLS Cup with the Sounders in 2019. Often deployed as a winger back home – indeed, Cooper stuck him wide on the left this evening – Morris has the sturdy build more normally associated with a traditional, hold-it-up centre-forward than with a lightly skipping winger, suggesting he could take a central role should injury befall either Lowe or Ayew. He appears to be another judicious Cooper signing.

The Swansea winner tonight, though, didn't come from its triumvirate upfront. With four minutes left, and the match still goalless after Forest had enjoyed the lion's share of chances,

Jake Bidwell's hanging cross was met by a beautifully timed, and decidedly athletic, leap by right-back Connor Roberts, who planted the firmest of headers past the Forest keeper. The excited words of former Swansea striker Ian Walsh, engaged as co-commentator for BBC Radio Wales' coverage of the game, rang out across the Liberty. 'He gets the sweetest nut on it!'

When it comes to assists, Roberts and Bidwell are currently the most productive full-back pairing in the entire Championship. But that's not the only way that Roberts stands out among other players. A Swansea-supporting local lad from the Dulais Valley above Neath, for starters he's teetotal ('Never tasted it'). This is not a footballer who'll ever be found staggering from pub to pub on the Mumbles Mile. He's more likely to be at home, in the workshop he's set up in the garage. A devoted woodworker, Roberts is adept at making dining tables, desks and birdhouses, often commissioned by team-mates or other members of the Swansea staff. On the team bus, while everyone else watches Netflix or plays computer games, Roberts studies how-to videos on YouTube to hone his carpentry skills.

Whether or not Steve Cooper has been the recipient of one of Roberts' creations is unclear, but he's a huge admirer of his wing-back's athleticism. 'We're a really fit group,' says the manager, 'but Connor catches the eye because he's up and down the flanks. By all accounts, he's always been the athlete that he is. And he can jump too.

'Lucky bugger, isn't he?'

*

Back down on the south coast, the saga concerning the identity of Jason Tindall's replacement was taking more twists and turns than an Agatha Christie whodunit. With the dawning of each new day, a fresh suspect was named. A week after Tindall's departure, there were reports that Patrick Vieira, David Wagner and John Terry were all due to be imminently interviewed over Zoom. Terry sounded highly unlikely; putting an untested assistant into the job was the mistake the hierarchy believed they had made six months earlier.

A few days later, a yet more unlikely candidate emerged when the Cherries were believed to be seeking permission from the board of CF Montréal to speak to their head coach about the vacancy at the Vitality. But as glamorous as the appointment of Thierry Henry might have sounded, it was an illogical one. Not only did Henry have precisely zero experience of Championship football, but the managerial record of this most elegant of players was notably inelegant. At Montréal, his win ratio stood at a less than impressive 31 per cent. That ratio was even lower during his earlier reign at Monaco, where he mustered just four wins in twenty matches. By contrast, Tindall had won 42 per cent of his games in charge.

Whether denied permission from Montréal or choosing to listen to the mood-music coming from the Bournemouth fans, the Cherries opted against Henry's appointment. Instead, having won three of his five matches in charge as interim boss, Jonathan Woodgate was handed the job until the end of the season. 'Having concluded an extensive search for a new manager,' the club announced, 'we believe Jonathan is the best candidate to lead the team for the final fifteen games of the season.'

The following day, Bristol City also opted for a short-term appointment until May, plumping for the well-travelled Nigel Pearson as Dean Holden's successor. Fortune might well favour the brave, but both clubs had recently felt the sting of what inexperience can mean. As the sharp end of the season approached, the conservative hedging of bets was the order of the day.

*

## Championship table, 28 February

|    |                      | P  | W  | D  | L  | F  | A  | Pts |
|----|----------------------|----|----|----|----|----|----|-----|
| 1  | Norwich City         | 33 | 21 | 7  | 5  | 45 | 25 | 70  |
| 2  | Brentford            | 33 | 18 | 9  | 6  | 61 | 35 | 63  |
| 3  | Watford              | 33 | 17 | 9  | 7  | 43 | 24 | 60  |
| 4  | Swansea City         | 31 | 17 | 8  | 6  | 39 | 22 | 59  |
| 5  | Reading              | 33 | 16 | 6  | 11 | 45 | 37 | 54  |
| 6  | AFC Bournemouth      | 33 | 14 | 10 | 9  | 47 | 32 | 52  |
| 7  | Barnsley             | 32 | 15 | 6  | 11 | 38 | 36 | 51  |
| 8  | Cardiff City         | 33 | 14 | 8  | 11 | 49 | 35 | 50  |
| 9  | Middlesbrough        | 33 | 13 | 8  | 12 | 38 | 35 | 47  |
| 10 | Stoke City           | 33 | 11 | 12 | 10 | 38 | 37 | 45  |
| 11 | Bristol City         | 33 | 14 | 3  | 16 | 35 | 44 | 45  |
| 12 | Millwall             | 33 | 9  | 16 | 8  | 32 | 30 | 43  |
| 13 | Preston North End    | 33 | 13 | 4  | 16 | 37 | 42 | 43  |
| 14 | Luton Town           | 32 | 11 | 8  | 13 | 27 | 37 | 41  |
| 15 | Blackburn Rovers     | 32 | 11 | 7  | 14 | 46 | 38 | 40  |
| 16 | Nottingham Forest    | 33 | 10 | 10 | 13 | 28 | 32 | 40  |
| 17 | Queens Park Rangers  | 31 | 10 | 10 | 11 | 31 | 36 | 40  |
| 18 | Derby County         | 32 | 10 | 8  | 14 | 25 | 33 | 38  |
| 19 | Huddersfield Town    | 33 | 10 | 6  | 17 | 38 | 50 | 36  |
| 20 | Coventry City        | 33 | 8  | 11 | 14 | 30 | 44 | 35  |
| 21 | Birmingham City      | 33 | 8  | 10 | 15 | 25 | 41 | 34  |
| 22 | Rotherham United     | 31 | 8  | 5  | 18 | 33 | 42 | 29  |
| 23 | Sheffield Wednesday  | 32 | 9  | 7  | 16 | 23 | 38 | 28* |
| 24 | Wycombe Wanderers    | 33 | 5  | 8  | 20 | 23 | 55 | 23  |

*Includes six-point deduction*

**Leading scorers**

Ivan Toney (Brentford), 25
Adam Armstrong (Blackburn), 19
Teemu Pukki (Norwich), 17
Lucas João (Reading), 17
Kieffer Moore (Cardiff), 15

**Manager of the Month**

Mick McCarthy (Cardiff)

**Player of the Month**

Teemu Pukki (Norwich)

**Managerial departures**

Jason Tindall (Bournemouth), sacked
Dean Holden (Bristol City), sacked

**Managerial appointments**

Jonathan Woodgate (Bournemouth)
Nigel Pearson (Bristol City)

# March

*'If I'm being honest, I haven't got a
Scooby-Doo what my best team is'*

— ALEX NEIL

It's been a busy Wednesday in the East Midlands. This afternoon, Derby owner Mel Morris called off the sale of the club to Derventio Holdings, the company through which the United Arab Emirates businessman Sheikh Khaled bin Saquer Zayed Al Nahyan was bidding to buy the Rams.

An announcement that the terms of the deal had been struck was made as long ago as early November, with the club declaring that all the paperwork would be completed 'very soon'. But four months on, Morris appears to have lost patience with the prospective buyers. They hadn't shown him the colour of their money and reports are that Morris is 'furious'. It is the third attempted takeover of an English football club by Sheikh Khaled that has failed. He disappears from view, but Pride Park is engulfed in further uncertainty, the stock-in-trade of Derby County Football Club.

This evening, sixteen miles to the east along Brian Clough Way – the portion of the A52 named after the man who brought league titles both to the Rams and to Forest – Championship royalty has come to town, as ten-points-clear Norwich visit the City Ground. They've won eight in a row, in the process scoring eighteen and conceding just three. Head and shoulders above the chasing pack, their coronation as champions is surely just a matter of time.

The Canaries arrive in Nottingham in the golden glow of early spring, all late sun and lengthy shadows. After the long hours of winter, we're now at the very welcome time of year when dusk doesn't make an appearance until early evening. The sky is a deepening blue, dotted with wispy clouds above the River Trent. And the floodlights are on.

The City Ground has known some classic nights under these lights. Take the 1978–79 season, for instance, and the side's march to European Cup glory. There was the 2-0 win that disposed of Liverpool, the reigning champions of Europe; the 4-1 crushing of Grasshoppers of Zürich; and the seesawing three-all draw in the semi-final against FC Köln on the scruffiest of late '70s pitches.

But those nights are generations ago. These are legends talked of by ghosts. The intervening years, the intervening decades, have been barren ones. Forest haven't graced the top flight since the last century. But there's one throwback to those times of European success tonight: thanks to gambling website Football Index having just gone into administration, Forest's shirts will not be troubled by a sponsor's logo.

Such is his way, Chris Hughton – the man who, in past lives, took both Newcastle and Brighton into the Premier League – has stabilised Forest since he arrived in October. However, there's a major issue holding them back from putting more distance between themselves and the relegation zone. It's quite a fundamental one in the sport of football. They seem allergic to scoring goals. They've managed just twenty-nine in thirty-six league games.

It's not as if they're lacking in quality and experience upfront. Their captain is Lewis Grabban, a well-travelled striker with nearly 150 league goals to his name. Then there's Lyle Taylor, another player with plenty of miles on the clock and who reached double figures in each of his previous five seasons for AFC Wimbledon and Charlton. Neither, though, has troubled the leading goalscorers' charts this campaign; they've mustered just seven between them in the league.

During the January window, Hughton returned to his old club Brighton to rescue evergreen veteran Glenn Murray from an anonymous loan spell at Watford. The result was instant: Murray scored twice on his first Forest start. But, since then, nothing. Nada. Zilch.

The contrast with Norwich is stark. Goals come from right across the team, but especially from the boots of Teemu Pukki. Over the last three seasons combined, no one has scored as many goals in the Championship as the Finn – and this is despite him spending one of those seasons in the Premier League.

Pukki is in his customary solo striker role this evening, but Murray is on the bench for Forest, with Hughton opting to recall Grabban to the starting XI. It's Grabban's first start for exactly a calendar month, but the prospect of him also returning to the scoresheet tonight against the runaway league leaders remains slim. Forest's three most creative players – Joe Lolley, Anthony Knockaert and Filip Krovinović – are on the injury list.

It doesn't take Pukki long to show Forest what they're lacking. Just nine minutes, in fact. After the kind of swift passing move that's become Norwich's trademark, the striker's tidy feet and unerring eye for the bottom corner reap another dividend. It's his eleventh goal in the last nine games alone. This early lead wasn't unexpected. In these opening nine minutes, Norwich have enjoyed 86 per cent of the possession.

Four minutes later, a Kieran Dowell twenty-five-yarder

doubles the lead. The familiar figure of Hughton – short, spindly, salt-and-pepper hair – switches between arms folded and hands deep in pockets. Either way, his demeanour is clear. Dejected, disappointed, and praying that Norwich go easy for the remaining eighty-odd minutes.

The Canaries do indeed avoid going for the jugular. But the rest of the first half is like a training exercise, a scratch game of defence versus attack. When Forest actually get a touch of the ball, they give possession away both quickly and cheaply. Norwich come again. And again.

Half-time can't come soon enough. Norwich have had seventeen shots in the first forty-five minutes, while Forest have mustered just two, both of which were off target. Long-serving BBC Radio Nottingham commentator Colin Fray tells his listeners that Forest have been second-best in all areas, before correcting himself. 'Third-best . . .'

Norwich remain rampant after the break, effortlessly chopping their path through Forest at will. The home side does get a rare chance to score, but the unmarked Grabban ponders on the ball and fails to get his shot away quickly enough. It's their best opportunity of the night. The second half has seen an improved performance, but the bluntness upfront is plain to see.

Lyle Taylor replaces Grabban with quarter of an hour left and is joined ten minutes later by Murray, whose (polite) two-fingered gesture to Taylor tells him they're going two up top. But the dice has been rolled too late. There's little time for the new formation to affect anything and Norwich settle for the 2-0 win that maintains their double-digit lead over the other promotion hopefuls.

Alongside Colin Fray in the commentary box tonight has been the former Forest legend Steve Hodge. In his post-match appraisal, he points out that, at best, Forest are currently treading water, able to beat – or, at least, not lose to – those around and below them in the league. It's a different matter against those at a higher altitude.

'The strikers certainly haven't been good enough this year,' he sighs. 'At the moment, it must be soul-destroying for the fans that we just can't score a goal. It's on and on and on and on.

'It's monotonous, it really is.'

\*

If Steve Hodge is one seriously underwhelmed former player, over at his home near the north Norfolk coast, a certain ex-Canary is gushing over the way his old team are playing, at how they keep racking up win after win. Tonight's victory puts them three points closer to the promised land, a destination that's getting nearer with every game.

As a Norwich City legend, one might expect Chris Sutton's appraisal of the team's season thus far to be slightly presented through mustard-yellow-tinted glasses, but such is their continuing domination of the league that no bias touches his words. There's not a single objective observer who could disagree with the former striker's verdict.

'It's a brutal league, but their consistency has been absolutely remarkable. Compared to last time out, they're much more solid defensively. That's been the key. Ben Gibson has been an excellent signing. He went to Burnley with a bit of a reputation and a £15m price tag, but didn't really get a game there. His partnership with Grant Hanley has been crucial. So too has the goalkeeper, Tim Krul. They've gone a bit more robust in midfield as well. They got Oliver Skipp in on loan, the boy from Spurs, and he's been really excellent. It'll be really interesting to see, when this season is all done and dusted, whether he'll go back to Spurs or whether Norwich can get him for another season or possibly even on a permanent.'

And then there's the Canaries' irresistible attacking

force, personified by the trio of Pukki, Emi Buendía and Todd Cantwell.

'Cantwell – the Dereham Deco – has come on to his best game, after looking like he wanted away at the start of the season and after Daniel Farke made a point of leaving him out. But Buendía's been the best player in the Championship this season by a stretch. His link-up with Pukki has been top drawer. And, once again, Pukki's been prolific. His movement is first class. He's not necessarily super-quick, but it's all about his intelligence, the timing of his runs and the telepathic understanding that he and Buendía have.' No one is more qualified to judge how difficult attaining such a level of consistency is, week in, week out. Before the Finn rolled into town, Sutton was the last Norwich player to score twenty-five goals in a league season.

That these flair players have freedom and confidence to express themselves on the pitch is down to the faith that Farke has in them – and the faith they have in his coaching methods. And this is the result of the stability in the way the club is run, despite the yo-yoing between divisions over the last few seasons.

'I take my hat off to them regarding how they run the club. The last time Norwich got into the Premier League, a lot of people said that they had to chuck money at it. But who can you spend £30–£40m on at this moment in time to bring guaranteed success? So Norwich have done it their own way, nurturing young players, giving them the opportunity.

'They're not going to change this model. Well, I'd be surprised if they do. No doubt there'll be people over the summer saying, "We're back in the Premier League. Let's go and gamble fifty million quid. We need to spend, spend, spend." But Norwich aren't a club who can afford to work that way. They don't have a rich owner. Delia Smith is wealthy within her own right, but I don't think she's football-wealthy. Norwich don't have a huge war chest.

'Plus, I think lessons have been learned in the past, when they signed players like Steven Naismith. There was a big outlay on him and he was a good player when they signed him. I thought things would work out, but they didn't. Players were put on large contracts and the club paid for those mistakes. Now, theirs seems to be a sustainable model that would be the envy of many clubs across the country.'

And they've not been hindered by selling off some of the family silver last summer, in the shape of those young defenders Ben Godfrey and Jamal Lewis. 'You could argue that Norwich were worse off after those sales, but they didn't flinch, they didn't get flustered. They've just got on with the way they work. They still play an attractive brand of football, but they've been more watertight too.'

In the world of football, where short-termism increasingly determines and dictates the agendas of clubs, the patience shown by the powers-that-be at Carrow Road is welcome and impressive. Perhaps it's related to geography, to the city being away from more heavily pressured football heartlands, but they do things differently here.

'We're in those times where three bad results translate into social media calling for managers to be sacked, so the patience is an admirable thing. Last season, after they came back in June after the enforced break, Norwich had a nightmare of a run. They lost all remaining nine games and went out of the Premier League with a whimper. But there was no panic. It was all about the big picture and having faith in both the squad that Daniel Farke had built and his coaching methods. They trusted a manager who'd been there a while and it's borne fruit. I think that's a lesson to clubs out there who make snap judgements and quick changes.'

The success at Norwich is also born out of a pragmatic realism, both in the boardroom and in the stands. 'The supporters are very, very patient. I didn't see a large part of the fanbase calling for Daniel Farke's head. There's a good understanding of where the club is actually at, what their current level is. They want to be successful, but the truth of the matter is that they're never going to be able to compete with the Manchester Citys and the Chelseas and the Liverpools over the long course of a season.

'They'll strive to do that, of course, but it's small steps. Small steps ...'

\*

This should have been Tyrese Campbell's season.

This should have been his chance to shine over the course of its nine months, to be among the high-climbers in the goalscoring charts – the likes of Ivan Toney, Teemu Pukki and Adam Armstrong. After all, the Stoke forward hadn't been far behind them during the autumn, thanks to a rich vein of form that saw him score six in eight games as the Potters rose up the table to nestle close to the play-off places.

In his fifth season at the Bet365 Stadium, twenty-year-old Campbell was earning rave reviews from all quarters. Each of his goals had been scored with aplomb. There wasn't a single tap-in or scuffed shot among them. And he was scoring against the league's best teams. Whether the solo effort against Brentford, the low drive at Reading or the beefy header against Norwich, Campbell was mixing it with the cream of the league.

But then, in early December in a home match against Cardiff, disaster struck. Ten minutes into the second half, with the ball running out of play, Campbell went in for a 50/50 shoulder charge. 'For some reason, though, I sort of jumped into it. When I landed, I heard a crack in my knee. I tried to jog but it wasn't right. I was thinking, *Why? Why did I do that?* To this day, I still tell myself that I shouldn't have done so. I started walking, but all I could hear was this cracking and crunching in my knee. I knew it couldn't be good.'

Campbell hasn't played since. He's barely jogged since. And he won't play again until next season.

It was a cruel incident that confirmed football's frailty, its fickle finger of fate. Of late, Campbell had rejuvenated his career under manager Michael O'Neill. During the tenure of O'Neill's predecessor, Nathan Jones, he had felt under-appreciated and unloved. Celtic and Rangers were reportedly circling above, beady eyes on their prey, talons out. For a player failing to catch his manager's eye ('It was never that I wanted to leave. I just wanted to play football'), these would have been attractive suitors. But the fates changed when the Ulsterman replaced the Welshman in the dugout. Campbell didn't just sign a new contract. He signed one keeping him in the Potteries for the next four and a half years. It was quite the turnaround, especially as Stoke were propping up the table at the time.

'Things weren't great. The team wasn't performing anywhere near its potential, and there were still a lot of egos around, which didn't really help. Relegation went through our heads, but no one really spoke about it. Michael came in and was just really honest with us. He played a formation that everyone was comfortable with, playing players in their preferred positions and letting us get on with it. Results turned around and we started winning games.'

O'Neill steered Stoke to the safe harbour of fifteenth place by the end of the season, with Campbell among the goals and assists. After the short close season, that form stayed with him into the pre-season schedule and beyond. 'It was a quick turnaround. We had something like eight to ten days off and then we were back at it. You can't really lose too much fitness in that short space of time. You've got to be doing a lot of bad things to get out of shape.'

With O'Neill settled into the job and a few choice acquisitions made over the short summer break, the eyes were fixed on the prize of making the play-offs, if not higher. A sense of unity and collectivism pervaded the training ground. 'Everyone was on the same page. We'd got that team cohesion back. We had a good mix of youth and experience, and had brought in players like John Obi Mikel and Steven Fletcher. Both are great players. John's won everything there is to win in English and European football, and Fletch has had a great career too. When players like them come in, they can only improve the team.'

Stoke's trajectory remained upward, fired along by Campbell being in the form of his life. 'I was on a great run. I was playing on the right side, on the left side and had a couple of games upfront. But wherever I played, I was involved, whether with goals or assists. I was so confident. I was going into games thinking that no one could stop me.'

What did stop him was that shoulder barge in the Cardiff game. 'I went for a scan the following day and found out I'd torn my meniscus. The day after that, a specialist told me I was unlikely to play again this season. Hearing that was hard, obviously. I did get emotional and upset initially. It was my first significant injury.'

Campbell sought counsel from those around him, most notably his father Kevin, the former Arsenal, Forest, Everton and West Brom striker. Campbell senior had been no stranger to the treatment room, particularly during his time at Goodison Park, and was able to dispense advice that came shot through with experience.

'He told me it was part of my journey. "There's nothing you can do about it now. Obviously it's not nice as you were in great form, but you're young, you've got age on your side and you'll heal quickly." I took that in my stride and accepted it. After all, it's unlikely that a footballer, or any professional sportsman, would avoid injury during their career.'

But the story doesn't end there. At times over the past few

months, Campbell's healing process hasn't been as quick or as smooth as hoped. After undergoing surgery ten days after the Cardiff game, he largely rested up over Christmas. Then, come the New Year, he tested positive for Covid, requiring a period of recovery and isolation that derailed a finely orchestrated rehab programme.

No sooner had Campbell recovered from coronavirus ('I was quite ill with that for a while') than the specialist delivered another setback: the swelling on his knee hadn't reduced because it had become infected. Two further operations were required. 'Infections like this are really rare and it was hard to take. It was, "Why has this happened to me?" When I came out of hospital, I had to do another two weeks of antibiotics, so I had an IV line put into my arm. Then I was taking tablets for another month after that.

'But I've never lost sight of the bigger picture, of getting back to playing football. That's what's driven me on. I've loved football from the day I was born, so getting back to playing will be a great day. You have little goals in your head. One of mine was just to get walking again. And when I was, I was buzzing. You'd normally take something like that for granted.'

Campbell has largely had to experience the second half of Stoke's season with his leg up at home, watching on iFollow. For a player previously taking to the pitch with supreme confidence and scoring at will, it's been a frustrating time. 'It's not easy. You want to be playing, but instead you're feeling how a fan feels. But at the back of your head, you're thinking, *I should be part of this match.* I've been to a couple of games too, but that's even harder. It's all there in front of you and you'd love to be on the pitch. But you've got to appreciate even being able to go to the games. When I was in my brace and on my crutches, I could only dream of being there.'

Since that early progress, Stoke have had an indifferent

season. Defensively strong but missing Campbell's attacking edge, they've been permanent residents of the Championship's no-man's land, its demilitarised zone. There's no danger of relegation, but there's no troubling the promotion race either. The season is winding down early for them.

From the vantage point of his sofa, Campbell has been able to study his team-mates over the past few months. What's his verdict? 'We've got a great team with plenty of players who've played at the highest level. We've played well, but there have been a lot of times when we could have played better. The team thinks the same.' He's too modest to highlight a conspicuous correlation: Stoke's upward progress began to level off pretty much at the point at which he hobbled off the pitch against Cardiff.

Now back on course for a return to action in time for pre-season in July, Campbell is the kind of positive figure who won't try to jettison the memories of the dark winter months and the bad news they brought. Instead, he'll use it as a reminder of the fragility of the life of a footballer, a reminder to not take being fully fit for granted.

'I would never want to forget about it,' he concludes. 'I've had some great times this season. I can't complain.'

\*

Ian McMillan presses his nose up against the fence and sighs. 'I'm slightly disappointed there's no blue plaque.'

Beyond the fence, the green, green grass of a football pitch remains unacknowledged, uncommemorated. McMillan, the celebrated poet and broadcaster, rightly feels it should be. For it was here that the most famous football match ever held in Barnsley took place. But it wasn't a game involving Barnsley FC, McMillan's beloved Tykes. It wasn't a match en route to their sole FA Cup win in 1912, nor one that aided their ascension to the Premier League in the mid-'90s. In fact, we aren't even currently standing outside Oakwell, the club's field of dreams.

Instead, we're next to a perimeter fence that guards the playing fields of a secondary school a couple of miles north of the town centre. It was here in 1968 that Ken Loach filmed a PE-lesson game for the film *Kes*, starring a bunch of local schoolkids and the actor Brian Glover. It's arguably the best-known football scene in British cinema history, eclipsing those in *Escape to Victory* and *Bend It Like Beckham*.

So many aspects of the scene can be instantly recalled. Glover's games teacher appointing himself referee, captain, centre-forward, penalty-taker and Bobby Charlton wannabe. The twig-like protagonist Billy Casper, stuck in goal, choosing to climb up onto the crossbar rather than attempt to save any goal-bound shots. Glover's undisguised dive to win a spot-kick – and his commentary after converting it at the second time of asking, having ruled that the keeper had moved too early for his first (saved) attempt.

For McMillan, a few years younger than Billy Casper at the time and a man who's lived in a former mining village outside the town for almost all his life, the film – and the book it was based on, Barry Hines's *A Kestrel for a Knave* – has remained a touchstone.

'The book is our *Things Fall Apart*. It's our *Moby-Dick*. It's our *Great Gatsby*. It told us that our lives were worthy of art, of people making dramas out of them. And it was fantastic to see people up on the screen who talked like you, who didn't put on a kind of mock accent and who were living in streets that you knew.

'Everybody in Barnsley claims to be in the film. People who weren't born back then. People who've moved here from Kettering. Even people who've never seen the film.

'"I'm in *Kes*."'

'"Are ya? Where are ya?"

'"You watched that football match? There's a kid who walks past. That's me."'

Today, though, once we've paid our respects to a staged, fictional football match from more than half a century ago, we need to get back to life, back to reality. Down the hill at Oakwell, there's a genuine game that needs our attention – and hard wooden seats in the press box that need our backsides on them. Sheffield Wednesday, Barnsley's rivals from across the M1, are in town.

We set off on foot, happy to be descending this sharp hill rather than trying to climb it. McMillan is particularly thrilled to be heading to Oakwell today. This is the season-ticket holder's first game since the gates were closed to fans last March and he's bagged himself a pew in the press box, thanks to closed-doors football being the subject of his next *Yorkshire Post* column.

It's a fine time to be a Barnsley fan. Aside from nine-wins-on-the-bounce Norwich, the Tykes are the league's form team, currently on a twelve-match unbeaten run. The streets might be quiet, but there's a carnival breaking out in McMillan's head, dreams of an unlikely return to the top flight – even though he's been forced to watch the team's progress from the sofa in his front room, iPad perched on his knees.

'Last season, we stayed up by the skin of our teeth – the last kick of the last game at Brentford. So I didn't have much hope for this season, but it's been exhilarating. It really has. To see this rise up the table, to see us keep winning and winning, is amazing.

'But not to be there is heartbreaking. It's like there's a fantastic party happening next door and you can't go. I'm sat there on my own, when what I really want to do is turn around and shout at the bloke next to me. I miss that so much, the closeness of being with people at an event that is unrepeatable. Being at a match is an astonishing thing. You can guess the end of a film. You can guess the end of a play. You can't guess the end of a match. A team can score in the last minute of extra time, but you wouldn't write it in a script.'

As we reach the noisy A61, exceedingly busy despite it being a Saturday lunchtime in lockdown, McMillan gives me chapter and verse about his affinity with the club. Somewhat surprisingly, it doesn't stretch far back into ancient history. He rarely went to see them as a kid and then, as a jobbing performance poet, would usually be working when Saturday came, 'doing gigs all over the place. I was never around and it passed me by. So I'm not a bloke who's followed them all my life. Sometimes I feel a bit of a fraud.

'A lot of people say, "My dad took me to the match", but it was my kids who took me, back when Barnsley were doing well in the mid-'90s. Then I got hooked, absolutely hooked on it. I'd go to all the away games on the bus with my kids and my nephews. There were loads of us who'd all go together. My wife would make all these sandwiches and they'd have our names on them. Of course, we'd eat them before we even got out of Barnsley . . .'

It was at the end of the Tykes' promotion season of 1996–97, when Danny Wilson led them to the Premier League, that McMillan's connection to the club was cemented further. All it took was a quick phone call to the general manager.

'"Do you fancy having a poet-in-residence?"

'"Will it cost us owt?"

'Normally you'd want paying, but I said I'd do it for nowt because I knew it would get a load of publicity. And it did. The Press Association put this little, tiny bit in the *Yorkshire Post* – "Barnsley's first Premier League signing: Ian McMillan" – and it went absolutely bloody crackers. I got phone calls from all over the world. I did loads of telly and radio. I did a series for Yorkshire TV following Barnsley around. I wrote a big thing for Radio 4 called *It's Just Like Watching Brazil*. It was so exciting to see that poetry could go anywhere, that it could do what it wanted. It didn't have to be in a certain place.

'Then the *Barnsley Chronicle* asked me to write a poem about football every week. "It's got to be sixteen lines long and fit in that space." Sometimes, if I wrote one that was a bit longer, they just didn't print the last couple of lines. People would say, "That poem ended a bit abrupt. Is it that modern poetry?"'

McMillan is no longer in the informal, unpaid position of poet-in-residence, but its effect still lingers. 'To this day, if something happens at a match, someone will still go, "Get thee notebook out! Put that in a bastard poem!" Once, when we were doing well, this guy behind me called John, who comes down from north of Newcastle, said, "He'll not write a poem about this. He'll write a sonnet!"'

'My ambition was to get a poem sung by the crowd. We once had this German goalkeeper, Lars Leese, and I once wrote this poem that went:

> *Lars Leese*
> *Tall as the trees*
> *That grow in Wombwell Wood*
> *Lars Leese*
> *Listen please*
> *We think you're very good.*

'At one point, I heard some folk singing, "Lars Leese / Tall as the trees ..." I thought, *Ah, I've arrived*. It was only later that I found out his name was actually pronounced Lay-zer ...'

We're close to Oakwell now, the point at which we need to turn left onto the quieter streets leading to the ground. It's at this juncture that McMillan starts to list the sights and sounds which would be there on a usual match day. For starters, there's the absence of his grandson Thomas, his nephew David and his mate Mick, with whom he always goes to the game. There's the lack of a police presence in the underpass from the railway station ('If there's any argy-bargy, it normally happens under there'). And there's the absence of 'the dawdlers, those fans taking their time to get there at exactly the same time every week for superstitious reasons'.

Nor can the calls be heard of those on the corner selling programmes, selling raffle tickets. Ever the performer, McMillan opts to fill the silence himself. 'Half-time draw. Pound a go. Half-time draw. Pound a go . . .'

One familiar aspect of the ritual and route that is being upheld is McMillan's diversion into the corner shop to get his favoured Kit-Kat Chunky. He's out of luck and has to make do with the classic four-fingered version, but an optimist like him will gladly welcome a sign wherever they can. 'Four fingers! We're going to score four today!'

The streets are ghost-town silent. Even the music from the stadium PA is inaudible. It could just be a normal weekday afternoon in lockdown. 'It doesn't make you think there's a match about to happen. And it makes you realise that much of our love for football is the anticipation. It's ninety minutes on the pitch, but it's a week of getting excited. When your team's doing well, you can't wait. I like going to the theatre, but you wouldn't start getting excited about it on the Monday.'

At the crown of the hilly street, looking down over the Oakwell pitch, McMillan tries to pick out his usual seat in the lower tier of the East Stand. Today, though, his position will be high in the West Stand, the first time he'll have experienced that particular vantage point. He does know all about the facilities on this side of the ground, though. 'We used to have a fanzine called *West Stand Bogs*, named after the notorious – guess what – West Stand bogs.'

The wooden seats of the press box are as unforgiving as the legendary stench of the toilets, but McMillan hasn't a care about comfort as he lowers himself into place. Today will be the first time that he can study Barnsley's manager, the appointed-five-months-ago Valérien Ismaël, in the flesh. 'We like the fact that he seems to be some kind of hard man who shouts and swears a lot from the touchline. And he gestures. We like a gesturing manager. We don't like stoics. We like windmill-armed bosses.'

It will also be a first chance to run the rule over Barnsley's on-loan American striker Daryl Dike, who swapped Orlando for Oakwell in January and who has since been a regular presence on the Barnsley scoresheet. 'Dike the Tyke!' notes the poet, well aware that, as with Lars Leese, the correct pronunciation of his name doesn't lend itself to rhyme. It's pronounced 'Dee-kay'.

When the match kicks off, McMillan momentarily forgets he's among the objective, unpartisan journalists and broadcasters, and just manages to stifle a 'Go on, then!' under his face mask as Barnsley make their first foray along the near touchline. As well as the on-field action, McMillan is intrigued to be among the press pack – the radio commentators, the print journalists, the invariably young online reporters seemingly constantly live-tweeting with barely an eye on the game. In the column that he'll go home later to write, McMillan likens the work ethic and industry here to that of New York City's Brill Building, 'where offices full of songwriters wrote hit after hit'.

When Jordan Rhodes heads Wednesday into the lead towards the end of the first half, one thing McMillan doesn't miss is the 'gloating and singing and shouting' that his usual corner of the ground would be subjected to by nearby away fans. But, come the break, there are more pleasurable elements of the ritual that are conspicuous by their absence.

'I'm missing the fierce half-time debate downstairs – my mate Mick saying, "It's rubbish. I'm going no more." There'd be blokes threatening to throw their season tickets onto the pitch. Or actually doing so and then having to ask a steward to retrieve them. I do miss the melee, the Rabelaisian farce of half-time.'

Another absence is the regular cup of coffee served at a volcanic temperature ('You could bring it to the next match and it'd still be warm enough to drink'). Instead, McMillan has to make do with a Swizzels lolly from the goodie bag that each inhabitant of the press box has been issued with.

McMillan's regular game-goers might not be here, but he points out one of the ballboys charged with retrieving balls that stray into the empty stand before giving them a thorough dousing with anti-bacterial spray. In the times of Covid, these ballboys are middle-aged men. The one serving the touchline in front of us is actually McMillan's window cleaner. In normal circumstances, he'd be manning the turnstiles, but he's now been redeployed – and seemingly in the perfect vocation. He's currently polishing a ball to the kind of shine he'd normally reserve for the patio doors of one of his customers.

Dennis the window cleaner is one of the lucky ones, able to still watch his beloved's home matches. Everyone else is denied entry. But some are decidedly imaginative when it comes to sidestepping the restrictions. At the far end of the West Stand, two cherry-pickers have been parked on the street outside, their cages elevated towards the skies. Four fans, looking the part of workmen in their day-glo jackets, are enjoying the best view in the house.

Jordan Rhodes adds another in the second half and although Barnsley pull one back, it's merely a consolation. The 2-1 defeat is Barnsley's first loss in thirteen games. But any disappointment felt by McMillan at the scoreline is more than compensated by being back inside Oakwell on match day.

'I'm a happy man, despite the fact that we lost and the great run ended. It feels like it's my fault, but I did enjoy it and I'll feed on that for the next few months. It was an odd spectacle. I like being able to hear the players and the subs cheering, but it was more like going to see a dress rehearsal rather than the actual performance. I did like watching Valérien Ismaël, though. He's excitable. He's a very cross man. I love it when a linesman tells a manager to calm down.

'Unlike the people who reckon they were in *Kes*, I can say that I was actually there today. I can bore my grandson to death later.

'"I know we lost, but I was *there*."

'"Grandad, put another record on, for God's sake . . ."'

As McMillan slips his programme into his pocket and heads for the exit, I spy a flag stretched out over the seats behind the South Stand goal, on which is printed the familiar image of Billy Casper flicking the V's. His two-figured gesture is in the direction of the imaginary Wednesday fans in the away end. More than fifty years on, the skinny lad is still having his say.

\*

The graffiti on the wall on Catch Bar Lane outside Hillsborough is still calling for Garry Monk's removal. It's well out of date. Wednesday have had three managers since then. After Tony Pulis's briefer-than-brief tenure, first-team coach Neil Thompson stepped up in an interim capacity, his initial success dissolving into the kind of underwhelming results that have been all too frequent this season. Darren Moore is now the keeper of the technical area, appointed on the first day of the month, having made the short trip down the A630 from Doncaster Rovers.

Today at Oakwell was Moore's fifth game in charge, but his first win. A victory over the league's form side is particularly sweet, but as he bathes in the dual warmth of the Barnsley sun and the glow of a rare away win, the quietly spoken, level-headed boss doesn't even allow himself a smile, let alone confirmation that Wednesday are remotely close to turning the corner.

Some pleasure, though, must surely be derived from Jordan Rhodes's resurrection. After his two goals today, he is officially the most clinical striker in the Championship this season, despite the paucity of games he's started. Thirty-two per cent of Rhodes's shots have been goals, slightly ahead of Barnsley's hero Daryl Dike. Fewer than one in five shots taken by the goal chart-topping Ivan Toney and Teemu Pukki have been converted.

Moore and Rhodes are on simultaneous media duties on the Oakwell touchline, ten yards apart. Just as the manager stays subdued and contained, his in-form striker fends off all questions with the kind of forward-defensive stroke beloved of the most dogged Yorkshire opening batsman. All his answers are modest and on the level; this is no rampant self-publicist stood in front of us. Asked whether, with three goals to his name in less than a week, the real Jordan Rhodes had finally revealed himself after three and a half less than prolific seasons at Hillsborough, the bat stays straight. 'I'm just trying my best in every game, whether that's contributing goals or assists, or working as hard as I can.'

Certainly a purple patch of goal-heavy form from Rhodes would do the club the world of good as they scrap for Championship survival. Judged solely on the tone of his voice, the fire in his belly might sound like it's barely smouldering, but he does insist that the passion is high. 'Everyone at Sheffield Wednesday Football Club is fighting the best that they can,' he insists. 'We'll absolutely keep going to the very end.'

One journalist points out to Rhodes that he's now close to becoming the Championship's all-time highest-ever scorer. Over the course of the remaining games, could the striker achieve the double accomplishment of both reaching that per-sonal milestone and steering the Owls away from the drop? To do so, there's just the small matter of notching up eight more goals in the eight remaining games. Rhodes, well aware of his disappointing scoring record in the blue-and-white stripes of Wednesday, allows himself a little smile.

'That's some ask, that . . .'

\*

Nowhere else in the Championship, possibly not even anywhere else within the ninety-two-club league, does one team continue to be defined by a single figure in the way that Preston North End do.

Liverpool might have Shankly, but they also have Paisley, Fagan, Dalglish, Benítez and Klopp. Matt Busby is seen as the godfather of the modern Manchester United, but his record is knocked into the shade by that of Alex Ferguson. But one man is also untouchable when it comes to being synonymous with the Lilywhites.

Here at Deepdale, he is inescapable. Standing on the pavement of the A6063 adjacent to the stadium, the evidence of this single player's hold over the history and heritage of the club is overwhelming. For starters, the road is better known as the decidedly more poetic Sir Tom Finney Way. Across the street is The Splash, the sculpture-cum-water-feature that replicates the most famous photograph of this legendary winger: that of him deftly evading the challenge of a Chelsea defender at a waterlogged Stamford Bridge in 1956, in the process sending a beautiful arc of spray up from the soggy turf. Beyond the sculpture is a café/sports bar attached to the stadium concourse. You can guess its name. Finney's.

That Tom Finney continues to be revered so heavily round these parts is testament to the artistry that not only bagged him two Footballer of the Year gongs during the 1950s, but also fired Preston to twice finish runners-up in the First Division that decade, along with being losing FA Cup finalists. His beatification and continued worship in this corner of Lancashire is also testament to the fact that Preston have had very little to shout about during the intervening years. Finney retired in 1960 and Preston dropped out of the top flight at the end of the following season. They've not been back since.

Dave Seddon went to school a couple of miles from Deepdale. For the past twelve years, he's been the PNE correspondent for the *Lancashire Evening Post*, a man able to study the workings of the club from the closest of quarters. So to what degree does the club remain a prisoner of the past?

'There is still a generation of fans who watched North End and Finney in the top flight, but they're the minority now. I think what's frustrating round here is that Blackburn, Bolton, Wigan, Blackpool and Burnley have all had a taste of the Premier League, but no one here has been able to go to work or to school and say, "I've seen Preston in the Premier League."'

Like Nottingham Forest, like Derby County, Preston are increasingly seen as a quintessential Championship club – and a mid-placed, comparatively anonymous one at that. The last time they troubled the play-offs was in 2009. Seddon sighs when asked about the main reason North End haven't been able to cross, or even get near, the threshold to top-flight football.

'It's probably down to money. They're a well-run club, but they're never going to be one to splash a big budget. They're never going to get themselves into a position like Derby where they're having to look at foreign consortiums to go in and buy them. But unless they can have a season where everything aligns – a good group of players all pushing in the right direction, the star players performing, everything and everyone gelling together – it's always going to be difficult for them to compete against the teams coming down from the Premier League who are able to pay their players twenty, thirty, forty grand a week.'

This reluctance to reach for the cheque book is an ongoing source of frustration for a large section of Preston fans – and for one good reason. The club's owner is the billionaire businessman Trevor Hemmings, one of Britain's richest people. A self-made man born into a working-class family, Hemmings also looks like one of Britain's least likely billionaires. Now in his mid-eighties, he is never seen not wearing his trademark flat cap and tweed jacket – an outfit more suited to horseracing than football. That makes perfect sense. Hemmings has owned three Grand National winners in a life that's seen him be the proprietor of holiday camps, casinos and even Blackpool Tower.

'Hemmings is a very private man,' explains Seddon. 'As the North End correspondent, I've probably spoken to him about half a dozen times over the last twelve years or so. When you do get to speak to him, he's very straightforward and very modest. He's almost like a grandad or uncle figure.

'He's also very asset-rich and owns a lot of companies. But he made it clear when he took over that he was never going to chuck money at the club like, say, Jack Walker did at Blackburn. Even though he realises that football can't be run like other businesses, he still wants it run properly, without stretching the boundaries too much. It does prove frustrating to a good section of the fans who know that that little bit more of a push could just make the difference, could just tip it over the edge.'

Hemmings' empire is based on prudent economics, of building up assets slowly over time. And that's the case with the football club. 'He doesn't believe in throwing money around. There's no debt to the bank. There's no list of creditors. I don't think Hemmings would ever want to be known as the man who put North End out of business, the man who overspent and then it all went badly wrong. And maybe that's viewed as more important than success on the pitch.

'Come the time, it'll not be a bad club for someone to buy.

Vulture-type owners tend to take over clubs that are teetering on the brink of administration and which they can buy for a pound. With North End, you've got an established Championship club with a nice stadium that's in good nick. It's not a bad club to take over. It really isn't.'

While Hemmings tends to spend his days shuttling between his horseracing stud in nearby Chorley and his home on the Isle of Man, he has entrusted the day-to-day running of the football club to one Peter Ridsdale (even if Ridsdale's official role is that of 'advisor'). For anyone conversant with the way that Leeds United spent well beyond their means while he was chairman, Ridsdale might seem a curious appointment for a club based on caution and prudence. But Dave Seddon points out how steady the Preston tiller has been, at least financially, under his stewardship.

'It was different at Leeds. It was the club's money being thrown at trying to win the Champions League. It's Trevor Hemmings' money at Preston and Peter Ridsdale has to account for every single pound of it. And he's been here nine years now. To be fair, they work pretty well together. Ridsdale is like the voice of Hemmings. The staff know his authority is coming down from above.'

Allied to the reluctance to throw money towards emboldening and improving the squad has been a willingness to cash in on their better players to ensure the accounts are balanced and tidy. Lifelong supporter Seddon puts the policy into historical perspective. 'They're averaging a big sale every six to twelve months to keep the books looking respectable. But this has always happened over Preston's history. They've always had to sell, going right back to Michael Robinson being sold to Manchester City for three-quarters of a million in 1979. It's nothing new.'

It's a policy that continues at Deepdale. In the January transfer window, Preston were involved in no fewer than sixteen deals – eight players in, eight players out. And it was the departures that received the most scrutiny, with a trio of key first-teamers being moved on; Ben Davies went to Liverpool, Ben Pearson to Bournemouth, and Darnell Fisher to Middlesbrough. At present, they've only been replaced by loan players, suggesting a lack of ambition in the corridors of power when it comes to the playing side of the club. After all, the January window is supposed to be a time of enhancement, of strengthening what a club already has ahead of the struggle of the next few months, be it promotion push or relegation scrap. Preston's jettisoning of some of their best players appeared to be a retrograde step and has indeed been borne out by their subsequent descent down the table. 'It's definitely wounded them,' confirms Seddon.

Since those January departures, Preston have slid – slowly, but inexorably – towards the quagmire of the relegation zone. In the eleven games since Transfer Deadline Day, they've managed just two wins and two draws. That's eight points from a possible thirty-three, with no sign of this downward trend being arrested. 'It's not up for debate. It tells its own story.'

Such a record has consequences. At the start of the latest international break, and in the immediate aftermath of a home defeat to Luton, manager Alex Neil was sacked after nearly four years in the job. The club currently sits in sixteenth place, having been tenth little more than a month previously. Yes, they're still a seemingly comfortable nine points clear of Rotherham in twenty-second place, but the Millers have four games in hand. The net is possibly tightening.

Before his dismissal, Neil had already waved the white flag. After the Luton defeat, he told the media that, 'If I'm being honest, at the moment I haven't got a Scooby-Doo what my best team is.' Seddon, the veteran of hundreds of pre- and post-match press conferences over the years, can instantly recognise when a boss has run out of road. 'When a manager is saying that, he might as well write out the P45 himself.'

It was no surprise when Neil's departure was announced the following day.

'Some fans will argue that it should have been a touch earlier. Others would argue that, because of what happened in January, he'd had his legs cut from under him and that he deserved the chance to try to rebuild in the summer. But they'd lost four of their last five, taking just one point. The style of football had gone very negative. Neil had lost confidence in his players. And he'd lost confidence in himself.'

Neil's faithful assistant Frankie McAvoy – a man who'd been his second-in-command at Hamilton Academical and Norwich City before the pair rocked up at Deepdale – was placed in interim charge until the end of the season. McAvoy had no experience as the big boss, and it was perhaps something of a surprise that Preston hadn't appointed a seasoned firefighter, as Cardiff had with Mick McCarthy, to douse the flames of potential relegation. After all, a few Championship clubs had already had their fingers burned this season by promoting assistant managers and/or first-team coaches to the top job.

'Preston have a tradition of doing well having promoted from within over the years. David Moyes took over from Gary Peters; Billy Davies succeeded Craig Brown. But it's also a case of who's out there. For instance, if you started going down the Tony Pulis route, I don't think that would appeal either to Preston or to the fans. McAvoy might not have been a number one anywhere, but he's been in coaching a while. And they don't need six wins in eight or anything like that. Only two or three wins should put them safe. So they're probably hoping there's enough in the tank for that . . .'

With the international break offering the chance to come up for air, the *Lancashire Evening Post*'s Preston North End correspondent has time to consider the club's options when it comes to finding Alex Neil's permanent successor. Plenty of rumours are circulating; there have already been five different favourites for the job.

'When Preston fans look at some of the names out there, they'll be saying, "Wouldn't it be great to get someone like Chris Wilder?" And, yes, someone like him would be brilliant, but I'm sure he would get snapped up by a club with a bigger budget who could offer him a bit more. Lee Johnson would have been a nice fit, had he not gone to Sunderland.

'From a personal point of view, I'd like to see Gareth Ainsworth get it. That might raise a few eyebrows with Wycombe being bottom of the Championship, but he got them there, he got them two promotions, on one of the smallest budgets. He had three spells as a player here and was well-liked. He was a big fans' favourite who would put his head in where it hurts. He might just be the one to galvanise the club. Everything points to Ainsworth for me at the moment.'

While such speculation might cause distress to the Wycombe faithful, appointing someone who served Preston's right flank with such dedication and passion makes perfect sense to the casual observer. With the Chairboys looking doomed to a return to League One, the opportunity to stay in the Championship, at a club on sturdier financial footings, would surely be an enticing prospect for Ainsworth. Even the EFL's longest-serving manager would give any offer some serious thought.

It could be the forging of a new dynasty, the birth of a new era in the club's history, the chance to escape its ancient history. Who knows? In decades to come, Tom Finney might even be joined outside Deepdale by another former Lilywhites winger immortalised in bronze.

*

# Championship table, 31 March

| | | P | W | D | L | F | A | Pts |
|---|---|---|---|---|---|---|---|---|
| 1 | Norwich City | 38 | 25 | 8 | 5 | 56 | 27 | 83 |
| 2 | Watford | 38 | 22 | 9 | 7 | 55 | 26 | 75 |
| 3 | Swansea City | 37 | 20 | 9 | 8 | 45 | 29 | 69 |
| 4 | Brentford | 37 | 19 | 11 | 7 | 65 | 39 | 68 |
| 5 | Barnsley | 38 | 19 | 7 | 12 | 49 | 42 | 64 |
| 6 | Reading | 38 | 18 | 8 | 12 | 52 | 41 | 62 |
| 7 | AFC Bournemouth | 37 | 16 | 11 | 10 | 55 | 37 | 60 |
| 8 | Cardiff City | 38 | 16 | 10 | 12 | 55 | 37 | 58 |
| 9 | Middlesbrough | 38 | 16 | 8 | 14 | 46 | 39 | 56 |
| 10 | Millwall | 38 | 12 | 16 | 10 | 38 | 36 | 52 |
| 11 | Stoke City | 38 | 13 | 13 | 12 | 42 | 42 | 52 |
| 12 | Queens Park Rangers | 37 | 13 | 11 | 13 | 39 | 43 | 50 |
| 13 | Luton Town | 37 | 14 | 8 | 15 | 31 | 41 | 50 |
| 14 | Bristol City | 38 | 15 | 4 | 19 | 39 | 50 | 49 |
| 15 | Blackburn Rovers | 38 | 12 | 10 | 16 | 50 | 42 | 46 |
| 16 | Preston North End | 38 | 13 | 5 | 20 | 39 | 49 | 44 |
| 17 | Nottingham Forest | 38 | 10 | 12 | 16 | 30 | 28 | 42 |
| 18 | Huddersfield Town | 37 | 11 | 9 | 17 | 41 | 52 | 42 |
| 19 | Derby County | 38 | 10 | 10 | 18 | 27 | 42 | 40 |
| 20 | Coventry City | 37 | 9 | 12 | 15 | 32 | 48 | 39 |
| 21 | Birmingham City | 38 | 9 | 11 | 18 | 28 | 50 | 38 |
| 22 | Rotherham United | 34 | 10 | 5 | 19 | 38 | 47 | 35 |
| 23 | Sheffield Wednesday | 37 | 10 | 8 | 19 | 28 | 47 | 32* |
| 24 | Wycombe Wanderers | 38 | 6 | 9 | 23 | 25 | 61 | 27 |

*Includes six-point deduction*

## Leading scorers

Ivan Toney (Brentford), 28
Teemu Pukki (Norwich), 22
Adam Armstrong (Blackburn), 19
Lucas João (Reading), 18
Kieffer Moore (Cardiff), 16
André Ayew (Swansea), 14


## Manager of the Month

Xisco Muñoz (Watford)


## Player of the Month

Alex Mowatt (Barnsley)


## Managerial departures

Aitor Karanka (Birmingham), resigned
Alex Neil (Preston), sacked


## Managerial appointments

Darren Moore (Sheffield Wednesday)
Lee Bowyer (Birmingham)

# April

*'When you get to my age, you're impatient.*
*You want to do everything yesterday'*

— NEIL WARNOCK

It's a Thursday afternoon in early April and, in the manager's office at Rockliffe Park, Middlesbrough's training ground set in the depths of the County Durham countryside, Neil Warnock is in reflective mood. Oozing warmth and charm, he's considering the past ten months on Teesside, the time that's elapsed since he was parachuted in to save Middlesbrough from relegation last June.

On the one hand, Jonathan Woodgate's replacement looked like a safe, even obvious appointment, calling on all the gnarled experience of a man devoted to football management for almost forty years. On the other, the words 'logistical' and 'nightmare' might have been on people's lips. Warnock lived in the Tamar Valley in Cornwall, where he was seven months into a quiet retirement. Middlesbrough was nearly 400 miles away, the furthest Championship club from his Cornish idyll. But the itch to be back in the dugout was just so strong, so in need of being scratched. Overwhelmingly, it was an itch to work with the long-serving Middlesbrough chairman.

'I must have come out of retirement three or four times

now, but I wouldn't have come back to football again for anybody other than Steve Gibson. I've known him for so many years and have always wanted to work for him, but we missed out on numerous occasions one way or another. When he rang up that morning, I had no intention of going back to work. But I wanted to help him because I think he's a fabulous chairman.

'I told Steve that it might take me a few hours to talk to my wife Sharon about it. I went straight upstairs and within five minutes she said, "Go on, get off now. I don't mind that. You're not doing anything round here with all that's going on."' The pandemic-induced lockdown meant that Warnock was largely twiddling his thumbs down in Cornwall.

'So I was off. I rang Steve when I got as far as Bristol. He asked me whether I'd decided to come or not. I said, "I'm already an hour and a half on my way, pal!"'

Gibson had told Warnock it was a four-and-a-half-hour drive. Anyone making that journey and wishing to adhere to the strictures of the Highway Code is advised to set aside a couple more hours than that in order not to attract the attentions of traffic cops or speed cameras. The distances involved meant that even a semi-regular commute to Teesside was a non-starter, so the Warnocks swiftly decamped to the North-east.

'That drive is a nightmare. It was all that I needed at my age. But within a week of taking over and moving up there, Teesside Airport started flights to Newquay. I could have got home in just two and a quarter hours. It would have been wonderful.'

Having arrived at the Riverside with only goal difference separating Middlesbrough from the relegation zone, Warnock calmly guided the club to a seventeenth-place finish. The short-term deal he'd signed then turned into a longer-term arrangement, since when he's reshaped Boro into promotion hopefuls. They were riding as high as fifth in the autumn, and have been sniffing around the fringes of the play-offs ever since. What's been the difference between the side he inherited and the side now?

'The team spirit, I think. All the lads have improved and everyone's playing to their potential now. It might have helped some of the lads who were written off that there have been no crowds. One or two in particular were lacking in confidence when I came here, players like Anfernee Dijksteel and Marc Bola, but they came on board, listened and really grew. Within a few weeks, I was very pleased with them. The lads have done well and we're not that far away. We just need a strong transfer window this summer to pick up three or four good players to add to what's already a decent squad.'

One judicious mid-term acquisition has been the free agent Duncan Watmore, whose goals have been a highlight of Boro's season. 'Duncan trained for two or three weeks without getting a penny as we couldn't sign anybody at that time. He had an offer from India, but I said to him, "Give it another two weeks here with me," and I was pleased to give him a contract. He's such a genuine lad and he's done really well for me. He works his socks off.' It hasn't just been his manager whom Watmore has impressed; he was named Championship Player of the Month for December.

Warnock's decision to come out of retirement one more time might have been made rather swiftly, but it was clearly the correct one for him personally.

'I must admit it had been nice to go out with Sharon and visit a few places, to walk the dogs, to go fishing in my fishing pond. But the pandemic changed it all. We couldn't do anything. If anything, I was safer in a job. Not being able to do anything or go anywhere would have probably driven me daft – and driven Sharon daft and all.' (Warnock seems to have forgotten that it was being back in a job that resulted in him catching coronavirus in September.)

That he was able to see off the virus was probably helped by his regular appearances on the training pitches here at Rockliffe Hall. Slipping on the tracksuit helps both his physical condition and his mental wellbeing. 'Being on the training ground with the lads keeps me fit – and it keeps me young. I let the lads laugh at me when I put my sweatband on.'

In a season when young assistant managers have made the step up to being the number one but found themselves out of work within a few months, Warnock is proof that the presence of a ship-steadying older hand – even in an assistant or advisory role – is vital in the second tier. 'I think some of the young lads probably worry a bit too much about their own jobs and so they bring in someone that they know or someone in the same age group as them. But the Championship is such a tough league and they need experience alongside or around them – someone who's seen it all and done it all. It's a different league to any other because of its intensity. There's no other league in the world where the bottom club can beat the top club on a regular basis. In most leagues now, you pretty much know who the top two are going to be most of the time in every country. But in the Championship, you really haven't got a clue.'

Despite a much-improved league position this season, Boro's campaign is beginning to fade. Their results over the previous weekend – a 3-1 defeat at Bournemouth on Good Friday and an Easter Monday draw with Watford – haven't completely shut the door on a berth among the play-off places come early May, but they have left it only slightly ajar. With just half a dozen games left, though, for Warnock it's as good as closed. The white flag has been raised.

'Nah, realistically I don't think it will happen – not unless we go on a run and one or two teams really slip up. Normally I would be really thriving at this moment in time with six games to go. Unfortunately, the squad isn't really good enough in certain departments to warrant a late run. We needed everyone to be fit, but we've now lost four or five good players more or less for the rest of the season. To win three or four, our lads have to hit top form. The strikers have to put the chances away and we have to defend well.

'We know that, if we have no injuries, we've got a great chance of beating anybody. But the injuries to our most important players are what's stopped us making a real push for it. And we haven't scored enough goals, either. If we'd have had Ivan Toney on our side when we played Brentford, I think we would have won. Just one player made all the difference. So it's not as if we're looking for a lot of players. Steve wants to help me and I won't be spending stupid money. He knows that. But he also knows that it's my last shot and wants to give it a crack. I'm seventy-two now.'

The chairman certainly isn't regretting that call he made to Cornwall last June. 'Steve's like me. He's delighted with what's happening. The only thing is that people say, "You can do it next year." But I wanted to do it this year. And with a bit of luck, we could have done. We just missed out on a few three-pointers for one reason or another.'

After forty years in the dugout, the veteran with countless promotions under his belt remains hungry for success – and for that success to arrive sooner rather than later.

'When you get to my age, you're impatient,' he confides, flashing a final grin. 'You want to do everything yesterday.'

\*

A few hours earlier on that same Thursday – and despite his Cardiff side being just one point above Warnock's Boro – Mick McCarthy was a little more optimistic than his fellow South

Yorkshireman about his own team's chances of scraping into the play-offs. But only a little.

'It's going to prove very difficult now. We'll never give it up, of course. We'll do whatever we can.'

The task has been growing more difficult with each game; the Bluebirds have won only once in their last six matches. The buoyant run that greeted McCarthy's arrival has hit the buffers, no more dramatically than in their last match, a 5-0 thumping on Easter Monday by bottom-of-the-table, desperately-seeking-resurrection Sheffield Wednesday. It was almost as if, like Samson, McCarthy having his untidy lockdown locks trimmed had removed Cardiff's strength.

Eight points off sixth-place Reading with six games left, it's a tall ask. Not impossible (especially considering the faltering form of both Brentford and, in particular, Swansea), but unlikely. A win today against visitors Blackburn would be the minimum requirement.

In case McCarthy's men needed motivation for the occasion, the PA pumping out a male voice choir singing 'Men of Harlech' ahead of kick-off should gird Cardiff loins, especially when it segues into Fatboy Slim's 'Right Here, Right Now', the tune that, played in a thousand sports stadiums on any given weekend, keeps Norman Cook's pension pot handsomely topped up. However, the inspirational effect is somewhat lessened when Fatboy is swiftly faded out in order to observe the two-minute silence for the Duke of Edinburgh, who died yesterday.

It's a lively start to the game, with both teams keen to play and anxious to win. Cardiff need to put themselves in the best possible position should any of the top six derail, while Blackburn are aiming to halt an eleventh-hour slide towards the relegation zone. It's certainly one of the noisiest behind-closed-doors matches in the Championship this season. These are two extremely vocal sides, both loudly protesting every challenge, every perceived injustice. To be fair, they're just following the examples set by their respective managers; McCarthy and his opposite number Tony Mowbray are both proper old-school shouters.

Kieffer Moore, the Bluebirds' leading scorer this season, is particularly lively in the early stages – this despite being, in McCarthy's medically precise words, 'knackered'. Moore played three times for Wales during the recent international break, including scoring the winner against Mexico, and throughout the season has linked up brilliantly with his compatriot Harry Wilson in the blue of Cardiff. The pair, key protagonists of their side's mid-season recovery, are off and roaring this afternoon.

Wilson is one of those playmakers – like Emi Buendía over at Norwich or Arnaut Danjuma down at Bournemouth – who should be playing at the highest level, as he was last season during a loan spell at the Vitality. This afternoon, in the battle of the on-loan Liverpool wingers, Wilson puts in a more accomplished performance than Blackburn's Harvey Elliott. Elliott, who only turned eighteen on Easter Sunday, is a dazzling player for the future, but today he catches the eye – or, rather, the ear – mostly for a remonstration with the linesman that reveals he possesses the vocabulary of the saltiest sailor.

Wilson is at the heart of every Cardiff attack, such as the move in the eighteenth minute where, played in one-on-one against the Blackburn keeper Thomas Kaminski, he's unceremoniously taken out. But, despite a goalscoring opportunity clearly being denied, the Belgian escapes with a yellow card. Once it's issued, he swiftly departs the scene of the crime and heads back to his goal. He knows he's swerved a bullet there.

Inevitably it's Wilson who sets up Cardiff's opener, a back-heeled free kick that Will Vaulks hits low and hard into the net before charging off for a somersaulting celebration. The memory of the capitulation at Hillsborough at the start of the week gets a little duller. But Blackburn rally during the second half of the first period and, shortly before half-time, their compact and free-scoring striker Adam Armstrong creates the kind of space he's been finding all season and levels. It's his twentieth league goal of the campaign, and his fiftieth in the blue-and-white quarters of Blackburn.

After the break, Blackburn pile on the pressure and hit the Cardiff woodwork three times. The home side are living dangerously, but ride their luck and retake the lead when substitute Joe Ralls – assisted by Wilson, naturally – slips the ball past Kaminski.

In a desperate move to arrest the decline that's seen Blackburn win just once since January, Tony Mowbray takes drastic action. With fifteen minutes left, he brings on all five permitted subs in one fell swoop. It's the kind of change rarely seen outside of kids' football. Indeed, it takes a good two minutes for the fourth official to input all ten player numbers into his electronic subs board.

But the mass substitution pays off. Not only does it mean the appearance of the twinkle-toed Tyrhys Dolan, but also the introduction of former Spurs and Germany midfielder Lewis Holtby. The latter makes an immediate impression on the match, oozing talent and composure every time he gets the ball. And, in stoppage time, it's his threaded through-ball that plays in Armstrong. No second invitations are needed by the voracious Geordie. In the blink of an eye, goal number twenty-one is chalked up.

On the final whistle, McCarthy accepts what a two-all draw means. If this were the Grand National – which kicks off in twenty minutes' time – Cardiff's passage into the play-off spots would have been seen as an outside bet. The top six have all won, either last night or this afternoon, and are now disappearing down the home straight. Only calamity befalling one or two of them at the final couple of fences could favour Cardiff now.

McCarthy offers his loyal lieutenant Terry Connor a gentle handshake. No words. They both know the meaning behind it. As do the players when their boss acknowledges each and every one as they leave the pitch. Mission Unlikely is now almost certainly Mission Impossible. Each handshake is a gesture of gratitude for their toils and their triumphs during the two and a half months under his command. The general salutes his foot soldiers.

Twenty minutes later, McCarthy re-emerges from the dressing room, trudging with all the athleticism of a snail towards the obligatory TV interview. But before the camera starts rolling, the half-dozen members of the ground staff need to turn off their noisy machines that are currently sucking up the loose debris of the turf. They're oblivious to what's happening at the side of the pitch. McCarthy sticks two fingers into his mouth to issue a whistle that would register a decibel reading as high as that of his match-long bawling. The ground staff remove their ear protectors and look across in puzzlement. The boss runs a finger across his throat. The machines fall instantly silent. McCarthy smiles his first smile of the afternoon.

'It feels like a defeat,' he will admit later. He's specifically talking about squandering that winning position in stoppage time, but the comment also applies to Cardiff's season running out of steam. That said, on his arrival in the Welsh capital back in late January, recovering so dramatically to reach eighth place would have looked like an unrealistic pipe dream. He's done a commendable job.

'I know we had a great start and everything was going particularly well, but I was never fooled by it, that we were suddenly one of the best teams in the league. We were just having one of the best runs.'

*

The sun is setting on the woodlands of High Wycombe. And the sun may well be setting on the Championship life of Wycombe Wanderers.

It's an hour into the club's penultimate home game of the season and the trap door is opening wider with each minute that passes. It's do or die. The facts are stark. With four games left, they're nine points shy of twenty-first-placed Derby County. If they lose tonight against Bristol City, Wycombe must win each of their three last games and hope that Derby lose all their three. Even if that unlikely scenario unfolds (bear in mind that Wycombe haven't won three on the bounce all season), they need a fourteen-goal swing to stay up on goal difference. And, of course, they must also hope that in the meantime neither Sheffield Wednesday nor Rotherham stage their own revival and leapfrog Derby.

A glance at the scoreboard offers further confirmation of the near-vertical uphill task. Bristol City are one-nil up.

The irony is that Wycombe are currently enjoying their best patch of form of the whole season. They've only lost once in the last five games, a run that includes two wins, plus a draw with high-flying Swansea after the Chairboys had surrendered a two-goal lead. It's a sequence that even knocks the form of champions-elect Norwich into the shade. And it's a sequence that's had the more optimistic residents of Adams Park whistling the opening bars of the theme tune to *The Great Escape*. In private, at least.

But this purple patch has almost certainly come too late. Had they hit the ground running back in September and not waited until their eighth game to register their first

Championship point, Wycombe might have been lounging in mid-table comfort by now. Instead they've spent most of the season at the very bottom of the table, propping up the other twenty-three clubs.

Tonight is realistically the last roll of the dice – a dice that's been loaded against them all season. It would be the harshest observer who didn't acknowledge the bad luck and unjust decisions that have come their way over the past eight months. Legitimate goals not given. Penalties awarded against them that simply weren't. Red cards that represent gross miscarriages of justice. These balance themselves out over the season, so the received wisdom goes. But there's been no such equalling-out here this campaign.

This evening, though, Wycombe are a goal down not because they've been wronged. Nor because they're the victim of their own folly or mistake. Bristol City's goal was a wonder strike from Tyreeq Bakinson who simply strolled onto the ball to caress it into the top corner from outside the area. No team would feel ashamed at conceding a goal of that quality. But, with half an hour left, that's no consolation. It won't make relegation any less painful.

As the second half deepens, Gareth Ainsworth shuffles his pack, putting on as many attacking players as he's got on his bench. The lull in play causes the Adams Park pitch to fall silent, ensuring that the battle cry of midfielder Curtis Thompson – 'Come on, let's fucking lift it!' – rings out loud and clear. Up on the hill above the ground, in the blue light of dusk, the chanting ultras who've made it their lofty perch this season respond in kind. Some of the ultras have drums.

Ainsworth's switches pay swift dividends when two subs – David Wheeler and Anis Mehmeti – neatly combine down the right and Uche Ikpeazu converts the resultant cross with a brave diving header. The equaliser emphasises what Wycombe have been lacking this season. Ikpeazu has just become their leading scorer. It's the club's forty-third league match, but it's only his fifth goal of the season.

Hope is renewed, dreams revived. Squeezed into his cramped space in the press box, 5 Live's Will Perry updates the nation. 'Wycombe's Championship dreams are still alive!'

If ever a team were up for being overturned, it's surely Bristol City, a side that – despite now being under the stern rule of Nigel Pearson – have maintained a steady downward trajectory since the heady, table-topping days of autumn. They've not won in six matches. And now, with the scores level, they show little evidence of wanting to break that sequence.

It's all Wycombe as they lay siege to the visitors' goal. Another sub, Adebayo Akinfenwa, now a couple of weeks shy of his thirty-ninth birthday, comes closest when he holds off four Bristol City defenders, pivots daintily and fires in a shot that City keeper Dan Bentley tips around the post. 'I was moving like a young Messi,' the big man will later report.

Into the dying seconds of the match, the dying seconds of hope, Wycombe get a corner. Their keeper David Stockdale looks towards Ainsworth to get permission to head up field. His pass is granted. It's a wise decision. When the ball comes to him on the edge of the box, Stockdale's less-than-ferocious half-volley strikes a City arm. It's a temporary reprieve, a chance to slam that trap door shut. For a few days at least.

But it's not reliable Joe Jacobson stepping up to the spot, the man whose penalty won the play-off final last season. Instead, he's given the nod to someone else. Akinfenwa is marching up, ball in hand. Survival, however fleeting for now, is in his hands. And, without nerves, he sends Bentley the wrong way. Close to the end of what may well be the only Championship season of his entire, labyrinthine career, Akinfenwa has finally got his first second-tier goal.

And Wycombe have all three points. Relegation resisted, demotion deferred. At least until the weekend.

The substitutes, and the substituted, sprint onto the pitch as if absolute survival has been secured, rather than there being three tricky games still to negotiate. Midfielder Garath McCleary rides Stockdale's back as Madness's 'Our House' pours out of the speakers. The rest mob Akinfenwa. These are the two clear heroes tonight. The drums are pounding up on the hill, the Rio carnival transplanted to some common land in Buckinghamshire.

And in what's been a testing day for American owners of English football clubs – with the proprietors of Liverpool, Arsenal and Manchester United all issuing mealy-mouthed apologies for their attempts to launch the European Super League – Wycombe's Chief Operating Officer is ecstatic. Pete Couhig, a dapper-dressed native of New Orleans, wears a smile as wide as the Mississippi.

Ainsworth is smiling too. Of course he is. This is a man who – regardless of the abyss his side have been staring long and hard into all season – can't fail to be positive in his post-match appraisals. The smile hasn't left his chops all season. A photo of a grumpy Ainsworth is a collector's item.

'The drive and belief the boys had right until the end there made me so proud of them. I always am proud. We are a real force at the moment. The second half of our season has been really brilliant.'

There's also some reassurance for those Wycombe fans concerned that relegation would signal Ainsworth's departure from Adams Park after more than twelve years as both player and manager. It looks like those admirers of his up in Preston can strike his name off the wanted list. 'I'm absolutely devastated the fans aren't here to see that. They deserve it. And do you know what? It's my job to make sure they get these nights in the

Championship again, whether it's next year or the year after. I am focused on making that dream happen.'

After an ecstatic interview for Sky Sports in his flip-flops, Akinfenwa makes the rest of us wait while he showers. Twenty minutes later, he emerges, now dressed head to foot in black. But the joy hasn't been scrubbed from his face.

Akinfenwa – aka Bayo, aka The Beast – reveals that he was given a standing ovation in the dressing room for his first Championship goal, 'like it was my debut, like I was nineteen. But that's just what this club is about. For me, that was the most humbling thing, how excited everyone was. From the kitman to the CEO, everyone had a big-arse smile. And that means a lot to me. I'm humbled.'

The match-winner also reveals that he and regular penalty-taker Jacobson had a pact. 'JJ said to me a couple of games ago, "Listen, B. If we get a penalty late on in a game and you want to take it, I'll be up for allowing you to." I did ask him tonight. "Are you good with me taking it?" "B. I back you. Take it."'

Just as he was fearless from twelve yards out tonight, Akinfenwa carried little fear that his search for that elusive first Championship goal might never be completed. 'If it didn't come, I wouldn't have allowed it to besmirch my career. But I really wanted to say that, at every level I've played, I've been able to score, and tonight I did that.'

Football's in-built jeopardy and high drama – qualities that had been stripped out of the proposals for what Akinfenwa calls 'that silly-arse Super League' – were on clear display tonight. 'This is real football. It was a beautiful way to end the week. Well, it's only Wednesday, but you know what I mean.'

But does this much-travelled player, Wanderers' wanderer-in-chief, believe the season will end in a similarly beautiful way?

'Trust me, we're going to be swinging in every game. Our gaffer exudes energy and belief. That's what we're built on.

We'll go to Cardiff and we'll swing. We'll play Bournemouth and we're going to swing. And we'll go to Middlesbrough and we're going to swing. And come the end of it, we'll see where we're at.'

Extraordinarily, if the Championship table were arranged by current form, Wycombe would now be third. No one is still daring to whistle The *Great Escape* theme tune, but that chink of light now shines a little brighter.

'My wife texted me at the final whistle,' explains the club's head of press, Matt Cecil.

'She said, "What are the chances of avoiding relegation now?" "Well, it was one per cent at the start of the game. It's two per cent now . . ."'

But euphoria is an emotion that's quick to evaporate. Less than three days later, Wycombe's outside chances of Championship survival are reduced to a fraction of a single per cent, having just narrowly lost to Cardiff. However, other results – the bottom four all lost this afternoon – have ensured that the executioner's blade has yet to strike, even if it's hovering closer than before, all sharp and shiny. Despite its proximity, the Chairboys will reach May, the final month of the season, with their fate still unsealed. That in itself is a commendable achievement after that long points-free run that opened life in the Championship for them.

For the executioner to turn his blade elsewhere, Wycombe must win their two last games – the daunting visit of Bournemouth to Adams Park, followed by a tricky trip up to Middlesbrough on the final day – and pray that Derby continue their losing streak. While the Rams' ongoing fragility suggests the latter to be perfectly possible, the former remains a long shot. And even then, if both sides end up level on points, there's that double-digit swing in goal difference to achieve.

Of course, Ainsworth the eternal optimist won't accept the

fates. His verdict after the Cardiff defeat? 'Yeah, we need to score a few goals in our next couple of games . . .'

*

Sunday, high noon. Gunfight at the Madejski Corral.

Yesterday, Brentford secured their place in the play-offs for the second successive campaign. Bournemouth and Barnsley are practically there too. If Reading are to sneak into the season's period of extra time, they have but one realistic target: they need to overhaul sixth-placed Swansea, this lunchtime's visitors to the Madejski Stadium. It's a straight shoot-out.

Even so, it's not a fair gunfight. Anything less than a Reading victory will give the last play-off slot to the Swans, two weeks before the end of the regular campaign. A season that started so brightly with all those early victories would have the lights shot out. Furthermore, a home win will only wound the visitors, who would very much retain the upper hand in the run-in.

The first thirty minutes are slow and cagey. Gunfighters sizing each other up; no one reaching for the trigger. There are nerves from each side. Swansea haven't come to Berkshire with a strut in their stride. Should they lose today, it would be their sixth defeat in their last nine games.

Right on the half-hour mark, Reading draw first blood. A looping John Swift cross is met meatily by the head of Yakou Méïté and planted in the far corner. But the Royals aren't content to sit on their lead. Four minutes before half-time, Lucas João pounces onto a poor Conor Hourihane back pass, but keeper Freddie Woodman saves the Irishman's blushes. Based on the razor-sharp form of earlier in the season, you'd expect João to bury that chance. But he's not quite the player he was. In recent times, he's been making the headlines for his lack of ruthlessness in front of goal. Three weeks ago, he put in a contender for miss of the season against Barnsley, contriving to miss the target from twelve yards out with a completely open goal in front of him. 'João's accuracy escapes him again today. Swansea are fortunate to go into the break just a goal behind.

After twenty minutes of a goalless second half, down in the Swans' technical area Steve Cooper gives his pack a shuffle. Three subs come on in one go, among them the returning-from-injury André Ayew. That they've missed him today is evident within three minutes when a fabulous piece of skill from the Ghanaian – holding off three players before launching an attack via a nutmeg – sets up Jay Fulton whose drive and shot is parried away, only for Jamal Lowe to follow up and equalise. Other than tearing a strip off Ben Cabango for a minor misdemeanour, it's Ayew's first contribution to the game.

And it's not the last. With seven minutes left, he fires home after a tidy move down the left. Swansea are in pole position now; Reading need to score twice to save their season. Curiously, it takes another five minutes for Reading boss Veljko Paunović to sacrifice a defender for a striker when Sone Aluko comes on for Omar Richards. They do manage to equalise deep into added time, but it's too little, too late. A season that began with the loudest of bangs ends with the quietest of whimpers. Swansea, meanwhile, confirm their presence in the play-offs in the same stadium they did so last season.

It was a strange performance from the home side. Had you not known what was at stake, you would have presumed that the past ninety minutes merely represented an inconsequential mid-season match. Nothing particular to gain, nothing particular to lose. In contrast to the blood and fire shown by Wycombe four days earlier, this was a team devoid of any sense of passion or spirit or fight. Once Swansea had equalised, it was the tamest of surrenders.

Still, the season in general has been a distinct improvement on last, when the Royals finished in fourteenth place. And, somewhat remarkably, it's been achieved despite the turmoil the club put itself through on the eve of the season when it sacked manager Mark Bowen and appointed Paunović, a decidedly unknown quantity. These are times not so fondly recalled by Simeon Pickup, the editor of the fan-produced website/podcast/ YouTube channel The Tilehurst End and a man bemused by a new sheriff riding into town at such a late juncture.

'It was all so eleventh hour. We just assumed that Bowen would be getting a proper chance this season as manager. There had been no real sense that he'd done too much wrong. He was a safe pair of hands and seemed to be getting us on the right track. No one had really heard of Paunović. Looking at his record, he'd done well with Serbia's U20s, but not particularly at Chicago Fire. That league experience wasn't encouraging. And he was yet to manage in England.

'Fans were keeping an open mind, but the mood was pretty downbeat. Ripping up our plans just before the start of the season felt very chaotic. Paunović barely got any time in pre-season because he had to quarantine when he came over here from the US. His first game was a League Cup tie against Colchester and he had to deliver his half-time team talk over Zoom as he was holed up at the club hotel attached to the stadium.

'The club has made some bad decisions over the last couple of years, but this just seemed to top them all, with this sheer, chaotic, comedic ...'

Pickup struggles for the appropriate noun.

'... clusterfuck.'

But then something remarkable happened, something magical that lit up the eyes of Reading fans. Their team shot out of the traps, winning seven of their first eight games. The view from the top of the Championship table, an altitude not experienced for many a summer, was an enthralling one.

'We were living on cloud nine. We were top of the table for

nine weeks or so and we were loving it. But those first eight results were better than the performances might have suggested. We weren't dominating games, but when we had chances, we tended to take them. In our next four games, we were better going forward and created more chances, but we lost all four, most of them heavily. And after that, we were inconsistent, even if we were picking up enough points.

'Things came off the rails at the end of January. Injuries held us back massively – I think we've lost pretty much every member of the first-team squad to injury at some point this season. We've been stretching a small squad too thinly and they've all got too tired in the last few months. When you're playing a more expansive, more energetic style of football, it shows in the fatigue that builds up.'

The players might be fatigued both mentally and physically as the curtain begins to fall on what's been arguably the hardest Championship season of them all, but that doesn't excuse the lack of hunger and desire in that make-or-break encounter with Swansea. For Pickup, that's down to the inadequate reserves of experience in the first-team set-up. 'It's a young squad. We lack leaders badly, especially in the final third.'

But there's been a reason the squad is thin, why players of experience haven't been signed. Earlier in the month, Paunović revealed that Reading are – and have been since he joined – under a transfer embargo imposed by the EFL because of their financial situation, having made significant losses over previous seasons. This is the real reason that, while those around them recruited and strengthened during the January window, ready to launch a campaign for automatic promotion, not a single new arrival came through the door at the Madejski.

'We've been under various "soft" transfer embargoes for a while,' explains Pickup, 'under some kind of extra oversight from the EFL. We can't spend money. We can't tie players down to new contracts. The irony of this is that we've got really rich owners who want to spend an awful lot of money, but it's Financial Fair Play that's holding us back.'

While seeing their promotion challenge deflate will have been disappointing for their fans, the state of play behind the scenes at the club changes the emotion to deep concern. Less than a fortnight before the Swansea game, the annual accounts were published, covering up to June 2020. And they made for grim reading.

The club registered operating losses of £43.5m during this twelve-month period, which, when added to the existing debt, shows them to now be in deficit to the tune of a cool £138m. This is especially concerning with the knowledge that that accumulative figure includes the income generated by the sale of both the training ground and the Madejski Stadium. Selling off the family silver has made little dent in the debt. And bear in mind that the time period covered by this latest set of accounts doesn't include the tail end of last season and the entirety of this. With bums not on the Madejski's seats, there's a fair chance that next year's accounts will make for even grimmer reading.

The day after the 2019–20 accounts were published, the Tilehurst End team invited football finance expert Kieran Maguire, author of the illuminating book *The Price of Football*, onto their podcast to analyse and contextualise the figures. His diagnosis cut right to the heart of the matter.

'The problem is wages. The average wages Reading are paying is about eighteen grand a week. If you spread that across the squad, immediately we find that the club is paying more than twice the amount in wages than it is generating in income. So, before you stick the floodlights on and pay the electricity bill, and before the groundsman puts petrol in his mower and mows the grass, the club has already lost a huge amount of money.'

Reading's losses over recent seasons have found them with

little wiggle room when it comes to FFP. Despite being owned by a seriously rich man, the Chinese shopping-centre magnate Dai Yongge, the club can't splash his cash. They need to reduce these annual debts before they can do so, and an obvious way of doing so would be to sell off their best and most promising players when their value is at its highest. But, as Simeon Pickup explains, there's a problem here.

'Our owner is notoriously stubborn when it comes to selling players. It seems that no one has properly explained to him that he needs to do that to have money to reinvest. He's well-meaning and he's got a lot of money to put into the club, but he doesn't seem to understand Championship finances. I guess his thinking is that he wants to keep hold of our best players to get us into the Premier League, but it's a naïve approach. It often ends up with us not getting any money for players whose contracts have been run down. We're lucky to get a million for anyone we sell.'

With the training ground and stadium sold off, the most conspicuous assets left are the players. The expectation is that the jewel in the Royals' crown, the playmaker Michael Olise, will be snaffled by a Premier League side during the summer transfer window. What price he might command, in this pandemic-induced buyers' market, is another thing. That is, as Pickup observes, if he goes at all.

'It could very well be that the owner is so stubborn that he'll say, "No, we're not going to sell Olise for £20m. I want to keep him and see if we can get promoted." That really wouldn't surprise me. The usual business logic would be to sell him for as much as you can and try to balance the books.'

Contrast this approach with that of Brentford, masters of moving their players on at the point at which they hit their optimum value. The case of Ollie Watkins is the shining example of this. Signed for less than £2m from Exeter City, when the striker left for Aston Villa after three years at Griffin Park, the Bees banked a 1,500 per cent profit on the player. No one there worried about whether their subsequent push for top-flight football would be irreparably damaged. They simply repeated the process, reaching down into the lower leagues for some guy called Ivan Toney.

It's not as if Reading haven't had success at identifying and nurturing cheaper talent. 'The irony is that our better signings tend to be players who we haven't spent very much money on. Two of this year's Player of the Season candidates are Josh Laurent and Michael Morrison. Laurent was a free transfer from the lower leagues and Morrison was a free transfer from Birmingham.

'When we have spent more money – such as £7m on Sone Aluko – they tend to be a flop. George Puşcaş cost around £7m too and has yet to get going. This season we've cut our cloth, spent less and done better. Now that we're behaving like a more sensible club, we're competing at the top end. About fifty-one per cent of all players who've played this season have come through the academy. For a Championship club, that's really impressive and something to be proud of.'

The current cloth-cutting aside, the after-effects of the actions of a previous CEO – generous to a fault when it came to player salaries – will continue to have a lingering legacy until those players are removed from the wage bill. And while a couple of the big earners are scheduled to leave the Madejski this summer with their contracts having expired, the still-parlous state of Reading's finances puts the fear of a points deduction into the minds of everyone associated with the club.

'Going by the rulebook, it would seem that we're going to get a points deduction, but it would look like a mean move by the EFL if there were a number of clubs hit with deductions at a time when everyone's struggling because of the pandemic.

But whether we get a points deduction or not, someone's going to be upset.'

But even if Reading did find themselves in negative equity points-wise at the start of next season, the fidelity of one person in particular wouldn't be tested. 'Dai Yongge has invested a lot of money into the academy, so we know he's committed. Losing all that money would be concerning if you didn't have a committed owner. It's worrying to look at our balance sheet, but the fact that we do have an owner who is seemingly reliable is reassuring, especially when you see how other clubs have gone.'

Nonetheless, for a season that started so brightly under a new manager who's since shown himself capable at this level, there is a discernible sense of concern about on-the-pitch matters too, as the man from the Tilehurst End concludes.

'The mood among fans is very split at the minute. Everyone can acknowledge that Paunović has done a better job than we thought he would have done, and to be in the promotion race at all was very surprising. But to have had such a big slide during February, March and April is obviously very frustrating, to put it mildly. There's very much a sense that this season was a flash in the pan.

'To be completely honest, I have no idea what to expect with this club. Next year, I genuinely don't know whether we'll finish first or twenty fourth . . .'

*

Today is a rare day for Jed Wallace. Football doesn't need him.

Instead, the Millwall winger – the club's current top scorer and a man who's been enjoying arguably his best season as a professional footballer – is on domestic duties at home in Camberley. 'I've had a man's sort-out day,' he reveals. 'The car needed a service, and then the garage needed a clear-out, so I've been up the tip and back. All those jobs that I've had an excuse to put off.'

This particular Championship season, this *peculiar* Championship season, has demanded every player's full attention. They've barely come up for air. It's been a continual cycle that's rarely slowed. Travel, play, rest. Travel, play, rest. Repeat to fade.

Now, with just two more games, two more Saturdays, left before the regular season closes, home life can get more of a look-in. And that's not just sorting out household junk. Once Wallace has returned from the tip, the boot of his car now empty, there's the opportunity for some boisterous quality time with his two pre-school kids. 'It's like wrestlemania round here.'

Wallace has been Millwall's principal creative force this campaign, whether buzzing in crosses from the right wing, or helping himself to his highest goal tally in what is his sixth season in the Championship. His strikes are often spectacular; see here the Messi-like free kick against Reading or the snapshot that saw off Rotherham.

But, of course, those goals aren't the only thing that sets this season apart for Wallace. While his form's been strong, the empty stands have been a real downer.

'Without the fans, you don't really remember key moments, like goal celebrations. As a footballer, you thrive off the atmosphere of the crowd, so even winning goals late in the game haven't felt the same this season. It's felt, to be honest, a little bit boring.

'Normally I'd look forward to going somewhere like Watford – a tight stadium with a decent atmosphere – but it's different knowing there'll be no fans. It's the same with cup draws. Normally ours is a giddy household when it comes to the cup draw. As a Millwall player, you always hope to be drawn against West Ham. But this year I was dreading us getting them. I didn't want to have waited six years but then have to play them at the Den in front of no one.'

In a more typical season, Wallace would be feasting off the adoration of the Millwall faithful. A roar of excitement and expectation would invariably rise every time this fans' favourite received the ball wide on the right, forty yards out. This season, though, at best Wallace might receive the encouragement of half a dozen subs up in the stand.

'When the fans are in and it's a flat match, you just need some-one to win a tackle and it lifts the crowd and it lifts the game. We definitely need fans back next season, however many we're allowed. We had 2,000 against Derby and, after having no one in, it felt like 20,000 were there.

'We're not the best team in the league. Nowhere near it. But we are hard to beat and we have a fanbase that gets right behind us. If you asked any Championship team which ground they would most like to play at with no fans in, they'd pick the Den. In my experience as a Millwall player over the last six years, we've always done well against the big teams, especially at home. But we've not beaten anyone in the top six all season. Yes, we've not played as well as we needed to, but we've also not had the crowd there to help us.

'Also, I want to get my kids to the Den. Because they're growing, they've gone through three Millwall kits during lock-down without even going to the bloody stadium. My youngest was the size of a loaf of bread when he last went . . .'

Not only have the empty stands made for a depleted atmos-phere but, as Wallace confirms, they've also changed the nature of what actually happens on the pitch. There are clear tactical differences between this campaign and the last.

'For example, if we're losing 1-0 at the Den and we're shooting towards our fans in the last ten minutes, if I put a below-average cross in, it would get cleared, but because there's pressure in the stadium and there's pressure building on the opposition, it might be at the expense of a corner, from which we might score. This season, there's not that pressure and so other teams aren't being forced into making mistakes. So I've definitely had to change my game and almost play safer at times. Similarly, I don't think there have been as many red cards as normal this season. Without the crowd getting on top of them, not as many players are losing their composure and lunging in for tackles.

'Another tactical change has been a few teams sitting back more. At Birmingham, they sat as a back five. I don't think George Friend, playing at left wing-back, ran forward once in ninety minutes. They had no real intent to win the game, but if they had 25,000 Blues in there, they'd be egged on and spaces would open up.

'Also, because of the schedule, pitches have been of a lesser quality than normal and I think that's made the style of play worse. Last season, more teams were playing football. This season, everyone's got a long throw. QPR, who are a very, very good footballing side, have Lyndon Dykes firing in long throws. Swansea, another very, very good footballing side, throw everything in the box. Because everyone's so tired, teams have been concentrating on set plays. There isn't the energy required to open teams up.'

Astute in his analysis, Wallace also appears to possess a near-encyclopaedic knowledge of the Championship and its players. One minute he's effortlessly comparing the relative merits of Jake Bidwell and Ryan Manning, the two players fighting for the left wing-back slot at Swansea. The next he's dissecting – and also praising – the 'insane' high-press tactics employed by Barnsley. Wallace is engrossed by the second tier, the level at which he's played the majority of his football.

'I'm less obsessed than I was before I had kids,' he defends. 'When I don't play well, it's typically when I've overthought the game, when I've tried too hard. That's when I struggle. Having a welcome distraction off the pitch in the form of my kids has meant I've spent less time thinking about football, which has actually been a positive for me.

'But I do love football. I love watching any games in the Championship, but if, say, Barrow were playing tomorrow night, I'd be watching them on the TV. And I won't just have it on. I'll be watching players, I'll be watching different styles. A couple of months ago, I noticed that Newport were playing Exeter, and that Exeter were down to nine men in the first half. So I had to watch that on iFollow to see how it panned out. Exeter played a 5-3 formation with no one upfront. It was so intriguing to watch.'

The passion that Wallace holds for the game is quite possibly a by-product of whence he came. This is a player who's done plenty of time in Leagues One and Two, along with a couple of loan spells in non-league. Having not been exposed to the potentially desensitising nature of a Premier League academy, he's retained an appreciation for the pure pleasure of playing football for a living.

'There's definitely pressure from a young age when you're an academy player. It starts in the playground. "Oh, look at Rhys. He plays for Chelsea. He's going to be a footballer." Straight away, at ten years old, he has to be a footballer. Does that take some of the enjoyment out of it?

'I was never like that. There was never any pressure from my parents and so I just enjoyed playing. I only ever trained twice a week until I was sixteen. A good friend of mine – George Saville at Middlesbrough – came through at Chelsea and he was training four times a week from the age of nine or ten, so I can see why people fall out of the game. Maybe some kids do get bored. Maybe it becomes a chore. For me, it could never be a chore. Football should be fun. I still love training every day.'

Wallace also enjoys the experience of playing at grounds whose turf he's not previously graced. This season, one of those was obviously the spanking-new Brentford Community Stadium.

'The dressing room feels like it's in a five-star hotel. It's unbelievable, especially compared to what was there before. The away dressing room at Griffin Park was a disgrace, especially the toilets. If you wanted to sit down for a number two, the door wouldn't shut. So you had to leave it open in front of thirty other blokes as you went. They've gone from that to me thinking I was in the Shangri-La Hotel. They've gone full circle.'

While clearly loving life at a club whose Championship existence is not immediately in peril, at the age of twenty-seven, has the time dawned for Jed Wallace to leave his comfort zone and move on in order to fulfil his ambitions of Premier League football? He's certainly a player with both the credentials and the chops to hold his own, if not prosper, in the top flight. And does the fact that he's just about to enter the final year of his contract at the Den suggest that such a move is actually imminent? His answers to these questions are both diplomatic and honest.

'I've not really thought much about my own situation as I'm just looking forward to football being back to how I know it is. It's been on the back burner. And that's not me being a politician. I just want to get back to normality.

'I didn't even realise that there were only fourteen months left on my contract until people started tweeting me about it. There's not been a minute to think as we've been playing, playing, playing. I've certainly not overthought it. You typically overthink these things when you're unsettled. But I am so settled. And that's when these things take care of themselves.

'When I permanently signed for Millwall four years ago, my

target was to play in the Premier League. I believe I can do that and I want to do that with Millwall. Luckily I've got a manager who wants to do the same. Gary Rowett will not let the club rest on its laurels and will push us forward. And that's something that I'm more than happy to be a part of. I've signed for Millwall three times and we're a great fit. I love it.'

Wallace isn't alone in feeling this way, in cherishing the 'togetherness' that is life with the Lions. He cites a recent conversation with George Evans, a centre-back signed from Derby during the January transfer window. Despite having been at the Den for fewer than three months, and despite having yet to play in front of the club's passionate fans, Evans made the following pronouncement.

'Jed, this is the most I've ever enjoyed my football.'

'Mate, you came through at Man City with Yaya Touré and David Silva. And you're telling me you prefer playing with me and Ben Thompson on the terrible training pitch at Calmont Road? You're joking, aren't you?'

'Honestly, Jed. I love it, I love it.'

Wallace is also loving it, loving it. This is a man who's as balanced off the pitch as he is while dancing his way past opposition defenders – a man deeply appreciative of exactly where his commitment and application have taken him.

On his right forearm, there's a tattoo in neat, understated script: 'Family is a safe haven in a heartless world.' It appears that the notion of family isn't just found inside the four walls of his Surrey home. At the start of each working day, it's a concept that Jed Wallace also encounters in a certain corner of south-east London. There's pride in being a Lion.

\*

As April turns into May, some certainties have crystallised in this most uncertain of Championship seasons. The automatic promotion spots have been claimed, the golden tickets snaffled. Both Norwich and Watford will be making the swiftest of returns to the Premier League. The clock has run down and no one can catch them now.

The identities of the four clubs who will extend their season with a little play-off action have, of course, also been confirmed: Brentford, Bournemouth, Swansea and Barnsley are the ones to go into extra time. With two games of the regular season left, though, the final standings in the table – and thus the make-up of the two-legged semi-finals – remain undetermined.

The real intrigue of the last two Saturdays of the regular season will now be focused on the league's bottom-feeders, those hoping to push themselves off the seabed and poke their heads above water. With Rotherham still playing catch-up after multiple Covid-related postponements earlier in the campaign, the game they still have in hand over their rivals could be crucial.

It promises to be the nerviest of fortnights for all concerned, from Huddersfield in twentieth place down to Wycombe in twenty-fourth. Quite possibly the nerviest of all will be Wayne Rooney. For a man with dreams of being a top-grade manager for decades to come, his ambitions could take a serious bash should Derby fail to make the cut. And a record of just one win in their last fourteen matches suggests that his Rams could be heading for slaughter.

Their final game of the season, at home to Sheffield Wednesday, could well turn out to be the kind of winner-takes-all shoot-out hated by the fans of the respective teams. The neutrals, meanwhile, will be salivating at the prospect.

\*

# Championship table, 30 April

| | | P | W | D | L | F | A | Pts |
|---|---|---|---|---|---|---|---|---|
| 1 | Norwich City (P) | 44 | 28 | 9 | 7 | 69 | 33 | 93 |
| 2 | Watford (P) | 44 | 26 | 10 | 8 | 61 | 28 | 88 |
| 3 | Brentford | 44 | 22 | 15 | 7 | 74 | 41 | 81 |
| 4 | AFC Bournemouth | 44 | 22 | 11 | 11 | 73 | 43 | 77 |
| 5 | Swansea City | 44 | 22 | 11 | 11 | 54 | 36 | 77 |
| 6 | Barnsley | 44 | 23 | 8 | 13 | 56 | 46 | 77 |
| 7 | Reading | 44 | 19 | 12 | 13 | 59 | 48 | 69 |
| 8 | Cardiff City | 44 | 17 | 13 | 14 | 61 | 48 | 64 |
| 9 | Middlesbrough | 44 | 18 | 9 | 17 | 54 | 49 | 63 |
| 10 | Queens Park Rangers | 44 | 17 | 11 | 16 | 52 | 54 | 62 |
| 11 | Luton Town | 43 | 17 | 9 | 17 | 39 | 48 | 60 |
| 12 | Millwall | 44 | 14 | 17 | 13 | 42 | 45 | 59 |
| 13 | Stoke City | 44 | 14 | 15 | 15 | 48 | 50 | 57 |
| 14 | Preston North End | 44 | 16 | 7 | 21 | 45 | 55 | 55 |
| 15 | Blackburn Rovers | 44 | 14 | 11 | 19 | 59 | 51 | 53 |
| 16 | Birmingham City | 44 | 13 | 13 | 18 | 35 | 52 | 52 |
| 17 | Nottingham Forest | 44 | 12 | 15 | 17 | 36 | 43 | 51 |
| 18 | Bristol City | 44 | 15 | 6 | 23 | 44 | 61 | 51 |
| 19 | Coventry City | 44 | 13 | 12 | 19 | 42 | 59 | 51 |
| 20 | Huddersfield Town | 44 | 12 | 11 | 21 | 47 | 68 | 47 |
| 21 | Derby County | 44 | 11 | 10 | 23 | 32 | 53 | 43 |
| 22 | Rotherham United | 43 | 11 | 6 | 26 | 42 | 58 | 39 |
| 23 | Sheffield Wednesday | 44 | 12 | 9 | 23 | 37 | 58 | 39* |
| 24 | Wycombe Wanderers | 44 | 9 | 10 | 25 | 35 | 69 | 37 |

*Includes six-point deduction*

**Leading scorers**

Ivan Toney (Brentford), 29
Teemu Pukki (Norwich), 25
Adam Armstrong (Blackburn), 24
Kieffer Moore (Cardiff), 20
Lucas João (Reading), 19
André Ayew (Swansea), 16

**Manager of the Month**

Jonathan Woodgate (Bournemouth)

**Player of the Month**

Arnaut Danjuma (Bournemouth)

# May

*'The club is at forty points. There's no
R next to our name. It's going to take
until the final whistle of the last day for
us to be relegated. If that happens . . .'*

— GARETH AINSWORTH

There was a danger that the Championship wasn't going to play ball, that there wouldn't be anything left to play for when the final day of the regular season came around. Twelve dead-rubber matches, twelve inconsequential encounters.

But that wouldn't account for the second tier's trademark erratic nature, for the tendency of one club in particular to implode and leave the escape hatch open for others. This year, that club is Derby County, a side whose absolutely woeful end-of-season form – six defeats on the trot, one win in the last fourteen games – has ensured that none of their relegation rivals has yet been condemned to League One football with the final Saturday upon us. Today they entertain Sheffield Wednesday, who also have their eye firmly focused on that escape hatch. Derby are still in the box seat. Beat the Owls and they're safe. Fail to beat them and all manner of scenarios might be playing out. The next couple of hours are going to be intriguing at the very least – and extraordinary at best.

As they have been for weeks, Rotherham are breathing down Derby's necks. The only problem is that they've been experiencing a similar abject run of form, having registered just one win in the last ten. The Millers, though, can claim extenuating circumstances. They've had four games in hand over their relegation rivals for much of the spring months and have been playing catch-up of late, the backlog caused by postponements due to two Covid outbreaks and poor weather. April alone saw them play eight games in twenty-two days.

If Rotherham fail to win, they'll return to League One after just this one season in the second tier. Their up/down, up/down pogoing between the Championship and League One will continue. Today they're playing Cardiff and even if they do pick up all three points in South Wales, the result of the shoot-out at Pride Park still needs to go their way – that is, for Derby not to win.

Neither Derby nor Wednesday have enjoyed the ideal preparation for the game. Last weekend, reports emerged that the Owls' first-team squad had yet to be paid their April wages. Perhaps even more significantly, some were still owed their March salaries.

Things have been no more stable at Derby. In the past couple of days, the word was that the latest takeover attempt – this one led by twenty-something Spanish businessman Erik Alonso, a former advisor to Dejphon Chansiri at Wednesday no less – was on the brink of collapse amid claims that the Spaniard intended to refinance Pride Park in order to complete the purchase. Alonso was quick to refute this speculation.

On-the-pitch matters haven't exactly been filling Derby fans with optimism either. In the days ahead of the game, the keyboard warriors of the fan message board dcfcfans.uk have been voicing their concern over both the tactics and the line-up for today's match. One fan suggests just a single change: Steve

McClaren in for Wayne Rooney. Another responds with: 'We could sub in the ghosts of Clough and Churchill, and I doubt it'd make a difference at this point.' A third sums up the prospect of the clash against Wednesday. 'It's like waiting for an operation with a 50/50 chance of success. The surgeon is Dr Crippen, ably assisted by Dr Shipman.'

At the foot of the table, Wycombe have – after a string of impressive victories, most recently in their final home game against Bournemouth – made it to the final day without being officially relegated. Admittedly it would be the greatest of great escapes were they to retain their Championship status today. They need Rotherham to lose at Cardiff, and Sheffield Wednesday to narrowly beat fourth-from-bottom Derby. And even then Wycombe would still need to go to Middlesbrough and win by a double-digit margin. For once, Gareth Ainsworth isn't seeing this scenario as a glass half-full. He actually sees it as a glass positively overflowing.

'The club is at forty points. There's no R next to our name. It's going to take until the final whistle of the last day for us to be relegated. If that happens . . .'

*12.25 p.m.*
Wayne Rooney hasn't smiled much this season, his first in management. But this lunchtime, as a hard rain falls in Derby – and possibly *on* Derby – he's laughing and joking on the touchline. Perhaps it's for show; perhaps this veteran of football at the very highest level isn't feeling the pressure. Or at least he's trying to kid the opposition that he's not. Down in the tunnel, though, the faces of his Rams are showing the gravity of the situation, all hard intensity and deep focus. Captain Graeme Shinnie leads them out, his face stern and unyielding. Colin Kazim-Richards lingers on the touchline, having a short word with a higher power before

crossing himself. The next two hours may need some divine intervention.

Up on the gantry, Sky Sports' man on the mic, Daniel Mann, makes what must be the first-ever reference to *The Thick of It* on a football commentary, when he repeats a much-cherished line from potty-mouthed spin doctor Malcolm Tucker: 'This is the fucking *Shawshank Redemption*, right? But with more tunnelling through shit and no fucking redemption.' Of course, for someone who will later apologise to viewers for audible swearing by the players, Mann delivers a decidedly family-friendly version.

Mann's viewers, at least those of a Derby or Wednesday persuasion, may well be viewing some of the match from behind their sofas. There's that much at stake. 'Steve Bloomer's Watching' blares out from the PA speakers. If this long-dead footballer is indeed watching, he too will surely be cowering behind some celestial furniture.

Darren Moore, a former Derby player, shares fist bumps with the Rams' backroom team. This is his first game back in the Owls' technical area after developing pneumonia and blood clots on the lungs as a result of an earlier bout of Covid-19. In Moore's absence, his assistant Jamie Smith has been picking the team, the fifth man to take charge of the Owls this season. It's the latest incarnation of the instability that's been a constant at Hillsborough since September.

Moore gazes out across the pitch where today's referee, the ever-colourful Mike Dean, is ready for action. The more superstitious Owls fans might have reason to be concerned. Dean was officiating on the day that Wednesday last got relegated to League One, eleven years ago. He blows his whistle to start the match a couple of minutes after the Cardiff/Rotherham game has kicked off 170 miles away.

*12.38 p.m.*
Over in Cardiff, it's Rotherham who provide the first twist of the day when Lewis Wing strikes a cleanly hit volley for the Millers to take the lead. There are only eight minutes on the clock but already Rotherham have, as it stands, lifted themselves out of the relegation zone.

*12.41 p.m.*
At Pride Park, Derby striker Martyn Waghorn misses a great opportunity at the far post after a corner is nodded on. But his header is off target and he spectacularly clatters into the post, his throat and chest making strong contact with the woodwork. He's treated for several minutes, during which time a stretcher arrives behind the goal. But Waghorn eventually gets back to his feet, ready to continue the fight. Significantly, though, for a match that already kicked off late, this long delay will put it even further behind the game in Cardiff.

*12.44 p.m.*
Wycombe take the lead at Middlesbrough through Fred Onyedinma.

*12.51 p.m.*
A header from Rotherham captain Richard Wood should have doubled the Millers' advantage in Cardiff. Chances are less frequent here at Pride Park. As expected, it's cagey and full of attrition in the early exchanges. Lots of niggly free kicks are being given away, most of them involving Wednesday's ever-combative midfielder Callum Paterson.

*1.03 p.m.*
Wycombe go two-up at Boro, this time through Garath McCleary.

*1.05 p.m.*

At Pride Park, there's a rare chance for Wednesday as Adam Reach's long-range effort comes down to earth on top of a Dave Mackay flag that's stretched out in the stand behind the goal.

*1.09 p.m.*

A low shot from Manchester City loanee Patrick Roberts is parried by Keiren Westwood but slotted home by Kazim-Richards, Derby's leading scorer this season. The whistle is instant, though, with the striker a clear couple of yards offside. Whoever is operating the music appears not to have heard the whistle and The Fratellis' 'Chelsea Dagger' blares out for an uncomfortably long time before being abruptly silenced.

*1.17 p.m.*

It's half-time in South Wales where Rotherham's single-goal advantage keeps them in the driving seat. On his forty-eighth birthday, the Millers' boss, Paul Warne, must be cautiously pleased with the state of affairs at the halfway point. His team have been on top for the first forty-five, creating plenty of chances that really should have been taken.

*1.19 p.m.*

Five additional minutes are signalled at Derby, all for that delay while Martyn Waghorn was being treated.

*1.22 p.m.*

A long throw by Paterson is directed at goal by the head of Jordan Rhodes. Kelle Roos saves it, but Wednesday defender Sam Hutchinson stabs it home: 1-0 to the Owls. It's a major step through the tunnel towards daylight. Things are looking decidedly gloomy for Derby. With Rotherham leading, the Rams must now score twice. There's no other way. But, in the twenty-three games in which they've found themselves behind this season, they've never staged a comeback and won. In fact, they've lost twenty-one of those matches. The omens for the home side are as dark as the clouds above. As things stand, Wycombe and Wednesday would be accompanying them down to League One.

*1.30 p.m.*
During half-time, the dcfcfans.uk forum continues to be a haven for pessimistic Rams supporters. Defeatism has well and truly taken over. 'We are a League One club playing in the Championship and coached by a Sunday League manager,' moans one fan. 'There are no words,' sighs another. 'We are down and deservedly so.'

*1.46 p.m.*
Within four minutes of the game restarting at Pride Park, that defeatism is proved to be misplaced. Tom Lawrence floats in a cross which is met by a beautifully guided Martyn Waghorn header for the equaliser. 'Chelsea Dagger' can now be rightfully played.

Meanwhile, Wycombe are heading for their fifth win in the last eight games. They're now three-up on Teesside.

*1.49 p.m.*
'Rampant' is a word that's been little employed to describe Derby this season, but the home side are now indeed that. Patrick Roberts waltzes through the middle of the pitch unchallenged and curls a shot around a diving Westwood. Now 2-1 down, Wednesday need to score two unanswered goals and hope Cardiff do them a favour against Rotherham. Derby, though, now hold the cards. If they don't concede again, they will remain a Championship club for another twelve months.

*1.59 p.m.*
But this is Derby, the 2020–21 version where defensive frailty is a leitmotif of their season. Craig Forsyth, the full-back who'd played Wednesday onside for the afternoon's opening goal, miscontrols the ball in his own box and presents Paterson with a simple chance to slot home from eight yards out. We're all square again and Rotherham are back in pole position. Rooney's smile of just a few minutes ago is back to a scowl.

*2.05 p.m.*
And it gets worse for Derby. The ball goes high in the area after a Barry Bannan corner and it's headed back across goal where the German Julian Börner, right on the goal-line and possibly offside, nods it home. Yet more paper-like defending. Rooney's scowl has transformed into a face of fury. They're on the ropes – cut, bruised and winded.

*2.14 p.m.*
With Derby having to score at least once to have any hope of survival, Rooney now has five attacking players on the pitch. One of his subs, Kamil Józwiak, powers into the Wednesday box and is brought down. Mike Dean points to the spot. The latest twist, the latest lifeline.

Before the penalty can be taken, though, a goal is scored at Cardiff. And it's an eighty-eighth-minute equaliser for the hosts from Marlon Pack. It's a body blow for Rotherham. As things stand, Wednesday are now the ones to occupy twenty-first place in the table, to feel the fresh air of salvation.

*2.15 p.m.*
But things only stand as they are for a short time. A very short time. Wednesday are outside the relegation zone for just *fourteen seconds*. Waghorn fires the penalty high into the net to make it

3-3. With both matches all square, Derby reclaim that precious position of safety.

*2.16 p.m.*
Four minutes of added time are signalled at the Cardiff City Stadium, four minutes in which Rotherham need to save themselves. But after playing so frequently of late, the legs are dead, the tank empty.

*2.19 p.m.*
Derby's Patrick Roberts has the chance to kill off the whole debate when he's clean through on goal, but as he shapes to go around Keiren Westwood, the Wednesday keeper smothers the attempt. On the touchline, Rooney is apoplectic. He sends on Curtis Davies, the highly experienced defender, to shore things up. This is Davies's first game since rupturing his Achilles back in December. He's on the pitch against the doctor's advice. The club's medical staff have not even allowed him to train, but Davies put himself forward for the match. It's later revealed that, before Rooney would consider selecting him for his cameo appearance, the defender had to sign a waiver absolving the club's medical staff of any blame or responsibility should he injure himself more severely.

*2.22 p.m.*
It's full time in South Wales. Cruelly reined in by that late equaliser, Rotherham are down, making a swift return to third-tier football. It's an unhappy birthday for Paul Warne. Later, as he faces Sky's cameras, one of the Championship's most erudite managers will be lost for words. 'Emotionally it's . . .' He will puff out his cheeks and take a deep breath. '. . . it's been tough.' He will appear a broken man. 'I'm absolutely exhausted.' A Pinteresque pause. 'I've got nothing more to give.'

It's now a straight slug-fest between Derby and Sheffield Wednesday. The latter have to score in the few minutes remaining.

Having been replaced by Curtis Davies, the substituted Martyn Waghorn now occupies the front row of the stand, leaning over the advertising hoardings to let his team-mates know the Rotherham result. Standing square-on to the Derby back line – now five-strong to protect the scoreline – he bellows instructions to stay solid, to stay tight. A draw will do.

*2.28 p.m.*
Six added minutes are signalled, six minutes for Wednesday to lay siege to the Derby goal. But the home side stay more resilient than at any point in their last ten games. With the finishing line in sight, their defence suddenly loses its porous qualities. Not even the presence of Westwood coming up for a corner fazes them.

*2.35 p.m.*
The final whistle of the regular season blows. Triumph and despair. Derby County are still members of the Championship. Sheffield Wednesday are no longer.

Waghorn, the hero of the hour, rushes onto the pitch, tears in his eyes. Over the next half-hour, he will give gushing TV interviews before heading out of the stadium with his team-mates – and clasping a foaming bottle of beer – to celebrate with the massed ranks of Derby fans. They've spent the past few hours in the rainy car park, their nerves shredded, their emotions raw.

Waghorn's team-mates are as ecstatic as he is. Rooney isn't, though. He's just relieved. The past few months have not been the most glowing of auditions for him as a manager; having done their darnedest to implode in recent weeks, Derby have survived by the skin of their teeth. This is not a reason for congratulation. It should never have come down to the final day.

'It is a relative success, but on one day,' Curtis Davies tells 5 Live. 'We've been a bad team over forty-six games of the season, let's not get away from it.' Davies has experienced relegations in his long career. Like Rooney, his overwhelming emotion this afternoon is that of relief, not celebration. 'There's no open-top bus tour for staying up from relegation, put it that way.'

At various points today, all three teams found themselves out of the danger zone, on dry ground. For Rotherham and Wednesday, though, it turned out to be shifting sands. Just one more goal from the Owls this afternoon would have kept them up. And, of course, without that points deduction, they'd have been safe too. Instead, they finish bottom, with Wycombe's masterful 3-0 victory at the Riverside lifting them to twenty-second place, a modest altitude that they've rarely experienced all season. They finish above both Wednesday and Rotherham, just a single point behind Derby, having – eventually – won the same number of games.

Barry Bannan squeezes his eyes tight to keep the tears at bay. As Wednesday's player of the season, he's been a rare beacon of consistency and calm in a disjointed, dysfunctional campaign. After this extraordinary, see-sawing game, the season – one pockmarked by managerial switches off the pitch and misfiring performances on it – has ended in chaotic fashion. It's been an afternoon that's mirrored the current chapter of the club's long history.

Bannan is the only player in the entire Wednesday squad known to have signed a new contract during the season; whether that contains a release clause in the event of relegation is undisclosed. But what is known is that there will be a widespread clear-out of players now that the Owls are heading back to League One, even if Darren Moore – in his post-match interview with Radio Sheffield's Andy Giddings – refuses the invitation to give more details on this. 'Nothing's been decided. And why's that? Everything, from day one, has been about staying in the league. I've not had one meeting. Other clubs have probably been working towards next season. We haven't. Why? Because it was all about staying up.'

Later that evening, Dejphon Chansiri, pilloried from all angles in the hours since the final whistle, issues an open letter to the Wednesday fans. His tone is decidedly more considered, and more self-aware, than that Tony Pulis-baiting press conference of his on New Year's Eve.

'As your owner and chairman, I take full responsibility for everything that happens at our club. I am the leader and in good times or bad, the responsibility for Sheffield Wednesday lies with me. I am sorry to you all that we have been relegated.

'You do not deserve this.'

*

Back in Jon McClure's kitchen in Sheffield, the atmosphere is even gloomier than on our last visit back in September. The singer and Wednesday loyalist is more despairing than ever about his football club, especially when a final-day escape was within their grasp.

At half-time at Pride Park, with Wednesday a goal to the good, there was cautious optimism in the McClure household. The family was nervously flipping between the games at Derby and Cardiff, when events late in the day in South Wales tipped towards the Owls' favour.

'Cardiff equalised against Rotherham and we were going barmy, jumping around the house. "We're staying up!" Then we switched back to the Wednesday game and we'd given that penalty away. It was, "Oh my God . . ." By the end, we were dead flat and mardy. "Urgh, I hate it!" But even if we had stayed up, we'd have gone down next season. That's the honest truth.'

Having been hopeful last autumn of venturing through Hillsborough's turnstiles at some point this season, McClure has had to watch the entire campaign unfold from a distance. Has that made the agony worse?

'If I'm really honest, I've been completely disconnected from it. It's almost like it's been happening to someone else. I remember when we were last relegated to League One. We played Crystal Palace on the final day and there was a visceral anger in the stadium. You could feel it. But this time it's been like watching someone or something drift away. You don't feel like it's real. It's been like a depressing, slow-mo car crash.

'My lad's six years old now and we've had a near-two-year break in going to matches. How am I going to get him excited again about watching Wednesday? You're supposed to be able to motivate the youth to carry that tradition forward, but why's he going to watch us when we're absolutely bobbins, when he can put the telly on and watch Man United or Chelsea or Man City smashing it?'

That slow-mo car crash has extended itself over nine painful months. For McClure, not even the halving of the points deduction in November meant the faint light at the end of the tunnel shone even a bit brighter.

'I saw this coming. There are still some fantastic footballers within the squad, but we've not replaced good players with players of a similar quality. The squad has been gradually weakened. But the problems go deep at Wednesday, the majority of which are off-field issues that are deeply affecting the players.'

One major issue that has clearly distracted and destabilised the squad is that of the non-payment of wages. 'The club signed these players up to contracts. They knew they would have to pay them. So who's doing the financial forecasting? I'm terrible with money, but I fancy myself doing a better job.'

And that issue is potentially more serious than mere inconvenience to the playing staff and their mortgage payments. Under FIFA regulations, a player is legally entitled to walk away from his contract and out of the club if two months' salary payments haven't been paid on time, as long as the club has failed to clear the arrears in the additional fifteen days' notice period the player gives them. McClure understands the gravity of such a clause should wages continue to be a problem. 'It's feasible we might start next season with no players,' he sighs. 'More than that, it's feasible we might not have a club. I don't know the way out. Well, I do know the way out. It's a new chairman.'

McClure's end-of-season diagnosis is consistent with the one he dispensed nine months ago: Dejphon Chansiri is to blame for the current ills affecting Wednesday. 'There's a rare thing in society nowadays where people confuse wealth with competence. They do it in politics, and they do it in football as well. "Oh, he's a rich guy so he must know what he's doing." Why? Because his dad's got money? I apply that rationale to the Prime Minister and I apply it even more to Wednesday's chairman. If your dad was Bill Gates, that doesn't make you Bill Gates, does it?

'One thing I'm certain of is that the club will never prosper under Chansiri. Never ever ever. And we've handed over this 150-year-old institution to him. "Here you go, mate. You have it." These owners forget they're the custodians. In their heads, these are *their* clubs.

'The ground is a mess. It's starting to look tatty. This is Hillsborough – a proper legendary ground. Euro '96 matches were played here, and the '66 World Cup, and FA Cup semi-finals... It's an historic place that's dying a slow death.

'And there's a problem with the fanbase. Some people are

incredibly deferential, or have been, to the chairman when there was no reason to be. For the longest time, they were saying, "We're lucky to have him." Why? What's he done? Get off your knees, man. It's embarrassing. If only people could band together for two minutes without being dickheads, to think about the bigger picture, we could do something amazing. But it won't happen. People are too divided.'

What the immediate future holds for Sheffield Wednesday is unwritten ('We don't even know who'll be playing for us next season, so how can you predict anything?'), but surely no season can be as turbulent as the one just completed, where the club's fundamental instability was illustrated by the frequency of the managerial turnover. But whatever the coming months hold for the blue half of the Steel City, McClure would never consider beating a hasty retreat. As soon as those turnstiles spin again, he'll be there, season ticket in hand and scarf around his shoulders.

'Like a mug, I'm still going to go, aren't I? It's like a family member. You might not be able to see them, but you can't stop caring about them. It's that, really. I love the club.

'And some of the away games in League One are just brilliant. Like Accrington, on the terraces, stood up – unbelievable. You can have some good times down at that level.

'But let's hope it's the start of a long journey back.'

*

Monday night and the fans are back at the Vitality Stadium. The food concession shutters are up, the deep-fat fryers have been dusted off, and the pie ovens are hot. Cherry Bear the mascot is back on the touchline after a few months' absence and the PA has been turned up to an ear-splitting level.

For twenty Championship clubs, the season is over, their players heading to summer beaches (although, with the ongoing travel restrictions, these are more likely to be the beaches of

Skegness or Scarborough than the Seychelles or St Lucia). The other four clubs, though, have been granted a fortnight's extension. Tonight is the first leg of the first Championship play-off, where sixth-placed Bournemouth are about to entertain third-place Brentford – and more than 2,000 excited home fans. These are the lucky ones plucked out at random by computer. Grandads and grandsons sit side by side, shared memories about to be made.

Bournemouth lost their last league game to Stoke, but Jonathan Woodgate has named an unchanged XI. When a side can leave such hugely experienced and talented players as Shane Long and Jack Wilshere on the bench for the home leg of a Championship play-off, you know that this is really a Premier League side in exile.

That we're just a couple of games from the so-called 200-million-dollar match at Wembley, from one team's ascension into the richest domestic league in the world, isn't necessarily clear from a glance at the match sponsors. They include such prosaic-sounding companies as BH Calibration and Castle Lane Barbers.

Sometimes this season – in empty, atmosphere-free stadiums across the land – football matches have had the luxury of starting slowly, of taking half an hour or more to get to anything close to a simmer. But the electric presence of the crowd, allied to what's at stake over these two matches, ensures we're in deep, straight from the referee's first whistle. The switch is flicked, the current is surging.

Football historian Richard Foster is the country's most eminent expert on the play-offs, as evidenced by his thorough and fascinating book *The Agony and the Ecstasy*. Unlike many, Foster is an unflinching champion of this end-of-season mini-competition. To him, it's 'less a lottery, more a high-grade laboratory providing the ultimate litmus tests of performance under pressure'.

Right now, Bournemouth fans would surely agree that the play-offs are a key component of the football calendar; without them, of course, their team's season would have been done and dusted nine days ago. Brentford supporters, on the other hand, would surely campaign to do away with them were their existence put to a public vote. The Bees have lost more play-off campaigns than anyone else. In all nine they've contested, they've never emerged from even one of them as victors.

Roared on by the faithful, Bournemouth are clearly after an early goal to settle any nerves. They need to press home the advantage they have tonight – the longer the deadlock, the heavier the pressure, the tighter the screw. An early drive from Jefferson Lerma flies just over. Within two minutes, a well-designed move down the right ends with Philip Billing fluffing his shot. A little later, a Dominic Solanke header strikes the post. The tide is in full flow, as are the singing elements of the Vitality's stands. A Cherries-themed adaptation of 'The Red Flag' breaks out.

And it's not just the home side's forward momentum that's being cheered. The biggest roar arrives for a brilliant tackle from captain Steve Cook which calmly defuses a Brentford counter-attack. That former England centre-back Woodgate has definitely tightened things up at the back over the last few months is beyond doubt; thirty-one-goal Ivan Toney isn't getting a sniff.

After around half an hour, rain starts to spit. One or two of those familiar with life in the unprotected front five rows of the East Stand know what effect that dark cloud approaching from the west will have in a few minutes' time. A couple of them reach for their waterproof trousers. Other front-row occupants who've not been quite as meticulous in their pre-match preparation improvise with black bin liners around their legs. When it comes, the rain comes hard.

But the weather won't distract them. They're reacquainted with their heroes who are, after a season's absence, within earshot of the on-first-names encouragement. 'That's yours, Phil.' 'Keep going, Lloyd.' 'Come on, Arnie mate. You've got him here.'

There's tension too. Bournemouth are penalised when full-back Lloyd Kelly does little more than breathe on an opposition player who collapses in a heap. The referee calls Captain Cook forward for a chat about Kelly's protestations, prompting 2,000 voices to reprise an age-old chorus that no official wants to hear. 'You don't know what you're doing, you don't know what you're doing . . .'

Tension turns to exasperation when Bournemouth have a two-on-one break, but Solanke fluffs the final ball through to his unmarked team-mate. Then a fierce Cook header is batted away by Bees keeper David Raya before David Brooks sees his follow-up blocked by Toney.

How the fans would wish for a repeat of the score when they last returned after a lengthy spell of behind-closed-doors football — that 5–0 cruise against Huddersfield back in December. Instead, it's 0–0 at half-time, a scoreline made worse by Captain Cook limping off shortly before the break.

Brentford come more into the game in the early stages of the second half, and threaten to open the scoring when Christian Nørgaard attempts an ambitious overhead kick that loops into the safety of the South Stand fans. Bournemouth are increasingly looking like the away side, soaking up the threat of Toney before hitting the visitors on the break. And it's a counter-attack that sees the first goal of the night when Bees captain and centre-back Pontus Jansson is caught in possession upfield; for some reason he's in an advanced position out on the right wing. In a sweeping move, the Cherries' two best offensive players, Brooks and Arnaut Danjuma, combine, with the Dutchman slotting home coolly. The place erupts. Dancing breaks out in the aisles and in the gangways. One supporter's moves cause his wet-weather poncho to billow up over his head.

It might be advantage Bournemouth, but it's surely premature to start singing Wembley-themed songs. That doesn't stop them, though – despite the margin being just a single goal and despite the opponents having the league's top scorer leading their line. Plus, an immediate triple substitution by Thomas Frank adds Emiliano Marcondes and the ever-tricky Bryan Mbeumo to Brentford's firepower.

And it's Mbeumo who is gifted the opportunity to become the Bees' hero when a low cross from Nørgaard skids across the six-yard box but the winger, with an empty net at his mercy, fails to hit the target. There seems to be an acknowledgement that this is the best it will get for Brentford tonight. And, indeed, after weathering the storm, Bournemouth push forward during the last ten minutes, with both Danjuma and Solanke going close.

The crowd meet the final whistle with both relief and jubilation. Might they just have witnessed the last Championship match here at the Vitality for the time being? Tonight has been a matter of timing. Bournemouth's win avoids a fourth successive defeat, while Brentford suffer their first defeat in their last thirteen games. Has that infamous play-off hoodoo returned?

The Bees won't necessarily be panicking just yet. In last season's play-offs, they overturned a 1-0 deficit from the first leg away at Swansea to reach Wembley. This is not unfamiliar territory. And this time, next Saturday, it will be in front of a few thousand of their own noisy fans.

Sky's mobile camera follows Danjuma around the pitch as he embraces his team-mates and consoles the opposition. Then, while not exactly a lap of honour, the team visit each corner of the ground to acknowledge the support their fans have given from a distance during this difficult season. Captain Cook's season might end earlier than that of his team-mates. He is currently limping around the pitch in a manner that can only be described as 'gingerly'. The second leg is just five days away.

A few minutes later, Danjuma walks through the stadium concourse in his flip-flops, his destination the press room. One young lad, already presumably thrilled to have been successful in the ticket ballot, can't believe his good fortune as one of his heroes walks by within touching distance. 'Nice goal' is all he can manage. He gets a smile in return.

In the press room, Danjuma – who didn't play in the two home games in December in front of Bournemouth's support- ers – explains the effect made by the stands being occupied. 'The fans helped massively. It's a different kind of feeling. A different pressure, a different atmosphere. It's twelve against eleven. You feel the fans helping when you're tired whenever they shout, whenever they scream.'

He's asked, as a player who has scored both in the Champions League for Club Brugge and for the Netherlands national side, what tonight's goal means to him. 'It ranks really high. The play-offs are massive to me. Even though I'm foreign, I know what they mean to the clubs and the players in England.'

As such, he knows it's far from mission accomplished. 'Don't get me wrong. I'm happy with the win, but I'm not satisfied yet. It's just half-time really.'

The 'half-time' cliché – rolled out whenever there's a two-legged tie in football, be it Champions League semi-final or National League play-off – gets another airing when Jonathan Woodgate takes the stand.

'Exactly. Half-time. We've got a slight advantage but we know we've got it all to do on going to Brentford. We know how good they are at home. We know how good their players are and how good the team is. They've been in this situation before. They've had that experience. So, yeah, slight advantage, but this tie is far from over.

'The atmosphere was unbelievable, electrifying. I felt that helped our players. The fans were constantly behind them. They liked the way we were playing and they've fully bought into what the team are doing. The team are working hard and attacking quick. That's what they want to see.

'But we're going to Brentford and the shoe's on the other foot. Let's see what their fans are like.'

Thomas Frank is next up and, bullishly, he's keen to reveal exactly what the Bees fans will be like. 'It was fantastic to have the fans out there. Really, really good. I think the Bournemouth fans did a really good job. But I expect our fans to be better.'

Where Woodgate is a fast talker but concise with his answers, Frank is more expansive and free-form. He talks of 'massive belief' in his dressing room, of how the experience of coming back against Swansea in last year's semi-final will be beneficial, of how he felt a draw would have been a fairer result tonight.

The press conference then goes quiet as the journalists use up all their questions. Frank doesn't like this silence.

'I have one more thing,' he says. 'You've not done your job well enough. Why is there not one of you who's asking about VAR and the penalty? Have you seen it back? One hundred per cent penalty. Another good example why there should be VAR in these games.'

No, no one has seen the incident again. There aren't any screens here at the Vitality for print journalists to watch replays. These are reserved for those working for TV and radio. In fact, most of us in the room don't actually know what incident Frank is referring to. Apparently it was a coming-together between Adam Smith and Tariqe Fosu-Henry in the first half. It evaded our collective consciousness because Fosu-Henry was the only Brentford player to appeal. Even his team-mates appeared not to see it.

The Championship might be a VAR-free zone throughout the regular season, but Frank – now in full flow – believes that a video referee should be employed in a match as significant as tonight's.

'Clear contact in the penalty box. Penalty. You can watch it back if you're in doubt before you write your article. And if you don't agree with me, you don't have to write it. But it's these situations we need to get bang-on.'

He rises from his seat and starts walking out. 'I think we're only playing for, what, one hundred and seventy million pounds. Oh my fucking God ...'

A smile.

'See you, gentlemen. See you Saturday.'

\*

When Saturday comes, and with it the inevitable post-match post-mortems, this time it's a shoulder-shrugging Jonathan Woodgate who's complaining about how a play-off semi-final should be officiated.

'I don't understand how he can give a penalty for that. It's beyond me, to be honest with you. The fans got on top of the ref. They were constantly at him. We played Norwich and got a Premier League ref. Give us a Premier League ref in a game of this magnitude.'

It's not hard to deduce, from both Woodgate's words and his demeanour, that he's the losing manager. In a thrilling and at times explosive second leg, Bournemouth have just lost 3-1 at Brentford, a result that sinks their dreams of returning to the top flight at the first time of asking. But the Cherries boss is choosing to focus on a handball decision early in the first half, one that was by no means the turning point of the match; Ivan Toney's converted penalty was merely the equaliser on the day. At that point, Bournemouth still held an aggregate lead having already doubled their advantage eleven minutes earlier when Arnaut Danjuma helped himself to another breakaway goal.

And it was a quite extraordinary goal so early in the game. Every single Brentford outfield player had gone up for a corner, leaving the Dutchman completely on his own near the centre circle – the kind of defence-free tactic usually employed by a losing side deep in the embers of added time, not by a side with plenty of time to nullify the first-leg margin. Bournemouth simply hoofed the ball clear and Danjuma's pace did the rest. A two-goal advantage calmed the away team's nerves.

Or you'd have thought it would have done. Twelve minutes after Toney's equaliser came the true turning point of the tie. Deputising in the centre of the Bournemouth defence for the injured Captain Cook, Chris Mepham lingered too long on the ball and the ever-bustling Bryan Mbeumo steamed in to gain possession. Straight through on goal, he was brought down by the Welshman, a tap-tackle with his hand of which his compatriots Justin Tipuric and Leigh Halfpenny would have been proud. An instant, undebatable red card for the former Bees defender. Bournemouth would now have to defend their slender advantage a man down against a team roared on by around 4,000 fans, by their twelfth man.

It proved too tough an ask, with Brentford grabbing two second-half goals to send them to the play-off final for the second year in a row. History was repeating itself. Last season's semi-final saw them return to west London 1-0 down but able to pull through thanks to a 3-1 home win. It's the same this evening.

For Bournemouth, a period of soul-searching and deep

reflection would ensue. Despite possessing arguably the best squad in the Championship this season, their race was run. Another second-tier season was their fate. And whether they'd have the best squad in the Championship next season became a heavy point of discussion. The likes of Danjuma and Brooks now looked certain to be leaving the south coast in search of life in the Premier League. Whether Jonathan Woodgate's time at the Vitality was also over would be another subject ripe for discussion.

*

When they finally came, they arrived from all over – from Skewen and Sketty, Townhill and Trebanos. They didn't come in their usual numbers, but they wore their colours of white and black. And they wore their hearts, full of hope, on their sleeves.

Four hours after Bournemouth had self-destructed after coming into their second leg with a one-goal lead, the Swansea faithful are sending prayers to their deity of choice that nothing like that happens this evening. Last Monday, the Swans returned from Barnsley with a vital away win, thanks to a peach of a goal from their talisman, André Ayew. Now, with the club having received special dispensation from the Welsh government to allow 3,000-odd of their fans in for the second leg, it's time for those in the stands to help push their side over the line. They've been away too long. They've been away for 441 days.

Fans are gathering outside the Morfa Parc, the Harvester pub in the shadow of the Liberty Stadium. The mood is a mixture of excitement and trepidation. 'I'm shaking,' admits Rob from Jersey Marine. 'When I see the green of the pitch, it's going to be emotional. It's going to be hard to keep it all in. I'll be a wreck before we even kick off.' Behind him, Sharon from nearby Llansamlet isn't quite as nervous. 'I don't want to jinx anything, but can I tell you last night I dreamed we won 3-0? A Jamal Lowe hat-trick. Or is it bad luck to have mentioned it?'

Inside the ground, expectation rides the air. 'This is a safety announcement,' barks a pre-recorded message over the PA system. 'Turnstiles are open. Turnstiles are open.' And in come the fans. They don't pour in. It's not a deluge, not a flood. And as they hunt for their seats, they're accompanied by The Tourists' 'So Good to Be Back Home Again'.

The crowd rise to their feet when the players come out for the warm-up. Ayew makes a point of jogging across to the fans on three sides of the pitch to applaud and salute them. He's the cult hero of this side, the totem player. Matt Grimes might wear the captain's armband, but no one is more a leader than the Ghanaian.

Flags and banners are raised; so too are voices. The massed choir sings along to The Monkees' 'Daydream Believer' and a wave of optimism flows across the crowd. The announcer, a local radio personality with a lung capacity that would rival that of Brian Blessed, introduces the Swans man by man with all the enthusiasm of someone announcing the participants of a heavy-weight title bout. The roar that greets each name is thunderous.

The game kicks off and the crowd launch into a fruity recital of 'Land of My Fathers'. If the Liberty is this loud at just a tenth of its capacity, your hearing must be seriously impaired when there's a full house in. I'm sitting just a row in front of the radio commentators, among them former Swansea strikers Ian Walsh and Rory Fallon, and 5 Live's chief EFL reporter Aaron Paul. They're just a few feet away, but for the next ninety minutes plus added time, I won't be able to hear a word they say.

The crowd soon burst into an enthusiastic rendition of 'Stevie C's black-and-white army!', but in his technical area, Steve Cooper looks unmoved. This week, following the announce-ment that Roy Hodgson is retiring from Premier League management, Cooper has been linked to the soon-to-be-vacant post at Crystal Palace. With Frank Lampard dropping out of contention, the Welshman is believed to be the preferred choice of the Eagles' American owners. If the Swans fail today – or if they fail at Wembley in a week's time should they get past Barnsley – there's a strong chance he might be interested in swapping South Wales for south London. This could be his last home game in charge at the Liberty. It may even be his last game in charge of Swansea forever.

Barnsley have won admirers, and climbed the table, as a result of the high-intensity, high-press game favoured by Valérien Ismaël. But it's Swansea who are in their faces in the first half-hour, sharp and snappy in the tackle, contesting each and every ball. In particular, the central defence pairing of Ben Cabango and Marc Guéhi is impenetrable and positionally immaculate. Both are putting in extremely mature performances in a high-stakes game. Both are only twenty years of age.

And then Swansea strike, creating a little breathing space. A free kick wide on the left is only partially cleared and it falls to skipper Grimes just outside the area. He feints to shoot and creates more space, before curling the ball into the far corner, in a not-dissimilar manner to Ayew's goal at Oakwell. Grimes signals up to the main stand where his girlfriend is on her feet, applauding her man. The bass drum in the far corner of the ground booms louder than ever. The momentum is building, the tide is flowing.

And the Barnsley bench know how hard it will be to swim against this tide. They start protesting every decision, their arms continually in the ten-to-two position. Ian McMillan, watching on his iPad back in South Yorkshire, will at least be enjoying Ismaël's angry arm-waving. One of his assistants is frequently out of his seat and in the ear of the fourth official, pointing out every minor infraction missed by the referee.

The half-time whistle is met by another roar that wouldn't be out of place at a title fight, the kind that would greet the bell after a round in which the champion had thumped the contender to the canvas.

Having curiously left Daryl Dike on the bench for the first half, Ismaël throws him into the fray for the second forty-five of what could be the American striker's last game in the scarlet of Barnsley. He's been the one charged with saving the Tykes' season. A hug from his manager tells Dike exactly what his task is. No words are necessary.

Wayne Routledge, now thirty-six and playing the central striker role for Swansea this evening, goes down heavily early in the second half and lies motionless for some time, much to Ismaël's annoyance. He clearly believes this is a wily old campaigner trying to slow the game, trying to run the clock down even though there's nearly a quarter of the two-legged tie to go. Ismaël's protestations are hushed when a stretcher is brought on. As Routledge is carried past the Barnsley manager and down the tunnel, the Frenchman offers a consolatory thumbs-up. If the Swans do hold their nerve and reach Wembley, it looks unlikely that Routledge will be gracing the famous turf.

With each minute that ticks by, each minute that Swansea edge closer to the final, the noise rises a few more decibels. The singing gets louder, the drum beaten harder. Until the seventy-first minute, that is. A swift Barnsley breakaway ends with their leading scorer, Cauley Woodrow, sweeping the ball home to equalise. We haven't yet had anything close to the drama that had unfolded earlier at Brentford, but we might now. Game on.

It's no longer a comfortable downhill roll to the final whistle for Swansea. The home fans have shifted out of their prematurely celebratory mood and now need to get back into inspiring their team to stay tight, to stay resolute. And on the pitch, the commitment cannot be questioned. At one point, Connor Roberts has his shirt completely wrestled off him by a Barnsley player, but this is no time for sartorial elegance. He throws it to the turf, playing on in his undershirt. Of course, the fact that he's doing so is another reason for Ismaël's assistant to be chirping in the fourth official's ear.

The tension around the Liberty could have been punctured had substitute Korey Smith kept his head when straight through on goal. Instead, he slips as he tries to round the Barnsley goalkeeper and the chance goes begging. His mistake ensures the five minutes of added time will be highly nervous ones. But, as they've been all evening – save for Woodrow's well-taken goal – Cooper's boys stay resolute.

The final whistle. The knock-out blow. The roar of all roars. Swansea are heading to north-west London.

The subs and backroom staff charge onto the pitch in delirium. Even Steve Cooper, one of the more taciturn presences in Championship technical zones this season, pumps his fist into the air and allows a wide smile to break out. (Within a few minutes, though, the calm and cautious manager returns. 'As soon as I get home, the laptop will be on and I'll be looking at the opposition.')

The Swansea fans, starved of seeing their team in the flesh for all that time, more than played their part this evening. And now, an hour after the final whistle, they continue to. 'Land of My Fathers' is still being belted out up on the main road, while a gaggle of teenage lads hang around the entrance to the players' car park, ready to cheer each of their heroes into the night. When Jamal Lowe's 4×4 approaches them, a mini carnival breaks out.

Just across from the lads, Rob from Jersey Marine is back outside the Morfa Parc. He doesn't feel like going home. 'What

an amazing evening. Extraordinary. I just want to milk this
moment. I wish I could bottle how I feel right now.

'After all, it could all turn to shit next Saturday.'

*

The Brentford coach driver doesn't need satnav to get to
Wembley. He's been here quite recently. Just nine months ago,
in fact, when the Bees last graced the Championship play-off
final. That occasion – a 2-1 extra-time defeat to Fulham –
marked their ninth attempt to get promoted via the play-offs.
They've not been successful on even one of those occasions.

This afternoon, they need to sidestep that hoodoo, undo the
jinx, break the chain.

Phil Parry, BBC Radio London's long-serving commentator/
presenter/reporter, is another who knows his way here. He's
seen this hoodoo in action from the closest of quarters having,
over the years, reported on six of those nine play-off attempts,
'this tale of utter woe and heartbreak'. How does he explain the
reliability of Brentford to implode at this stage of the season? Is
it some kind of self-fulfilling prophecy?

'It definitely adds to the legend. I'm no psychologist, but I
do wonder whether this constant talk just gets into people's
psyches, whether the squad just goes, "Oh, it's another one. It's
another one."

'But it's not just Brentford. In his fantastic book on the play-
offs, Richard Foster tells you, quite categorically, that if your
home kit is red-and-white striped shirts and black shorts, it's not
good news. Sunderland, Sheffield United, Exeter, Lincoln . . .
They all have ropey records when it comes to the play-offs. None
of them as magnificent as Brentford's nine, mind you . . .

'Italy have just won the Eurovision Song Contest, thirty-odd
years after they last won it. They've tried all sorts over the years.
So have Brentford – with different managers, different players,

different styles of play, different divisions. But there's no real reason for their repeated failure.'

The clubs they've lost to in their three most recent play-offs – Fulham, Middlesbrough and Swansea – all came with a Premier League pedigree. Brentford, though, don't have the strut of being a top-flight club in exile trying to regain their supposedly rightful place.

'Psychologically, is there a deep-down feeling of inferiority? I don't know. But it's not "little old Brentford" any more as they've had such good coverage for the way they've gone about things as a club. People talk plenty about Brentford now.

'Last season, they missed out on automatic promotion *and* in the play-offs. Two chances, two bites at the cherry. But they bit their tongue on both occasions. The statistics would suggest they are stronger than last year. They've got more points, they've lost fewer games, and Ivan Toney's broken the Championship goalscoring record. But Brentford fans are never going to be overtly confident because of the history. This is the play-offs, after all. I would imagine that today people are doing the reverse of wearing their lucky underpants. Maybe they're burning them because in previous play-offs they've not been very lucky.

'Who knows, when they come to excavate Griffin Park ahead of building those houses, if they churn up a bizarre crypt or find some kind of ancient burial site, that might explain it all . . .'

But it's not just the club that's on a bad roll. The play-offs haven't been a happy hunting ground for their skipper Pontus Jansson; the bearded, tattoo-heavy Viking is on an undesirable personal streak. It's not just the Fulham defeat in August that hangs heavy in his heart. Two years ago, Jansson was wearing the captain's armband for Leeds United. After spending the vast majority of the season in the automatic promotion places, Marcelo Bielsa's men stumbled in the final few games of the regular season and finished third. Then – with Jansson on the bench through injury – they stumbled further, losing to Derby in the play-off semi-finals. The second leg was a humiliating 4-2 defeat at home. Jansson's replacement in the centre of the Leeds defence was sent off.

There's no doubt that Jansson rapidly became a totemic figure at Brentford. 'Leadership was what was required,' explains Parry, 'and he was a strong individual to come in. He was a marquee signing in some respects. It said that Brentford were able to go and get a player from a club like Leeds United. It was thinking bigger and it was thinking upwards. He connects with the supporters very well. And he'll be desperate to get to the Premier League.'

Those supporters are, in today's afternoon sun, sporting Brentford shirts of all different vintages, the unspoken suggestion being the older the shirt, the more hardcore the fan. In making their selections, none of them seem to regard the curse of the red-and-white stripes with too much credence.

'Hey Jude' is played over the PA and the combined choirs of both sides sing along, with Swansea fans seemingly unaware the song is the favoured pre-match anthem of today's opponents. Nonetheless, it's a bit of a moment, a collective statement of joy that everyone in the stands feels privileged to be back, to be here in the sunshine. What's that? No, it's nothing. Just something in my eye.

A twelve-foot-high plastic replica of the play-off trophy stands next to the halfway line. The real one sits in front of it, a modest prize. But the real prize isn't metallic. It's the invitation to join, or rejoin in Swansea's case, the top table of English football. The players march out, quite possibly within earshot of touchline-prowling Quest presenter Colin Murray barking into his microphone: 'There's no game in world football like this.'

Two national anthems later, it's game on.

If the script for the match was that it would be a tight, cagey affair, it gets ripped up as early as the ninth minute when the blue-booted Bryan Mbeumo latches on to a Sergi Canós pass, only to be hauled down by Swansea keeper Freddie Woodman. It's a stonewall penalty. Undeniable.

Also undeniable is Toney's precision from twelve yards. This might be the wearer of the Golden Boot versus the wearer of the Golden Gloves, but that trademark technique – slow and deliberate, passing it into the net from no run-up at all – hits the mark again. The eastern end of the stadium erupts. The western side is silenced and subdued.

It takes little more than ten further minutes for the effect to be doubled. A swift breakaway – inevitably featuring the ever-nippy Mbeumo – ends with Emiliano Marcondes finding enough space to sweep home Brentford's second. Despite finishing fourth in the table, Swansea have scored more than two goals in a game only twice this season. The gradient before them is a steep one.

We're not even a quarter of the way through the match but the two sub-teen boys in front of me are already in tears. Sat between them, their mum puts an arm around each. Her packet of Polos helps to soothe the pain.

Along from them, a twenty-something lad – who, up until the penalty, had been cheerily chatting away hands-free on his phone to a mate who's elsewhere in the stadium – leans forward, his head bowed. His phone is back in his pocket and he stares at his shoes, unable to watch what's unfolding on the pitch.

It means that he misses Brentford going as close as can be to three-up, when Toney's magnificent long-range volley cannons off the crossbar, onto the goal-line and away to safety, to collective sighs of relief from Swansea's quarters. A spectacular strike that only enhances Toney's growing-by-the-day reputation, it would have been one of the greatest goals ever to have graced a play-off final.

The game is all rather one-sided. Brentford have plenty of pep in their step, while Swansea remain very disjointed and show little gumption going forward. Thirty-two minutes have elapsed before the Swans earn their first corner, an achievement met with the first thunderous roar heard from their fans since kick-off. It comes to nothing.

Just before the break, an André Ayew header grazes the Brentford crossbar but that's as good as it gets from the Welshmen in the first forty-five. Stevie C's black-and-white army have very little to cheer as they leave their seats in search of half-time sustenance.

A veteran of play-offs, this afternoon Jed Wallace has swapped his usual berth on Millwall's right wing for a seat in the top row of the Wembley press box, where he's on summariser duties alongside 5 Live's Alistair Bruce-Ball. This gives Wallace a chance to showcase that encyclopaedic knowledge of the Championship during the interval. He points out to a grateful nation that, had Toney's volley gone in, it would have been the striker's first goal this season from outside the area.

After the break, Swansea are much more on the front foot. Steve Cooper, or one of his lieutenants, has clearly given them a rollicking at half-time. A diving Ayew throws himself at a Connor Roberts cross but sees the ball go agonisingly wide. On the hour mark, Liam Cullen comes on for Kyle Naughton – a striker for a full-back. But this attacking enhancement has only a handful of minutes before there's another setback for Swansea.

The midfielder Jay Fulton, who hasn't had his best game in a Swansea shirt, puts in an off-the-ground, two-footed chop on Mathias Jensen, earning him a straight red. It was an utterly unnecessary challenge to make in a benign area of the pitch – Brentford's right-back position – although the video replay does make clear that Fulton slips before making contact with the Brentford player. Had VAR been active – which, of course, Thomas Frank was very vocally calling for down at Bournemouth – Fulton may well have escaped with a yellow and Swansea would still be in the game.

Now, though, everyone in the stadium pretty much concedes that the task is too great, that gradient too steep. It would be the comeback to end all comebacks were Swansea's ten men to dramatically turn things around. And they don't. As he paces his technical area, Cooper shrugs at the lack of real invention from his players. Bearing in mind the rumours surrounding his future, are these the last few moments of his time as Swansea manager?

At the eastern end of Wembley, the Brentford fans bask in the sunshine. Down the other end, the Jack Army are in the shade. Figuratively, too. Into the ninetieth minute, they start turning on their heels to leave, although the announcement of six minutes of added time does cause a few to linger longer. Hope springs eternal, but the fates have been dealt. On the touchline, Frank is savouring these final moments of the season. His team are not only two goals to the good, but they're seeing the game out against ten men. It doesn't get much better than that. They're home and hosed, as Cooper acknowledges when he offers his opposite number his congratulations a minute or two before the final whistle is blown.

Were the stadium fitted with a roof, the roar would have blown it clean off when that whistle sounds. The gravity of the moment starts to sink in. Brentford are in the top flight of English football for the first time in seventy-four years. And, after seven seasons, they are waving goodbye to the Championship. They have scaled its walls. They're over and away. The curse has been lifted.

Swansea remain within the Championship's confines.

Shoulders slumped, the players acknowledge their disappointed fans before trudging down the tunnel. Marc Guéhi, that most impressive of centre-backs, is last off. But his time in the Premier League will come. That is certain. For Brentford, the newest chapter of their story had all been about the departure from Griffin Park. Now it's all about the departure from the Championship.

As the scenery-shifters turn a football pitch into a party venue, the players and staff charge around giddily, none more so than Frank himself. But when the squad takes to the podium to receive their winners' medals, another figure is ushered into the fray, an older chap in his civvies. And when Pontus Jansson raises the trophy to the heavens, he does so with this other man's hands on the silverware. The hands are those of Peter Gilham, Mr Brentford himself, a man born six weeks after his precious team played their last top-flight match. It's a lovely gesture. For the privilege, Gilham's face takes the full brunt of the champagne currently being sprayed by Ivan Toney.

Irresistible stories can be found everywhere. Ethan Pinnock, the former PE teacher once of Dulwich Hamlet, is now a Premier League footballer. Pontus Jansson, after three successive play-off campaigns, is now a Premier League footballer. And star striker Toney, after a single, record-breaking season in the Championship and earlier rejection by Newcastle, is back to being a Premier League footballer.

And Thomas Frank is now a Premier League manager. Phil Parry has just started the last of his innumerable interviews with the Dane this season when the Brentford players charge out of the tunnel to drench their manager in beer. It won't be his last brush with alcohol on this most celebratory of days.

'I just want to get very drunk tonight,' says the King Bee, his eyes widening. 'If I'm not home in the morning, my wife will have to look for me . . .'

*

High above the ecstatic Brentford players and staff, a father and his middle-aged son and daughter exchange hugs.

'You're crying. Oh, Dad ...'

'I'm not really crying. The tears in my eyes are because I'm so chuffed about it.'

Brian Sawyer has waited a long time to witness the scenes currently playing out in front of him. At the age of eighty-two, he's been a long-time Bees fan, a relationship cemented by his stewardship of the old Centenary Club – the social club at Griffin Park – and by his paint company supplying the maintenance team at the old ground. In return for his years of dedication, the club has now done the decent thing by moving to a stadium even closer to his home near Kew Bridge ('I'm bloody on top of it!'). From his front door, he can be in his seat in the ground in fewer than ten minutes.

Brian is also perfectly placed to put this triumphant season into context. 'Brentford have played some bloody good football this season. Years ago, we were terrible. We never got anywhere in the old days. I remember one particular match at Cardiff and ... oh my God ... it was pathetic, it really was. We paid all this money to go and you'd have thought that they would at least have a go. But they just didn't want to play. It was awful. But luckily, as the years have worn on, they got better and better and better. And we've had some very good managers who really put some effort in. That makes a difference.'

For his achievements this afternoon, Thomas Frank has arguably put himself at the top of the pile of Brentford managers. Hopes were high at kick-off, such is the faith put in the Dane by the Bees faithful, including Brian and his kids.

'I did feel optimistic beforehand. Had it been raining, I might not have done. We went two-up quite early, but I did think that they were going to come back and give us such a wallop. But one of the guys behind me said, "Swansea aren't anything like they used to be. They're not playing football. They really aren't." That went down well with me. Then I relaxed when Swansea went down to ten men. We were playing superbly and, once he got sent off, I think that was it.

'I was keeping my fingers crossed. And my legs. And everything else. I was praying we'd pull through. When you're eighty-two, you think, *Oh God, am I going to see this?* And, touch wood, there's more to come.'

Indeed, a season on the high seas of the Premier League awaits. 'It's going to be an adventure. Going to all these big stadiums will be wonderful. No disrespect to some of the teams we've played over the years, but it won't be tiny, tin-pot grounds any more. We deal with a company in Manchester and they've got a box at Man City. I'll certainly be after an invite up there ...

'It's a wonderful feeling, a very wonderful feeling. I know it's happened, but I can't believe it. And I don't think I will until we actually start playing in the Premier League.'

Octogenarian Brian will have still been in short trousers the last time Brentford graced the top flight. His attire may well have been significant today. He's wearing his trade-mark wide-brimmed, tan-coloured hat, one made in South Africa but looking quite similar to that of a cowboy. It gets him noticed.

'When we go to away games, people say, "I saw you, Brian. I saw the hat. I knew you were there." Years ago, I came out of the club and this little boy, a nice lad of about ten, came up to me.

'"Can I have your autograph?"

'"What do you want my autograph for?"

'"You're known as the Cowboy of Brentford ..."'

While Brian might see his headwear as some kind of talisman ('I wouldn't leave home without that hat on'), another item of his clothing is equally notable. Under his blazer, he's wearing a white shirt emblazoned with the images of tiny bees. Going by today's result, the shirt appears to have gained the instant status of good luck charm. 'I'm going to wear that to every game now.'

So, after the hard yards of forty-nine league and play-off games this season, it appears that it wasn't Brentford's much-admired recruitment, nor Thomas Frank's immaculately conceived tactics, that got Brentford over the line. It was Brian's choice of clothing.

'I'll go along with that,' he chuckles. 'That's not a bad idea at all ...'

*

Saturday evening, a couple of hours after the last kick of the ball of a Championship season unlike any other.

In the wild meadow on top of the hill above Adams Park, summer has officially started. The grass is tall and the buttercups stand high. The sunshine is golden. A pair of the resident red kites take their last exercise, circling the pitch from up above before returning to their roosts.

Down the hill, the stadium's car park is a scene of repair and renewal. A pile of rubble waits to be removed, while the main sign welcoming visitors to Adams Park lies damaged in a corner, needing some tender love and care before next season comes around.

Come August, Wycombe Wanderers — after making their brave bow in the Championship — will return to the familiar terrain of the third tier. But things aren't as cut and dried as they might be. There may yet be a twist.

Any doubts about the Chairboys' relegation centre, almost

inevitably, around Derby County. Back in August, the Rams were cleared by an independent disciplinary commission of financial wrongdoing. However, three days after those wild celebrations in the Pride Park car park on the final day of the season, it was announced that the EFL has won the right to appeal the verdict of one of the charges – that of how the club measured the value of their players across the length of their contracts.

If Derby are found guilty of this particular charge, the punishment would almost certainly be a points deduction. And if those points total two or more, then Wycombe – thanks to that late run and that final-day win up on Teesside that took them to twenty-second place in the table – would be the beneficiaries. They would remain a Championship club.

But this presumes a few factors going Wycombe's way: that Derby would be found guilty; that a points deduction would be the punishment; and that this deduction would be applied to the season just finished and not to the next one. It also presumes that the EFL will act fast. All the time that the slow cogs of football's machinery take to rotate, the less likely it will be that the Chairboys will benefit. And, of course, any decision would be subject to a Derby appeal. It could take months.

So, for now, on this gorgeous evening in bucolic Buckinghamshire, the eyes remain on League One. Wycombe will be hoping that their time there will be as short as their period in the second tier, that they'll get to taste the Championship again as soon as possible, that in twelve months' time they'll be celebrating promotion to the toughest league in the world.

They now know there's no better place to be.

\*

# Final Championship table

|    |                          | P  | W  | D  | L  | F  | A  | Pts |
|----|--------------------------|----|----|----|----|----|----|-----|
| 1  | Norwich City (C)          | 46 | 29 | 10 | 7  | 75 | 36 | 97  |
| 2  | Watford (P)               | 46 | 27 | 10 | 9  | 63 | 30 | 91  |
| 3  | Brentford (P)             | 46 | 24 | 15 | 7  | 79 | 42 | 87  |
| 4  | Swansea City              | 46 | 23 | 11 | 12 | 58 | 39 | 80  |
| 5  | Barnsley                  | 46 | 23 | 9  | 14 | 58 | 50 | 78  |
| 6  | AFC Bournemouth           | 46 | 22 | 11 | 13 | 73 | 46 | 77  |
| 7  | Reading                   | 46 | 19 | 13 | 14 | 62 | 54 | 70  |
| 8  | Cardiff City              | 46 | 18 | 14 | 14 | 66 | 49 | 68  |
| 9  | Queens Park Rangers       | 46 | 19 | 11 | 16 | 57 | 55 | 68  |
| 10 | Middlesbrough             | 46 | 18 | 10 | 18 | 55 | 53 | 64  |
| 11 | Millwall                  | 46 | 15 | 17 | 14 | 47 | 52 | 62  |
| 12 | Luton Town                | 46 | 17 | 11 | 18 | 41 | 52 | 62  |
| 13 | Preston North End         | 46 | 18 | 7  | 21 | 49 | 56 | 61  |
| 14 | Stoke City                | 46 | 15 | 15 | 16 | 50 | 52 | 60  |
| 15 | Blackburn Rovers          | 46 | 15 | 12 | 19 | 65 | 54 | 57  |
| 16 | Coventry City             | 46 | 14 | 13 | 19 | 49 | 61 | 55  |
| 17 | Nottingham Forest         | 46 | 12 | 16 | 18 | 37 | 45 | 52  |
| 18 | Birmingham City           | 46 | 13 | 13 | 20 | 37 | 61 | 52  |
| 19 | Bristol City              | 46 | 15 | 6  | 25 | 46 | 68 | 51  |
| 20 | Huddersfield Town         | 46 | 12 | 13 | 21 | 50 | 71 | 49  |
| 21 | Derby County              | 46 | 11 | 11 | 24 | 36 | 58 | 44  |
| 22 | Wycombe Wanderers (R)     | 46 | 11 | 10 | 25 | 39 | 69 | 43  |
| 23 | Rotherham United (R)      | 46 | 11 | 9  | 26 | 44 | 60 | 42  |
| 24 | Sheffield Wednesday (R)   | 46 | 12 | 11 | 23 | 40 | 61 | 41* |

*Includes six-point deduction*

## Leading scorers

Ivan Toney (Brentford), 33*
Adam Armstrong (Blackburn), 28
Teemu Pukki (Norwich), 26
Kieffer Moore (Cardiff), 20
Lucas João (Reading), 19

## Manager of the Season

Daniel Farke (Norwich)

## Player of the Season

Emi Buendía (Norwich)

## Team of the Season

Asmir Begović (Bournemouth)
Max Aarons (Norwich)
Grant Hanley (Norwich)
Sean Morrison (Cardiff)
Adam Masina (Watford)
Arnaut Danjuma (Bournemouth)
Michael Olise (Reading)
Alex Mowatt (Barnsley)
Emi Buendía (Norwich)
Ivan Toney (Brentford)
Teemu Pukki (Norwich)

## Managerial appointments

Frankie McAvoy (Preston)

*Includes two goals during the play-offs*

# Extra Time

**Matt Bloomfield** didn't play as often as he would have liked during Wycombe's debut season in the Championship – just sixteen times, including an eleventh-hour cameo in that final-day win at Middlesbrough. But his current contract runs for another twelve months, a deal that includes a coaching commitment. To all eyes, Bloomfield is a Wycombe manager of the future.

In that first season at Ewood Park, **Tyrhys Dolan** made ten starts in the Championship, plus a further twenty-seven appearances coming off the bench. 'It's exceeded my expectations completely,' he gushes. 'I really didn't expect everything that's come my way.' And with loanee Harvey Elliott having returned to parent club Liverpool, Dolan will be hoping to make Blackburn's right-wing berth his own next season.

Five weeks after being sacked by Bournemouth, **Jason Tindall** returned to the Premier League when he joined the coaching staff at Sheffield United under interim manager Paul Heckingbottom. With his old partner Eddie Howe yet to return to the dugout (despite being heavily linked with the vacancies at Celtic and Crystal Palace), it remains to be seen if the pair will join forces again.

With twenty-seven of his thirty-four appearances in QPR's hoops coming from the bench, **Albert Adomah** was reportedly considering the unthinkable: leaving his beloved W12 in search of more regular first-team football. Derby, Birmingham and Luton were among those rumoured to be interested – more Championship clubs to add to his collection.

**Ben Foster**'s season was somewhat curtailed in the New Year when he broke a finger, causing ligament and tendon damage too. Once fit, and with Watford's promotion push on schedule, he couldn't dislodge his replacement, Daniel Bachmann, until the final day of the season. Foster returns to the Premier League after just one season away. Back to the land of the dreaded VAR . . .

As of late June, nearly eight months on from his enforced departure from Hillsborough, **Garry Monk** had yet to be re-employed by a football club. But as long as the managerial merry-go-round continues to spin, opportunities will knock, as his former right-hand man showed. During the summer, **James Beattie** took an assistant manager role at Wigan Athletic.

**Joe Jacobson** wore the Wycombe captain's armband for the remainder of the season, leading them on that tantalisingly close survival bid. But having had a taste of the second tier, he's hungry to return for another helping. 'We loved every minute in the Championship and showed that we can compete at that level. I'm sure the club will be back there soon.'

After successfully completing his first injury-free season for many years – and helping Coventry to avoid the drop back into League One – **Matty James** was, as expected, released by Leicester at the end of the campaign. His performances in both South Yorkshire and the West Midlands during 2020–21 ensured Championship suitors formed a disorderly queue for his services. He ended up signing a three-year deal with Bristol City, now managed by Nigel Pearson, the man who originally took James to Leicester.

After reporting on twenty-seven matches during the season for various networks (as well as hosting Quest's highlights show a dozen times), there was little time for **Michelle Owen** to relax. She was swiftly announced as the ITV reporter who would be following the Wales squad around the continent at the European Championships shuttling between Baku and Rome.

**Josh Marsh** didn't take his time to bolster the Huddersfield squad. Before the end of May, he'd already arranged the free signings of two Championship stalwarts: midfielder Matty Pearson and striker **Jordan Rhodes**, the latter making a return to his old happy hunting ground of the John Smith's Stadium. And by securing a future in the Championship, Rhodes now has every chance of becoming the division's highest-ever goalscorer.

**Gary Sweet** was delighted with Luton's twelfth place, their highest finish in the league for fifteen years – and one that comes just seven seasons after the Hatters were a non-league outfit. The upward progression under his stewardship continues, with the club's move to that new stadium on course for 2024.

That easy life of fishing and dog-walking in Cornwall has again been put on hold for **Neil Warnock** as he prepares to lead Middlesbrough again next season and to improve on their tenth position from this campaign. 'I'd say it's a B,' he says, when asked to grade how the previous nine months have gone. 'I wouldn't be as harsh as a C. I think B is about right, with a "Could do better, Warnock", like I used to get on my school reports . . .'

On 23 June, an independent disciplinary commission handed Derby County a £100,000 fine for accounting irregularities, as well as ordering the club to file three years' worth of restated accounts. Suggesting dissatisfaction with the level of punishment, the EFL immediately announced they would be publishing fixture lists for the 2020–21 season in which Derby and Wycombe would be interchangeable. Not only did the announcement sound as if the league were preparing to appeal, but it also hinted that a retrospective points deduction for Derby was their preferred outcome, meaning Wycombe would remain in the second tier.

Wycombe's owner, Rob Couhig, was also disgruntled about a fine being issued. 'It is beyond disappointing that a club can systemically cheat and end up with a slap on the wrist. You have years upon years of violating the rules.' The lawyer from New Orleans also suggested legal action might be taken against the Rams if any appeals process hadn't been completed by the start of next season and Wycombe were forced to start the new campaign in League One.

However, on 2 July, the EFL did make a decision. But it wasn't the one Rob Couhig wanted to hear. 'While the EFL does not agree that those sanctions are commensurate to the breaches found, following consultation with our legal advisors, the EFL Board has regrettably determined that there are insufficient grounds to appeal the sanction imposed.'

Derby County breathed again.

# Acknowledgements

Huge gratitude goes out to the many and varied interviewees for their time and patience, and for their insights, which helped to both widen and deepen the story.

For getting me beyond the velvet rope (and other favours), big thanks and appreciation to Anthony Marshall at AFC Bournemouth; Andrew Clark at Barnsley; Dale Moon at Birmingham City; Rob Gill at Blackburn Rovers; Chris Wickham at Brentford, Dave Barton and Ed Lewis at Bristol City; Mark Denham and Sam Roberts at Cardiff City; Mark Hornby and Alex Lowe at Coventry City; Tom Loakes at Derby County; David Threlfall-Sykes at Huddersfield Town; Stuart Hammonds at Luton Town; Paul Dews at Middlesbrough; Billy Taylor at Millwall; Daniel Houlker and Charlotte Foster at Norwich City; Ashley Lambell at Nottingham Forest; Ben Rhodes at Preston North End; Paul Morrissey and Matt Webb at Queens Park Rangers; Mark Bradley at Reading; Sam Todd at Rotherham United; Trevor Braithwait at Sheffield Wednesday; Fraser Nicholson at Stoke City; Ben Donovan, Chris Wilson-Barney and Sophie Davis at Swansea City; Richard Walker and Jon Marks at Watford; and, most of all, Matt Cecil at Wycombe Wanderers.

Thanks to Mark Rowan and Billie Marshall at the EFL, and Oron Bristol at Football DataCo, as we got close to the final whistle.

For going above and beyond, Colin Murray, Michelle Owen, Phil Parry, Natalie Sawyer, Chris Sutton and Geoff Twentyman deserve special shout-outs.

At Simon & Schuster, my excellent editor Fran Jessop matched her impeccable taste in commissioning the book with her enthusiastic marshalling of the entire process under the strictest of time constraints. Thanks also to her colleagues Ian Marshall, Craig Fraser, Victoria Godden, Lorraine Jerram and Rhiannon Carroll.

A tip of the hat to my shrewd and perceptive agent Kevin Pocklington at The North Literary Agency, and to his faithful assistant Syd.

Finally, as ever, big thanks to Jane, Finn and Ned for their love and tolerance as I disappeared upcountry for yet another match. There's nothing remotely second tier about you guys.